Partnerships

STEP · BY · STEP

Partnerships

S·T·E·P · B·Y · S·T·E·P

David Minars, M.B.A., J.D., CPA

This book is dedicated to my wife, Iris Elaine Minars, for her *joie de vivre*. My thanks to Anna Damaskos for her inspiration, support, and wise counsel.

All inquiries should be addressed to:
Barron's Educational Series, Inc.
250 Wireless Boulevard
Hauppauge, New York 11788

International Standard Book No. 0-7641-0184-6

Library of Congress Catalog Card No. 97-2594

Library of Congress Cataloging-in-Publication Data
Minars, David.
    Partnerships step-by-step / David Minars.
      p.   cm.—(Barron's legal-ease)
    Includes index.
    ISBN 0-7641-0184-6
    1. Partnerships—United States—Popular works. I. Series.
KF1375.Z9M56   1997a
346.73'0682—dc21   97-2594
                          CIP

PRINTED IN THE UNITED STATES OF AMERICA

987654321

Contents

CHAPTER 1   Introduction

WHAT THIS BOOK IS ALL ABOUT

The objective of this book is not to make you into a CPA or an attorney. It is, however, for people who wish to start out in their own business, with minimum capital and the freedom to organize and dissolve without interference or approval by the state or federal government. One way to launch a business is in the partnership form. While forming a partnership is relatively easy, it does not come, as we shall see, without some risk. A partnership lacks continuity and exposes you to risky personal unlimited liability. Furthermore, the death, bankruptcy, or withdrawal of any partner causes the dissolution of the firm (see Chap. 7).

There are many reasons why people go into business today. Many people feel that they have the experience and "smarts" to "make a go of it." They may also want the personal freedom to reach certain economic and personal goals, as well as simply wanting their name on the door. This book will show you how to form your own partnership, using easy-to-follow steps, while suggesting to you various ways to invest only minimal capital. It will also help you avoid fundamental and costly tax mistakes if you choose to do business as a partnership. Remember that there are a variety of other legal forms through which you can conduct a business, such as the sole proprietorship and the corporation, but they too have their pitfalls.

HOW THIS BOOK IS ORGANIZED

In the next chapter, you will learn what is involved in the different types of businesses: i.e., the individual proprietorship, limited partnerships, joint ventures, the limited liability partnership, the family limited partnership, and corporations. The advantages and disadvantages of each form of business are itemized for you.

Chapter 3 clarifies who can enter a partnership and what types of partners there are (general partner, silent partner, etc.). This chapter goes on to discuss such details as how to set up your partnership, choose a name for your firm, what you need to know about the partnership agreement, and how to use the Internet to find a partner and develop economic opportunities.

The question of who owns the property of a partnership is discussed in Chapter 4. Here, you will also learn what happens when a partner assigns her interests in the firm as well as what rights partner has to use partnership property.

Chapter 5 discusses the relations between partners. This includes, the fiduciary obligations of each partner, how profits and losses are shared, salaries paid to partners, reimbursement and indemnity for expenditures, how to treat a partner's advances, the rights of a partner upon dissolution, a partner's rights to inspect the partnership's books and records, legal actions between partners, and a partner's right to worker's compensation.

The topic of relations is continued in Chapter 6. This chapter discusses the relations of partners to third parties and amending the partnership agreement.

Many people who enter a partnership want to know how they will be able to dissolve the partnership if circumstances call for it. This is addressed in Chapter 7, which also discusses the safeguarding of the going concern value of the partnership by use of a Continuation Agreement as well as who has the authority to wind up a partnership's affairs.

Chapter 8 discusses the limited partnership in more detail than Chapter 2 did. Here, you will learn what the nature of the limited partner's contribution is as well as what the rights of a limited partner are. In addition, the rights and liabilities of a general partner in a limited partnership are discussed.

Every business must deal with the reality of accounting and a partnership is no different. Chapter 9 discusses how to deal with partnership accounting. This topic is expanded on in Chapter 10, which explains how to get started with the day-to-day operations of the partnership (e.g., choosing the right accounting method and establishing employee benefit packages) as well as how to select an accountant.

Chapter 11 explores how various partnerships are taxed. Tax shelters and the selection of the partnership's tax year are also discussed here.

The question of how to buy and/or sell an ongoing partnership is answered in Chapter 12. Also discussed are how to value an ongoing business and how to set the terms of valuation for a partner's interest. A checklist of the differences between a large and small partnership as a determinant factor in selecting a valuation technique is provided here.

Important terms are defined in the Glossary.

Finally, our appendices begin with Fifty Commonly Asked Questions Regarding Partnerships. Here, each question is given a clear answer to help you understand the nature of partnerships.

Sample federal tax forms are supplied in Appendix B. Complete instructions for filling out these forms are also included.

Appendix C contains sample agreement forms, which you can use and modify to create and maintain your own partnership.

Our final appendix is a list of books that you may find helpful to you in starting and maintaining a business.

ACTING AS YOUR OWN LAWYER

"A person who acts as her own attorney has a fool for a client." Obviously, the author of this quote never had to pay a sizeable legal fee in return for a routine legal service. While creating a partnership is essentially very simple, most basic business situations can become complicated and require the guidance of an attorney. Thus, your lawyer, who knows you best, is in an excellent position to advise you in choosing whether to operate as a sole proprietorship, partnership, or corporation. He can also help you to establish the partnership, deal with any potential conflicts that may arise among partners, register trademarks, patents, and copyrights, file for licenses, purchase real estate for the business, negotiate a lease, deal with customer disputes and potential litigation, assist in estate planning for when you die, and handle possible liquidation or bankruptcy proceedings should the need arise.

However, many of these costs, and in some cases virtually all of your start-up costs, can be reduced or eliminated by carefully following all the many money-saving techniques discussed in this book.

Therefore, before entering into a partnership, you should understand all basic issues, determine what legal aspects, if any, can be handled without legal help, and then decide whether it is worthwhile in terms of time and money to launch your new business.

SELECTING A LAWYER

While wealthy individuals and businesses retain lawyers to answer their legal problems and to monitor unusual or complex transactions, a new partnership, which may consist of as few as two enterprising individuals pursuing their dreams, generally cannot afford this luxury. After analyzing the specific needs of the business, it would be wise to enlist the services of an attorney whose skills and experience can help solve both common and unforeseen legal problems. The attorney can assist you in setting up the type of enterprise that you need, such as a partnership, and can negotiate any loans, leases, and contracts applicable to your business. She also will advise your accountant as to what transactions must be recorded on your books and records for tax, environmental, health and safety regulations, and minimum wage requirements. If possible, avoid hiring an attorney on a costly monthly retainer basis. Find an attorney who bills by the hour, and determine which services comprise billable hours. For example, does she bill for a ten-minute phone call concerning a simple question? Thus, you will only be paying for services that you actually use rather than burdening your business with fixed monthly costs. Determine the attorney's rates in advance. Shop around for an attorney in whom you have trust and whose fees your new business can afford.

Selection is no easy task, but here are some suggestions for finding the right legal professional.

1. Talk to people in your community and ask who they use;
2. Talk to your accountant or banker;
3. Ask friends and relatives;
4. Look in the "yellow pages" for a listing of lawyers who specialize in business matters, and when you find one, ask to speak to some of her clients regarding the quality of her services;
5. In many states, the bar association will have a lawyer referral and information service. This service can provide you with the name of a lawyer in your area who can be contacted. An initial consultation may be obtained at a minimal fee or possibly free of charge if the attorney is seeking new clients.

In selecting a lawyer, just don't settle on the first lawyer on your list. Set up an interview, ask about her education, area of expertise, and prior experience in business matters. Also determine whether you are comfortable with this person. Are her fees reasonable? Does she return calls quickly? Also determine whether the person is practical minded and can fine tune your partnership, if necessary, without getting involved in complex legal issues that might prove costly.

CHAPTER 2

Selecting the Form of Your Business

FORMS AND FACTORS IN SELECTION

The selection of the best form of doing business is based on many considerations. From a strictly business viewpoint, there are several forms of doing business. They include the sole proprietorship, general partnership, limited partnership, limited liability partnership (also called an LLP; see Chap. 11), corporation, limited liability company (also called an LLC; see Chap. 11), and professional corporation. Each of these forms can be tailored to take into account the particular situation of one or more persons. For example, if a person wishes to start out with minimal federal, state, and city regulations and capital, it might be advisable to start off as a sole proprietorship. The individual proprietor retains all profits and absorbs all losses, but must bear all personal risk, such as using a savings account to pay off creditors. Later on, if the business grows and becomes more complex, the individual might consider taking in one or more like-minded people and choose to operate as a partnership. Furthermore, the successful sole proprietorship also can choose to incorporate to take advantage of limited shareholder liability, fringe benefits, pension plans, and perhaps to raise additional capital.

Factors that enter into the selection of the form of doing business include initial start-up costs, operating procedures that must be followed, capital and credit requirements, management and control, whether there is exposure to unlimited personal liability, the number of people needed to operate the business, the determination of salaries, the freedom to transfer an ownership interest, and whether the business can be continued if an owner dies or wants to sell his interest.

THE INDIVIDUAL (OR SOLE) PROPRIETORSHIP

Definition

As the name suggests, this is a natural form of doing business at the lowest initial cost. It is initially the simplest way of doing business in that there is no "sole proprietorship law" in any state that must be followed. Thus, the sole proprietorship can be a home-office undertaking where the owner is the "boss." Generally speaking, any kind of business, both big and small, can be operated as a sole proprietorship, for example, an art supply store, a computer service, or a bookkeeping and tax practice. A sole proprietor can sell goods and services, enter into business contracts, employ others, and take vacations when she wants to. She can get credit or raise capital by either borrowing based on the value of the firm's assets or on her own personal wealth. As the firm grows, the owner, if she wants to, has the flexibility to convert the firm into a partnership by admitting a new partner or can transform it into a corporation tax-free. The major disadvantage of a sole proprietorship is *exposure to unlimited personal liability* or legal responsibility for all obligations incurred while doing business. This means that any business contracts made by the owner, or any negligent acts committed by her or her employees while doing business, exposes her to unlimited personal risk of loss. Any personal assets, such as her home or car, may be seized to satisfy any claims should the business be unable to do so. Of course, personal liability exposure may be reduced by either express agreement in a contract with a customer or by purchasing substantial liability insurance.

EXAMPLE Myra Jennings operated a home improvement service as a sole proprietorship. With the help of an employee, Myra installed a new roof on an old house. During a subsequent rainstorm, the new roof leaked causing $30,000 in damage to the house and its contents. Myra's liability insurance covering her business was limited to $25,000 per project. Myra will be forced to pay $5,000 ($30,000 less $25,000) out of her own personal assets.

There are no formalities involved in starting a sole proprietorship beyond any capital requirements. Thus, this form is very suitable for an individual with some business experience who is seeking to start a one-person operation.

When operating as a sole proprietor, there is generally no continuity of existence. When the owner dies, the business generally will terminate. The firm's assets, if any, become part of the deceased owner's estate. However, the owner may, by will, permit the executor of the will to continue the business so that her heirs may receive a going concern. In effect, this technique permits a beneficiary, as a new owner, to continue what may be a thriving business.

In a sole proprietorship, the owner pays individual taxes on net profits that may run from 15 to 39.6 percent. The sole proprietorship is also subject to federal self-employment tax. Net losses generated by the business can be used to offset the individual's other taxable income, such as salary and wages from other sources.

EXAMPLE Charles Oak earned $100,000 in salary from his job as an accountant for a public accounting firm. He has also started a sole proprietorship doing business as a computer consultant. His gross sales for his first year of operation were $10,000 but his initial start-up costs were $14,000. Thus, his net loss was $4,000 ($14,000 in costs – 10,000 in income). Oak may offset this $4,000 loss against his $100,000 taxable salary as an accountant.

Thus, the sole proprietor enjoys minimal government scrutiny, a large degree of secrecy, and certain tax benefits but is subject to unlimited liability.

Advantages of a Sole Proprietorship
1. Requires minimal start-up capital.
2. Minimum legal and accounting fees upon start-up.
3. Lack of operating formalities, such as meetings of a board of directors. The individual is in complete control of the proprietorship.
4. Free access to trade in all state jurisdictions with minimum legal burdens.
5. A sole proprietor's protection as an individual by the Fifth Amendment's guarantee against self-incrimination.
6. Less governmental regulation than a corporation.
7. Possible availability of credit based not only on the business assets but also on the personal assets of the owner, proprietor.
8. Minimal legal and accounting problems upon termination.
9. Opportunity of a sole proprietorship to generate losses, which the owner can use to offset taxable income. This is particularly advantageous if large operating losses are expected in the initial years of operation.
10. Opportunity to operate under an "assumed" or "trade" name. If the sole proprietorship desires to conduct business under an assumed name, state statutes in many jurisdictions merely require that a certificate be filed in a public office.
11. Availability of certain types of pension plans to offset the effects of federal taxation.

Disadvantages of a Sole Proprietorship

1. Death of the principal automatically terminates the business.

....

OBSERVATION *Continuity may, however, be obtained in some jurisdictions by means of special statutes applicable to decedent's businesses.*

....

2. The owner is subject to unlimited liability in case of breach of contract or liability due to some negligent action on the part of the owner or her employees. However, this disadvantage can be mitigated somewhat by the use of various forms of liability insurance.
3. The amount of capital available for use in the business is limited to the resources of the owner.
4. Income obtained by the owner from other sources will put the owner of a profitable business into a tax bracket as high as 39.6 percent.
5. The sole proprietorship form limits the number of retirement and profit sharing plans that may be utilized.

In some cases, the sole proprietorship option can be very risky. For example, a high exposure to legal risks may require operation in the corporate form in order to provide greater protection against personal liability, as in the case of a manufacturer of potentially hazardous consumer products.

THE PARTNERSHIP

Partnerships and corporations are the two most common methods of operating a business by more than one individual. Corporations are independent legal entities; partnerships are not.

The Uniform Partnership Act (UPA) is the uniform law on partnerships and is in use in the District of Columbia and all states except Louisiana. The Uniform Partnership Act (UPA §6) defines a partnership as "an association of two or more persons to carry on as co-owners of a business for profit." A partnership is an association of persons as individuals, not, as in the case of incorporators, an association whose individualities become merged into a corporate entity. A partner is not an employee of the partnership.

EXAMPLE Vern Osprey and Tomas Callahan were partners engaged in clearing land sites for construction. Osprey was injured when his backhoe hit a gas pipe resulting in an explosion. He subsequently died, and his widow applied for workers' compensation benefits, including immediate medical benefits, wage replacement, and a death benefit. She argued that Osprey was an employee of the partnership and thus, entitled to these benefits. Her claim was denied since partners are not employees of the partnership for workers' compensation purposes.

A partnership must be carried on for a profit. Nonprofit institutions, such as religious or charitable groups, labor unions, or clubs, are not partnerships.

Partnerships are either general partnerships or limited partnerships (see page 9). General partnerships consist of partners who are all general partners while a limited partnership has both general and limited partners. The formation of a partnership must be voluntary. Individuals cannot be forced into partnerships. They have a right to select the persons with whom they wish to associate in business.

In a partnership, each partner is an *agent* (one who is authorized to act for another) of the partnership in dealing with third parties, and each partner is subject to joint and/or several liability. This means that each partner may be sued individually for the entire amount of the alleged debt or for his proportionate share. Thus, the *fiduciary* (a relationship of trust) character of the association between the partners and the risk of unlimited personal liability for the acts of the other partners within the scope (meaning within the range or area of business) of the partnership underscores the voluntary nature of the firm. No person can become a partner without the unanimous consent of all the other partners and the death of a partner dissolves the partnership. The fiduciary relationship among the partners requires that they act in good faith and with complete loyalty to the other partners.

The sharing of gross returns does not of itself establish a partnership. However, the sharing of net profits, due to a proprietary interest in the entity, is regarded as the most accurate test as to whether a partnership exists.

The sharing of profits may not, however, automatically characterize an individual as a partner. The joint use of property, or part ownership by itself, does not establish a partnership. In addition, profits received in payment of a debt by installment, wages of an employee, rent to a landlord, an annuity to a widow or representative of a deceased partner, or the consideration for the sale of the goodwill of a business or other property by installments or otherwise will not create a partnership (UPA §7). In all other situations, if the party who has received profits from the unincorporated business does not introduce evidence to the contrary, a partnership will be deemed to exist, and the individual will be held liable as a partner.

General partnerships are either trading or nontrading. Trading partnerships are those that are formed for ordinary or industrial purposes, such as the sale of goods. Nontrading partnerships are those formed for professional purposes, such as law, medicine, and accountancy. The practical effect of the distinction between trading and nontrading partnerships is that third persons are entitled to assume that members of a trading partnership have wider authority than members of a nontrading firm.

A partnership may sue or be sued in the firm name. When one partner is served with a court summons, it represents service of process on the entire partnership.

Advantages of a Partnership

1. Partnerships are easy to create and generally require no approval from state or local authorities.
2. There are no formal annual meeting requirements, such as those required for corporations.
3. Partnerships are generally simple to operate.
4. Partnerships are not subject to as many formal reporting requirements as are imposed on corporations.
5. A partnership also has a tax advantage because it is not directly subject to federal income tax. Profits and losses flow through to each individual partner on the personal level. Thus, the partnership acts as a "conduit" for partnership profits and losses.

6. Partnerships also can utilize various qualified pension and profit-sharing plans.
7. Partnerships may dissolve by mutual agreement while other types of entities, such as a corporation, require statutory compliance when dissolving.

Disadvantages of a Partnership

1. Members are subject to unlimited personal liability for all the liabilities of the business.
2. Death of a partner terminates the partnership, which can cause difficulties in the continued operation of the business. Besides the death of a partner, a dissolution may occur when any partner indicates an intention to disassociate from the partnership. Dissolution can also occur when a change in the law prohibits further operation or by judicial decree, such as where the partnership can only be operated at a loss or a partner perpetuates a fraud upon the other partners.
3. A partnership, because of its size and minimal assets, may find it difficult to raise any required capital.
4. A partner's interest in the partnership is not readily transferable.
5. Under the Internal Revenue Code, partners' profits are taxable to the partners whether or not there is an actual distribution of the profits to them. Thus, if the partnership decides to reinvest the partnership's profits, the partners must come up with the necessary cash with which to pay the applicable income taxes on the undistributed profits.

The Advantages of a Partnership Over a Corporation

A major advantage of a partnership over a corporation is the avoidance of additional income tax (the double taxation on original corporate income and on dividends).

In some respects, operating a partnership is simpler than operating a corporation. There are no mandatory annual meetings, such as those required for corporations. A partnership also has a tax advantage because it is not subject to the federal income tax and merely files Form 1065, which is an informational return. Profits and losses, as reported on the partnership tax return, flow through to each individual partner and are reported on their personal tax returns. Thus, the partnership acts as a "conduit" for partnership profits and losses. Partnerships can also employ various qualified pension and profit-sharing plans.

In a general partnership, unless the partnership agreement stipulates otherwise, each partner has an equal voice in the management of the partnership. Unless the UPA requires a unanimous vote for a particular transaction, normal operating decisions require only the majority consent of the partners. In some partnerships, one partner may be given more authority than other partners. For example, in some accounting firms, one partner might be designated as the "managing partner." A further discussion of the partnership's operation and liability of the partners is presented in the next chapter.

EXAMPLE The partnership of Clinton, Gore, and Socks reports a net income of $75,000 for the tax year 199X. If profits and losses are shared equally, each partner will report $25,000 on her personal tax return.

OBSERVATION *In the area of passive activities operated as limited partnerships, or so called "tax shelters," partners are permitted to offset losses from rental real estate activities in which they* materially *participate against income from all other sources. This area will be discussed in Chap. 11.*

The Risks of Doing Business as a Partnership

The most serious disadvantage of a partnership is the unlimited personal liability of each member for all the liabilities of the business, including those partnership obligations incurred by the other partners. Each partner is the agent for the other—capable of making decisions binding all other partners.

EXAMPLE Moe Degas, Robert Evans, and Millie Copper operated a furniture store. Degas issued a check to Cruise Manufacturing in payment of inventory purchased by the partnership. When the check "bounced," Cruise obtained a judgment against the partnership. When the partnership's assets proved insufficient to pay off the judgment, Cruise was able to move against Copper personally and seize her personal bank account to satisfy the deficiency.

Note that partners do have a right of contribution (reimbursement) from other partners to mitigate (reduce) damages. In addition, because the death, bankruptcy, or expulsion of a partner in accordance with the terms of the partnership agreement terminates the partnership, potential participants in this type of venture usually cast a wary eye on this form of doing business.

LIMITED PARTNERSHIPS

Limited partnerships, which are created by state laws, are formed by two or more individuals, of which at least one must be a general partner. Limited partnerships are governed by either the Uniform Limited Partnership Act (ULPA) or the Revised Uniform Limited Partnership Act (RULPA), which is the law in most states. Under both ULPA and RULPA, a limited partner's capital contribution may consist of cash or property, including a promissory note. The Acts differ, however, as to services. Under ULPA, a limited partner may not contribute services. Under RULPA, a limited partner may contribute both services rendered and the duty to perform services in the future, which will represent the partner's capital contribution.

Limited partners, as such, are generally not personally bound by the obligations of the firm, but their capital contributions are subject to the claims of outside creditors. A limited partner cannot obtain the return of her capital contribution until the claims of the creditors are either paid or safeguarded.

EXAMPLE If a limited partner contributes $10,000 and then, either before or after dissolution, withdraws it before the outside creditors are paid, such creditors may seek payment from the money withdrawn. However, by weight of court decisions, creditors must first exhaust their remedies against the general partners before seeking to hold the limited partner liable.

THE JOINT VENTURE

A joint venture is an arrangement formed for some temporary or limited purpose. Courts often have difficulty distinguishing between a joint venture and a partnership. Although joint ventures are usually formed for a single transaction while a partnership is usually formed for a series of continuing transactions, this distinction doesn't always apply because partnerships are sometimes formed to carry out an extended single transaction.

EXAMPLE 1 Sue Bally and Bill Cox pool their money and services in the purchase and resale of a certain real estate lot for their joint profit. This is a joint venture.

EXAMPLE 2 Ted Dark and Betty Grey pool their money and services to purchase a real estate lot for the construction of an apartment building. Upon completion of the project, they plan to dissolve the project. They have formed a partnership to carry out a single transaction.

Both limited partnerships and joint ventures are given the same tax treatment as a general partnership. This means that profits and losses flow through to each individual partner and are reported on his personal tax return. There is no tax at the partnership level.

THE LIMITED LIABILITY PARTNERSHIP (LLP)

The limited liability partnership (LLP) is a relatively new form of business entity that has grown rapidly in recent years. Under current state laws, the primary difference between a general partnership and a limited liability partnership is that in a limited liability partnership a partner is not liable for damages resulting from the negligent work of other partners or of the people supervised by other partners.

EXAMPLE Assume that an audit partner of a national accounting firm with headquarters in Chicago has been found liable for failure to perform a proper audit. A partner in the same firm located in Greensboro, North Carolina, who had no involvement in the Chicago audit, would not be liable for damages resulting from the negligent audit. Many large law and accounting firms have become LLPs in recent years. All of the "Big 6" accounting firms and a number of other national firms are LLPs.

THE FAMILY LIMITED PARTNERSHIP (FLP)

The use of family limited partnerships is an increasingly popular planning idea. In proper circumstances, a family limited partnership can provide meaningful tax benefits to a client in one or more of the areas of income, estate, and gift taxation, while also meeting the client's control objectives.

The term family limited partnership (FLP) is a term that has informally developed for a limited partnership under state law in which there is a family relationship among the general and limited partners.

An FLP can own any type of asset, including land and buildings, stock, life insurance, and cash. Thus, virtually any of the parents' assets can be transferred to a family limited partnership in return for partnership interests.

From a practical planning viewpoint, family limited partnerships planning tends to focus on substantial assets, like investment real estate and business interests, in which such benefits as lower valuation of assets for estate tax purposes, retention of control, and income-shifting to lower income persons are important. The tax benefits of forming an FLP will be discussed in Chap. 11.

CORPORATIONS

There are many definitions of what a corporation is. Some call it an "artificial person" having certain legal functions, rights, and duties. Being an artificial person, it can only act through its directors, who are elected by the shareholders.

Advantages of a Corporation

1. Unlike a sole proprietorship or a partner in a partnership, shareholders enjoy limited liability. For example, if they each invest $5,000 into the corporation and it eventually fails, they have lost no more than the amount invested ($5,000). Furthermore, under the Internal Revenue Code, they can deduct up to $3,000 per year in stock losses on their personal tax

returns, with the balance carried over to future years for further deductibility. The corporation may also elect Section 1244 stock treatment, which permits substantial tax deductions for stock losses in excess of the $3,000 per year in case the corporation fails.

WARNING *This limitation is not absolute. In many states, corporate shareholders of small business corporations are personally liable for unpaid corporate wages. For example, under New York State Business Corporation Law, the ten largest shareholders are personally liable for the unpaid wages and salaries of corporate employees. This rule does not apply to publicly listed corporations.*

2. It may be formed for a variety of purposes, both profit and nonprofit. Note that the thrust of this book is a detailed discussion of only profit-motivated corporations.
3. Ownership of corporate stock may be freely transferred by sale or gift, subject only to certain corporate restrictions.

EXAMPLE James Arnett owns 200 shares of Phoenix Mfg. Corporation stock. The shares had a total fair market value of $20,000. He sold 100 shares for $30,000 to Charles Raitt and gave the remaining 100 shares to his daughter Ramona. The right to sell or gift away an ownership interest shares is not readily available when doing business as either a sole proprietorship or partnership.

4. The corporation enjoys unlimited life and remains unaffected by the death of a director, officer or shareholder, no matter what the size of the shareholder's ownership in the corporation.
5. The company may purchase, hold, and sell property in the corporate name.
6. The corporation enjoys great flexibility in selecting the methods it will use in raising capital.
7. The corporation has numerous tax advantages available to it, such as pension and profit-sharing and the election of S corporation status (see Chap. 11).
8. A corporate employee, even if there is only one, can receive workers' compensation, an insur-

ance benefit not available to a self-employed person operating as a sole proprietor. This feature provides a strong incentive for a person to incorporate and operate as a single-shareholder corporation.

Disadvantages of a Corporation

1. The corporation is an expensive way of doing business. The cost varies based upon the amount and type of stock to be authorized and issued, the size of the planned corporation, the amount of business done, and the type of labor force needed. In addition, initial incorporation costs, including filing fees, organization taxes, and legal and accounting expenses, can be costly.
2. Shareholders have limited liability in most cases. This limited liability is not absolute and a corporate shareholder can still be liable for the full price of his corporate stock if the stock was originally purchased at a discount. As previously stated, shareholders are also liable in most states for unpaid wages.
3. The corporation is subject to greater governmental regulation and control than any other form of doing business. There are more rules and restrictions that must be followed.
4. The corporation is subject to double taxation, once at the corporate level, and again at the shareholder level when a distribution of profits, called dividends, are made to shareholders. However, the Internal Revenue Code offers certain tax breaks, such as the S corporation election, that can reduce and even eliminate taxes at the corporate level.
5. Majority shareholders (persons owing most of the shares) may be in a position to make business decisions that are not in the best interests of the minority shareholders. This danger is greater in close corporations that have three to five shareholders that may have different ideas about running the corporation and what product or services to sell.
6. The right to influence corporate matters by owning voting shares may be reduced where there is a widespread or increased ownership of corporate stock.

7. Management and control of the corporation rests with the duly elected directors and officers and are, thus, separate from the shareholders who are the true owners of the corporation.

8. The corporation is not protected by the Fifth Amendment's guarantee against self-incrimination. This privilege is purely a personal one available only to individuals.

9. Corporate operations are governed both by state law and the articles of incorporation, or charter of the corporation. Thus, a corporation may be liable for ultra vires acts (i.e., those not authorized by the corporate charter). It is essential that the lawyer who forms the corporation write the corporate charter in the broadest operating terms possible.

The Risks of Doing Business as a Corporation

There are several disadvantages to forming a corporation. The limited liability of a shareholder might limit the amount of credit that the corporation might be able to borrow. If the corporation has few shareholders, the majority shareholders have the ability to make decisions that may not be in the best interest of the minority shareholders. If the corporation is publicly traded, voting rights might prove insignificant due to the widespread ownership. Management of a corporation is in the hands of the directors and, therefore, separate from the shareholders who are the true owners. A corporation is subject to the laws of any state in which it does business.

OBSERVATION *A partnership may be treated as a corporation for federal income tax purposes if it possesses a number of corporate tax features. The Internal Revenue Code lists the following corporate tax traits:*

1. Associates (i.e., shareholders or partners);
2. A joint profit motive;
3. Continuity of life;
4. Centralized management;
5. Limited liability for corporate debts;
6. Free transferability of interests.

Because the first two characteristics are common to both partnerships and corporations, a partnership must possess at least three out of the last four corporate characteristics to be reclassified as an association and, therefore, taxable as a corporation. In 1996, the Internal Revenue Service (IRS) issued "check-the-box" proposed rules that provide a simplified elective procedure for firms to be classified for federal tax purposes as partnerships, even if they have corporate characteristics.

Regardless of these many handicaps, the corporation remains the safest form of doing business. One of the greatest advantages of doing business as a corporation is that it permits individuals who are stockholders to carry on business for profit without subjecting their personal assets to unlimited liability if the corporation incurs debts that it cannot pay.

CHAPTER 3

How to Form a Partnership

WHO MAY BE A PARTNER

Under the UPA, any person, partnership, corporation, and any other association can be a partner. In a majority of states a corporation may be a partner. Two or more persons must expressly or impliedly agree (1) to carry on (2) as co-owners (3) a business for profit. The UPA does not actually define the term "partner" but it is obvious that a partner is a member of a partnership association. An infant (generally anyone under the age of 18 in most states) can be a partner, but only to the limited extent of the infant's legal ability to enter into a contract. Thus, most state laws permit an infant to withdraw his or her partnership investment subject to the claims of the partnership's creditors.

EXAMPLE The partnership of HMG consists of Tom Herbert and Jack Monsey, who are adults, and Lina Gable, an infant who is 17 years old. Each individual has contributed $10,000 in cash at the initial operating stages of the partnership for a total capital contribution of $30,000. Partnership liabilities total $50,000 when Gable decides to withdraw. Although the creditors' claims are in excess of the partnership's capital, Gable is only liable for $10,000, the amount of her original capital contribution.

The fiduciary character of the relationship between the partners and the risk of unlimited personal liability for the acts of the other partners within the scope of the partnership underscores the voluntary character of the firm. As discussed in Chap. 2, every partner is an *agent* of the partnership in dealing with third parties. Each partner is not subject to control in her day to day activities involving the partnership, yet each must abide by the operating and policy decisions reached by a majority of the partners.

OBSERVATION *Unless the partnership agreement states otherwise, no one can become a partner in a partnership without the express or implied consent of all of the partners.*

HAVE YOU CONSIDERED THE RISKS OF BEING A PARTNER? *Since the chain of partnership is no stronger than its weakest link, it might be prudent to ask yourself whether you would make a dependable partner. Some questions to ask yourself are as follows:*

1. Do you have the financial ability to withstand financial reverses?
2. What are the financial resources of your prospective partners?
3. What is your age and what are the ages of the other partners? Note that death dissolves a partnership.
4. Are your partners trustworthy? Do you trust them to handle large amounts of capital including your own? Do you feel comfortable allowing them to borrow funds for which you may be held solely accountable?

5. What is your business acumen and skill? Do not confuse these vital traits with enthusiasm, which although commendable, is not a satisfactory substitute for competence.

6. Do you believe that you and your partners have the personalities required to get along? Can you tolerate dissent? Many partnerships are formed with the best intentions only to dissolve when dissent is viewed as disloyalty to the financial goals of the partnership.

TYPES OF PARTNERS

Partners may be classified as general, secret, silent, dormant, and nominal.

General Partner

A general (or active partner) is one who takes an active part in the management of the partnership and is subject to unlimited liability to partnership creditors. General partners may also have membership in a special or limited partnership.

Secret (or Undisclosed) Partner

A secret partner is one who actually participates in the management of the partnership but whose connection with the firm is not publicly disclosed. Third parties may hold a secret partner liable like any other general partner.

EXAMPLE Sloan Simpson and Harry Bartlett form a computer company to be conducted in Simpson's name. Simpson buys parts on credit from a seller who knows nothing of the partnership. Later the firm fails. The seller, on learning the facts, may hold Bartlett, as well as Simpson, liable.

A Silent Partner

A silent partner does not share in the management of the partnership. Unless he is also a special partner, he is still subject to unlimited liability for firm obligations.

Dormant Partner

A dormant, or sleeping partner, is one who is both secret and inactive. Upon discovery of his connection with the firm, his liability to third parties is the same as that of a general partner. Note that being a dormant partner does not prevent him from taking part in managing the firm's business if he so chooses, unless he is prevented from active participation by the partnership agreement.

A Nominal Partner

A nominal partner is one who appears to the world as a partner and who may be charged with the liabilities of a partner whether or not he has an actual interest in the firm. A nominal partner is sometimes known as a *partner by estoppel*.

EXAMPLE Jack Marlboro loaned Vera Fay $50,000 for use in an air conditioning and heating business and sometimes gave her business advice. In return of this loan, Fay agreed to divide profits equally with Marlboro. The loan was to be used strictly for business purposes. Fay was to conduct the business in her name alone and paid herself $20,000 in salary annually for her services. Royal Manufacturing, Inc. furnished building materials to the business but was not paid. Royal, after learning of Marlboro's relationship, sued him for payment and won. Marlboro was held liable as a partner by estoppel even though an actual partnership relationship did not exist.

Subpartner

A subpartner is a person who forms a partnership with one of the partners to share in the profits and losses due the actual partner. The agreement is a joint venture rather than a partnership, and the subpartner does not become a member of the main firm. A subpartner is therefore not liable to the partnership's creditors.

WARNING *This arrangement may not be as harmless to the subpartner as it appears.*

EXAMPLE Dick Calvin, a wealthy individual, refused to become a partner in the Josephson Company. Instead, Calvin suggested that his daughter Henrietta join the Josephson firm and loaned her $10,000 as her share of the capital. An agreement was drawn up making Henrietta a partner. It was also understood that all of Henrietta's share of the partnership's profits would go to Calvin. In a subsequent lawsuit by Josephson's creditors for nonpayment of the partnership's debts, the so-called "subpartner" (Calvin), who owned the *entire interest*, was considered the real partner subject to unlimited personal liability.

A Limited Partner

A limited partner is a member of a limited partnership whose authority to act and liability are limited by law, in contrast to those of the general partners who are active members of such firm with unlimited personal liability. Limited partners, as such, are generally not personally bound by the obligations of the firm, but their capital contributions are subject to the claims of outside creditors. Unlike the ULPA, (discussed in Chap. 2), the RULPA provides that a limited partner who participates in the control of the business is liable only to persons who do business with the partnership with *actual knowledge* of the limited partner's participation. Liability may be imposed without actual knowledge of participation, however, if the limited partner exercises powers substantially the same as those of a general partner.

HOW TO SET UP YOUR PARTNERSHIP

The General Rule: No Formalities

There are no particular formalities for setting up a partnership. Unless a state law requires that the partnership be set up in a particular way, a simple agreement is all that is necessary. The express contract, setting out the exact terms of the partnership agreement, may be oral or in writing. Of course, an oral partnership agreement is a prescription for disaster in that there are no definite written guidelines that can be referred to in case of a dispute between the partners.

When a Written Agreement Is Necessary

Any partnership agreement that cannot be performed within the space of one year must be in writing in order to satisfy the statute of frauds. The statute of frauds is a name given to a group of laws relating to agreements that are unenforceable unless there is a written memorandum signed by all of the

parties. If no definite time is specified in the agreement, the partnership can be dissolved at any time.

CHOOSING THE FIRM'S NAME

Unless there is a state law governing the selection of a partnership name, a partnership need not have a firm name although it is customary to have one. Most partners generally use the last name of one or more partners, such as Sandra Jones and Willa Norton adopting the partnership name Jones and Norton. Most states do, however, have some restrictions. The name cannot be similar to another operating partnership due to the concern that the sole purpose of the name is to attract the customers of the existing company.

Most states permit the registration of a fictitious name (e.g., Weight Reduction Health Spa). Because the name does not reveal the actual names of the partners, state law usually requires that a certificate be filed with either some state official, or in the city county clerk's office where the main office of the partnership is located, listing the assumed name of the partnership together with the true names of all of the partners. If ownership of the business subsequently changes hands, such as where a partner sells her interest or a partner is added or withdraws, a new certificate must be filed. This requirement protects the public by providing an up-to-date record of all people doing business in the state or county under a fictitious name.

....

NOTE *A business name, as well as trademarks, can also be checked through several commercial databases. Federal and state registers are available through TRADEMARKSCAN© Online and CD-ROM (Published by Thomson and Thomson 1-800-692-8833) which is part of the DIALOG® database, an on-line service. Most major corporate and academic libraries, as well as many public libraries, offer DIALOG searches to their clients. DIALOG can be contacted at 1-800-3-DIALOG (1-800-334-2562), 1-415-858-3785, or 1-215-241-0131: FAX 1-415-858-7069.*
....

....
WARNING *Failure to file this certificate can result in fines, possible criminal charges, or both. Furthermore, the partnership itself may be prevented from enforcing its*

legal rights in a court of law. Of course, upon learning that a name filing for a partnership is required, the partnership can meet its obligation prior to starting any legal action on behalf of or against the partnership.

THE PARTNERSHIP AGREEMENT

Many partnerships, although financially successful, have failed for the lack of a full agreement among the partners in respect to matters that normally arise in the ordinary course of an operating partnership. The partnership agreement, sometimes called the articles of copartnership, should aim to resolve, at the outset, every possible point of difference. Among the common provisions are the following:

1. Names and addresses of all of the partners;
2. The name of the firm;
3. Nature, purpose, and scope of the partnership business;
4. Location of the principal place of business;
5. When the partnership is to take effect;
6. The duration (life) of the partnership;
7. The required capital contributions of each partner, whether it be in the form of cash, property, or services; if cash, amounts to be invested and when payable;
8. Procedures to be used when additional capital is needed;
9. Interest (and rate), if any, payable on capital or other contributions;
10. The duties of each partner;
11. How profits and losses are to be shared;
12. How profits are to be calculated;
13. The amount of drawings that each partner can make, and whether it is to be weekly, monthly, or annually;
14. Whether each partner is to get a salary;
15. How much time each partner must devote to the business;
16. Whether a partner is permitted to engage in any other nonpartnership business, and any limitations on these activities;
17. The authority among partners to act on behalf of the partnership;
18. Limitations, if any, upon authority of partners to bind the firm by commitments;

19. Designation of a bank and who shall have the authority to both sign and countersign checks;
20. Where the books and records are to be kept and that each partner shall have equal access to them;
21. Right, if any, of a partner to withdraw, under what conditions, and how notice to the other partners is to be given;
22. Dissolution: right to continue business upon withdrawal, death, disqualification or incapacity of any partner, with procedures as to the adjustment of such partner's interest;
23. What happens to the partnership's name in case of dissolution;
24. How goodwill, if any, is to be determined in the event of dissolution;
25. Administration of partnership property and affairs upon dissolution and the rights of a partner or partners to conduct the process;
26. Provision for arbitration, if any, in case of a dispute among the partners;
27. Any other provisions deemed important to the partnership.

Sample Partnership Agreement

The Partnership Agreement, in Appendix B, can be used when forming your partnership.

OBSERVATION *Regardless of the method of accomplishing the task—and the bottom-line concern is money—a partnership can remain vigorous and profitable only by periodically reviewing and addressing the changing financial and personal needs of the partners, the partnership, and its clients and customers.*

HOW TO AVOID THE UNINTENTIONAL PARTNERSHIP

Generally, courts look to the intent of the parties to determine whether they are operating as a partnership. Of course, when there is an express partnership agreement, or when the parties refer to themselves as partners, there is little difficulty in determining that a partnership exists. However, where the intent of the parties is unexpressed, or not made perfectly clear, unforeseen problems arise. In making a determination whether you are a partner in a partnership with all of its advantages and disadvantages, consider the following points that the courts have taken into account in making decisions.

1. **Title to Property.** Do you and other persons hold property jointly or as tenants in common? Jointly held property is ownership by two or more persons. On the death of a joint owner, the remaining owners take the share of the deceased owner. The last surviving owner takes complete ownership of the property. Tenancy in common is a form of ownership by two or more persons. The interest of each owner may be transferred or inherited, in which case the recipient becomes the tenant (or owner) in common with the others. The mere joint ownership of property, even if the owners share the profits earned from the jointly held property, does not create a partnership.

2. **Sharing of Gross Profits.** The sharing of gross profits, even when the property is jointly owned, does not create a partnership.

3. **Amount of Activity Involved.** How much energy is expended by each person may be indicative, but is not conclusive, that a partnership exists.

EXAMPLE 1 Due to an anticipated rise in the real estate market, Regina Martinson and Susan Lupo each contribute $10,000 to purchase land for eventual resale. Their degree of activity is minimal and cannot be deemed a partnership.

EXAMPLE 2 Paula Knudson and Carl Winters each contribute $10,000 to purchase ten acres of forest with the intent of clearing the land and building a condominium for eventual resale. The considerable degree of activity will most likely be deemed a partnership even if the parties did not intend such a legal classification.

4. **The Sharing of Profits in Repayment of a Loan.** If an individual loans money to a business in return for a share of the profits and takes back a note, the lender will be treated as a creditor and not as a partner.

EXAMPLE Harry Collins loans $10,000 to a business taking back a note requiring repayment at designated intervals. Collins will not be treated as a partner.

5. **An Agreement to Reimburse Against Losses.** Where two persons enter into a venture in which one reimburses the other against loss, the arrangement is not necessarily a partnership.

EXAMPLE Minna Zip loaned money to Hilda Yamada, a stock broker, for the purchase of common stock with the agreement that profits are to be divided equally but that all losses would be absorbed by Zip. This is not a partnership agreement but a contract of insurance against loss in return for the right to share in any possible profits.

As a general rule, the UPA states that there is no inference that a partnership has been created if an individual receives partnership profits as repayment for a debt, as wages as an employee, as rent to a landlord, as interest on a loan even if the interest varies with the profit of the business, or as payment of an annuity to a surviving spouse or representative of a deceased partner.

EXAMPLE Georgina Haupt, a landlord, signed a lease with Restaurant Associates permitting them to rent space for one year. Rent is to be 10 percent of gross restaurant receipts from the sale of food with a minimal rental per month of $1,000. Although the rent is based upon the amount of the restaurant's monthly sales, Haupt is not considered to be a partner.

The above discussion illustrates how one can avoid being classified as an unintentional partner subject to unlimited personal liability in case of a possible lawsuit against a business.

WATCH OUT *The general rule is that a sharing of net profits, or advancing monies in return for participation in management, may result in an individual being classified as a partner in a partnership.*

EXAMPLE Roland Carron advances money to a business *without* demanding a note for the amount of the advance. Repayment is contingent upon profits. There is a strong inference that the loan was intended as an investment thereby making Carron a partner.

PARTNERSHIP BY ESTOPPEL

A person who appears to all the world that she is a partner in an enterprise may be charged with the liabilities of a partner whether or not she has an actual interest in the firm. This unintended partner is called a *partner by estoppel* and can create unforeseen personal liability for the individual who, through her unintentional negligence, holds herself out as a partner.

EXAMPLE Roberta Henshaw and Louis Blake are doing business as the partnership of Henshaw and Blake. Wishing to secure a potentially profitable government contract, they approach Fred Banner, who knows how the governmental bureaucracy works, and ask for his advice. Banner tells them that if they give him $10,000 and agree to put his name on the partnership's letterhead, directly underneath the names of Henshaw and Blake, he will do his best to secure a government contract for aircraft parts. Shortly thereafter, Banner secures a government contract, but the partnership produces parts of inferior quality that results in a lawsuit against them. Banner cannot escape liability because his name is on the partnership's letterhead making him liable as a partner whether the government was misled or not.

How to Avoid the Possibility of an Unintended Partner

It would be very advisable that, when hiring a new employee, the contract be written so that there is no question that you have hired an employee and have not created an unintended partnership. The following are some important points to consider when hiring that new employee:

1. The contract should state that the individual has been hired as an employee and not as a partner;

2. Any profits to be received by the employee are salary and/or bonus, and are not to be treated as a share of profits;

3. The employee is not required to contribute capital or to absorb any losses;

4. The employee is to receive a guaranteed weekly salary even if the partnership has an operating loss for the period;

5. The employee's name is not to appear on the partnership's letterhead in any way so as to suggest that she is a partner; and/or

6. The employee is not permitted to hold herself out in any way as being a partner.

USING THE INTERNET TO FIND A PARTNER

Many small companies are now using the Internet and on-line services to drum up new business, but some entrepreneurs are also using their computers to find like-minded potential partners. This has occurred because on-line communication is both efficient and effective. Internet and on-line services allow users to post messages and electronically converse with persons who have similar business interests. Of course, partners who initially met on-line say that they first developed face-to-face relationships before investing their time and money together. The drawback to this type of approach is that an individual may meet a principal who lives in a different city. Such long-distance partnerships are difficult because any new business partnership requires constant and spontaneous communication between partners.[1]

How to Arrange A Prudent Meeting With Potential Partners After Contact on the Internet

In today's somewhat unsettled society, it might prove wise to check out a potential partner that you plan to meet face to face before having a face-to-face meeting. One way is to check his personal profile on the Internet service that you are using. America OnLine, as well as other online services, have a personal profile of all of its customers. Of course, when checking this profile, you must always consider that

---

[1] "Entrepreneurs Connect With Each Other Electronically," *The Wall Street Journal*, July 2, 1996, pg. B2.

the information supplied to the online service might not be true and even fraudulent.

Secondly, make the initial contact over the phone, preferably not your own home phone, and question his business background and professional qualifications, if the proposed business requires a certain type of professional expertise. If you find his business acumen lacking, or something about him such as the sound of his voice is not to your liking, it is suggested that you do not pursue the meeting.

Should you decide to meet this individual in person, tell someone the name of the person that you are meeting, where you are going to meet, the time of the meeting, and a number where you can be reached. Arrange to meet in a public place such as a restaurant and not in some private hotel room or secluded area such as in a park. A word of caution to the wise is sufficient.

USING THE INTERNET TO DEVELOP ECONOMIC OPPORTUNITIES

Cities and states are now using the Internet to escalate their competition for new businesses and investment. More and more economic development agencies are now boasting on line about their incentive packages to attract companies to relocate to their areas. The World Wide Web's interactive nature allows companies and individuals looking for facts about different regions to get information that only used to be available, if at all, through the mail and in person visits.

Some of the leading publications in the business of relocating firms have made their way onto the Web and offer firms, such as partnerships, another source of information. *Area Development*, a magazine that deals with planning company relocations, has a site with reprints of its articles, as well as state-by-state economic profiles and a listing of state tax incentives. Site Net, a venture of *Site Selections* magazine, has a comprehensive site that allows corporate relocation planners to learn more about regions. The site also features a useful "tool kit" that provides a checklist for picking an optimum site,

along with in-depth lease information. Companies interested in learning more about the demographics of American counties and cities may find the University of Virginia Social Sciences Data Center's site useful. It offers extensive marketplace information that can be searched by more than 200 variables, including age groups and household incomes.

Unfortunately, many states and cities have not made good use of the interactive nature of the Web and have basically published their brochures on the Internet. As more and more businesses use this medium for their initial scouting, sites that are not current or well designed will lose traffic and business.[2]

Where to Go

- *AREA DEVELOPMENT* MAGAZINE
  http://www.area-development.com/
- ARIZONA DEPT. OF COMMERCE
  http://www.state.az.us/ep/commhome.shtml
- CITY OF SAN CARLOS, CALIF.
  http://.ci.san-carlos-ca.us/
- COMMERCIAL REAL ESTATE NETWORK
  http://.crenet.com
- COTE D'AZUR BUSINESS NET
  http://www.cad.fr/
- DELAWARE ECONOMIC DEVELOPMENT OFFICE
  http://www.state. de.us/govern/agencies
- ECONOMIC DEVELOPMENT PARTNERSHIP OF ROANAKE VALLEY VA
  http://www.roanoke.org/
- FULD & CO. WEB WARRIORS AWARDS
  http://www.fuld.com
- HOMEBUYER'S FAIR INTERNATIONAL SALARY CALCULATOR
  http://www.homefaircom/homefair/cmr/salcalc.html
- INTERACTIVE-ECONOMIC DEVELOPMENT NETWORK
  http://.iedn.com/iedn/business/
- *MONEY* MAGAZINE'S BEST CITIES FEATURE
  http://www.moneycom/

---

[2]"Taking In the Sites: Cities and States Go Cyber In Hunt for New Business," *The New York Times*, February 17, 1997, pg. 47.

- **NEW YORK CITY**
  http://www.ci.nyc.ny.us/
- **NEW YORK INFORMATION TECHNOLOGY CENTER AT 55 BROAD STREET**
  http://www.55broad.com/
- **OHIO STATE GOVERNMENT**
  http://www.ohiobiz.com

- *SITE SELECTIONS* **MAGAZINE'S SITE NET**
  http://.conway.comfindex.htm
- **SOUTH CAROLINA DEPT. OF COMMERCE**
  http://www.state.sc.us/commerce
- **UNIVERSITY OF VIRGINIA COUNTY AND CITY DATA BOOKS**
  http://www.lib.virginia.edu/socsci/ccdb/

CHAPTER 4

Who Owns the Property of a Partnership?

INTRODUCTION

Once a partnership is created, each partner will make his capital contribution according to the terms of the partnership agreement. Simultaneously, a decision must then be made as to which property belongs to the partnership and which belongs to the individual partners. After deciding what property will be owned by the partnership, the rights of each partner in the property must then be determined.

CLASSIFICATIONS OF PARTNERSHIP PROPERTY

Partnership Capital

Partnership capital consists of the cash and property contributed by each individual partner for the purposes of carrying out partnership business.

EXAMPLE 1 Dina Curtis and Mark Heller form a partnership. Curtis contributes cash of $10,000 while Mark contributes land with a fair market value (what the property is currently worth) of $30,000. The total partnership capital is $40,000.

EXAMPLE 2 Donald Olin and Margaret Simms form a partnership. Olin contributes cash of $25,000 while Margaret will merely contribute her services and skills. The total partnership capital is $25,000.

Partnership Property

Partnership property includes not only the initial capital contributed by all of the partners but all property subsequently acquired by the firm, either with partnership funds or through the performance of services and profits accumulated in the business.

EXAMPLE At the beginning of January 199X, Henry Olden and Rita Elks form a partnership with each partner contributing $1,000. During 199X, the partnership earns a profit of $30,000 and each partner withdraws $5,000. Partnership ending capital is $22,000 calculated as follows:

Initial capital contribution:		
Henry Olden	$1,000	
Rita Elks	1,000	$ 2,000
Profit for year		30,000
		$32,000
Less: Drawings		
Henry Olden	$5,000	
Rita Elks	5,000	10,000
Ending Capital		$22,000

Each partner still has reported ending capital of $11,000.

WHO ACTUALLY OWNS THE PARTNERSHIP PROPERTY?

Unless a partnership agreement states otherwise, there is no limitation on the kinds of property that the partnership can own. Unless there is an agreement to the contrary, property bought with partnership funds belong to the partnership. Secondly, if the partners have bought or acquired property with the *sole intention* of devoting it to partnership business, it is considered to be partnership property. Title to partnership property may be in the name of one or more partners, individually, who hold the property for the partnership, or it may be held in the partnership name. This rule applies whether the property is real (land and buildings) or personal (anything tangible and movable, such as trucks and office equipment). Title to property so acquired can also be conveyed only in the partnership name.

EXAMPLE Wanda Tillis and Enid Hazelton formed a partnership and using partnership cash, bought land and buildings for $100,000. Enid subsequently bought, with her own personal funds, office equipment for $15,000 with the intent of using it in the partnership's operations. The total property of the partnership is $115,000 consisting of land, buildings, and office equipment. The fact that Enid used her own personal funds to purchase the equipment does not detract from the rule that since her intention was that it be used in the partnership, it is to be treated as a partnership asset.

How to Avoid Those Messy Disputes as to Who Owns Partnership Property

Frequently, the intent of the partners is not clear as to whether an individual partner or the partnership itself owns specific partnership property. The following are some rules that beginning partners should consider:

1. Where do the funds to acquire the property come from? The UPA states that unless the partners intend otherwise, property purchased with partnership funds belongs to the partnership.
2. Who holds title to the property? If the partnership holds title, it is strong and convincing evidence that the property belongs to the partnership. Ownership in the partner's own name might indicate otherwise. Note that

sometimes a partner may hold partnership property in her own name as a matter of convenience thereby clouding the issue of ownership.

3. Has the asset been recorded on the books and records of the partnership? An accounting entry on the partnership's books is prima facie evidence (the best evidence) that the partnership owns the asset.
4. Is the property required for the successful operation of the partnership? The actual use of the property by the partnership usually means that the property belongs to the partnership. Furthermore, the fact that the property was improved, maintained, and insured at partnership expense is further evidence that the property belongs to the partnership.

What to Do

To avoid potential disputes, it is advisable to include a statement in the partnership agreement indicating that all assets acquired with partnership funds are to be treated as assets of the partnership. Secondly, what property, if any, belonging to individual partners is to be made available for partnership use. Finally, before a partner is to purchase assets for the partnership from her own personal funds, there is to be written notice to the partnership of the partner's intent to buy such asset(s) for the partnership and that the partner expects to be reimbursed by the partnership when she transfers title to the property to the partnership.

THE RIGHT OF A PARTNERSHIP TO OWN AND CONVEY LAND AND BUILDINGS

The UPA allows a partnership to own and convey land and buildings, called "real property." Where title is in the names of all of the partners, a transfer of title by all of the partners passes all rights to such property. However, a partnership might find it more convenient to permit the holding of title in one or more of the partner's names. Where title to such property is in the name of the firm, conveyance by one or more partners is voidable at the option of remaining partners provided that title to the property has not passed from the purchaser to an innocent third party.

EXAMPLE Thorson Timber Company, a lumber partnership consisting of ten partners, owned 10,000 acres of hardwood trees in northern Montana. Tex Rider, one of the partners, sold 1,000 acres to Clark Boone, a land speculator. If Rider was authorized to transfer the land, the sale is valid. However, if it is shown that Rider made the sale without authority, the sale may be cancelled.

Where title to the real property is in the names of all of the partners, a transfer of title by all of the partners passes all rights and title to the property.

In most states, a partner cannot mortgage the partnership's real estate without unanimous consent. However, in a minority of states, a single partner may create a mortgage (a lien) on the partnership's real property to make sure that a partnership's current and possible future debt is repaid.

THE RIGHT OF A PARTNER TO USE PARTNERSHIP PROPERTY

Under the UPA, a partner's ownership interest in any specific partnership asset is generally not that of an outright owner. Instead the partner holds the property as a *tenant (owner) in partnership*. This means that the partner is subject to the following rules:

1. The partner has an equal right with all the other partners to possess and use the property only for partnership business but cannot use the property for other purposes without the permission of the other partners.
2. A partner cannot assign (transfer) his or her right in specific partnership property unless it is part of an agreement made by all of the partners to assign their rights in the same property.
3. A creditor of an individual partner cannot, by lawsuit, reach that partner's right in specific partnership property. That is, a partner may not voluntarily or involuntarily assign his interest in specific partnership property. However, the firm's assets can be seized to satisfy the claims of unpaid *partnership* creditors.

OBSERVATION *To satisfy a personal debt of a partner, a judgement creditor can ask a court to issue a charging order against the debtor-partner's partnership interest. A charging order, which is a legal lien, entitles the judgement creditor to be paid out of the debtor-partner's partnership profits. The charging order does not make the judgment creditor a partner in the partnership.*

4. Upon the death of a partner, her right in specific partnership property transfers to the remaining surviving partners. Upon the death of the last remaining partner, that partner's rights vests in her legal representative. Such surviving partner or her legal representative has no right to hold the property for anything except partnership purposes.

OBSERVATION *A tenancy in partnership is subject to the claims of partnership creditors and cannot be "partitioned" (broken apart) between the partners unless the partnership's liabilities and other claims are paid first.*

EXAMPLE Cynthia Bacon and Jose Cruz are partners in an auto repair shop. Partnership property includes the building (contributed by Bacon) in which the shop is located and repair equipment (bought by Cruz with his own funds and contributed to the partnership). Bacon and Cruz hold the property as a tenancy in partnership. Both parties can use the property for partnership purposes, but neither has the right to use it for personal purposes without the consent of the other. Neither can they independently sell or otherwise assign any interest in specific partnership property (for example, an electronic diagnostic machine) to a third party. Bacon and Cruz, acting together, however, could transfer title to specific property. Personal creditors of Bacon or Cruz may not, by court order, possess or seize specific partnership property to satisfy an unpaid personal debt. Creditors of the partnership could, however, force a seizure and sale of the specific property to satisfy an outstanding partnership debt. On Bacon's death, title to the partnership property vests in Cruz. Bacon's estate receives no interest in the specific property now vested in Cruz, who may possess the property only for partnership purposes.

WHAT HAPPENS WHEN A PARTNER ASSIGNS HER INTEREST IN THE FIRM?

Although a partner cannot transfer specific items of partnership property without the authority of the other partners, a partner's interest may be freely assigned. The assignee (recipient) cannot become a partner without the consent of all of the other partners. The assignee is only entitled to receive the assigning partner's share of profits for the period of time stated in the agreement creating the assignment. Finally, the assignee cannot participate in management nor can the assignee inspect the partnership's books and records.

Relations Between Partners

FIDUCIARY OBLIGATIONS OF EACH PARTNER

Each partner is a general agent of every other partner in the firm for the purpose of carrying on the partnership business. Hence, each partner (or copartner) owes a fiduciary duty to the partnership and must use her powers only for partnership goals and not for the personal benefit of the individual partner. All profits earned by the partner within the scope or range of the partnership's business belong to the partnership. The UPA requires that all partners must account to the partnership for any benefits or "secret" profits derived by the partner from any transaction connected with the conduct, formation, or liquidation of the partnership or from any use of partnership property. Prohibited conduct includes using or diverting partnership property for a partner's personal gain, acquiring a partnership asset without the actual consent of the partners, competing with the partnership in a similar business, failing to disclose to the partnership personal business deals that pose a potential conflict of interest, and any other matters that might hurt the partnership. Thus, no partner can take unfair advantage of her copartners.

EXAMPLE 1 Helen Beal and Ben North operated a real estate partnership for both buying and selling land and buildings. The partnership, by agreement, was to end on December 31, 19XX. On December 15, 19XX, Beal learned of land in a downtown business area that could be purchased at a bargain price. Beal realized the possibility of buying the property and making a quick sale to Esterhazy, a customer of the partnership who was looking for just this type of property. Not wishing to share any potential profits, Beal waited until January 5, 19XX, just five days after the partnership ended, and then purchased the property on her own behalf. Beal then resold it to Esterhazy, keeping all of the profits for herself. When North learned of the transaction, he sued Beal for half of the profits. **HELD:** North could recover half the profits. The relationship of one partner to another is one of total trust. Since the information regarding the downtown property was learned during the course of the prior partnership's business, Beal was required to share such information with North for their mutual profit.

EXAMPLE 2 Norman Devorak and Barry Mailer were partners in the DM partnership for ten years. Mailer's duties regarding the partnership included complete control over the books and records. Devorak later discovered that Mailer had diverted partnership assets to his own personal use and used the monies to purchase stocks and bonds. Mailer claimed that the assets belonged to him personally but was unable to produce supporting personal books and records. **HELD:** Devorak could recover all of the profits for the partnership. Where a partner has dealt with the partnership's assets so as to raise a question of possible wrongdoing, it is the partner's responsibility to show where the assets came from. Having failed to do so, Mailer created the impression of having breached his fiduciary duty and must account to the partnership for all assets that appear to have been purchased with partnership funds.

EXAMPLE 1 Two out of five partners quit an existing partnership before the term of their partnership agreement expired. They then formed their own partnership and began taking customers from their former partnership. Both partners of the new partnership have breached their fiduciary duties to their former partnership and are liable for damages.

If all of the partners are deceased, the legal representative of the last surviving partner is legally bound, as a fiduciary, to liquidate the partnership and to distribute the partnership's assets to the survivors of the deceased partners.

HOW TO SHARE PROFITS AND LOSSES

In the absence of an agreement stating how profits and losses are to be shared, partners share profits and losses equally. The sharing arrangement generally bears no relationship to the amount of capital that each partner is required to contribute.

EXAMPLE John Quant, Melanie Brown, and Tony Arcadi own The Plumbing Outlet, electing to operate as a partnership. Quant contributes $10,000, Brown $6,000, and Arcadi $2,000. The partnership agreement is silent as to the division of profits. The partners will share profits equally.

The distribution of a partnership's profits will be discussed in Chap. 9.

MUST A PARTNERSHIP PAY SALARIES TO PARTNERS?

Profit sharing is the primary motive for forming a partnership. The sharing of profits does not mean the payment of salaries.

General Rule: No Salaries

Unless the partners agree otherwise, a partner is not entitled to any salary for services rendered to the partnership, even if the partner's efforts are more than the services provided by the other partners. A partner's right to share in the profits of the partnership is considered to be the total payment. The "no salary rule" must be followed even if one partner is forced to assume additional work that was not intended or contemplated when the partners originally entered into the partnership agreement.

EXAMPLE Joan Zorn and Jane Freed are partners in a bookstore. If Zorn, because of Freed's illness, is forced to assume additional responsibilities, the extra work assumed will not entitle her to additional salary.

Exception: Winding Up by Surviving Partner

If the partnership is forced to dissolve because of the death or physical or mental incapacity of the other partners, the last surviving partner is entitled to a salary for her services in winding up partnership affairs.

Breach of Agreement by Partner to Work for Partnership

The partnership agreement usually requires that all partners, unless otherwise agreed, must devote their full time to the partnership's business. If a partner fails to live up to her duties, she may be charged in an accounting for any losses suffered by the partnership. This includes any costs incurred in replacing the services of the delinquent partner, as well as any other losses that are incurred by the partner's failure to perform her partnership duties.

EXAMPLE Lana Barclay, Ted Holmes, and Regina Gooden formed an advertising partnership. It is agreed that Barclay will supervise the creative department in the firm while the other partners are to pursue new business and assist current clients in creating their advertising plans. Barclay always comes in late, and at times shows up drunk, thereby causing an estimated $100,000 loss in advertising project revenues. Holmes and Gooden are, therefore, forced to hire Victor Newell to take over Barclay's duties. Holmes and Gooden may charge Barclay for the $100,000 loss in revenues, as well as Newell's salary.

REIMBURSEMENT AND INDEMNITY FOR EXPENDITURES

A partner has the right to be reimbursed for all reasonable expenses incurred in the ordinary conduct of the partnership's business or for acts necessary to preserve and protect partnership assets. In addition, should a partner be forced to pay more than his share of the partnership's obligations, he may seek contribution from the other partners to the extent that he has paid more than his share according to the partnership agreement.

HOW TO TREAT A PARTNER'S ADVANCES

Unless required by the partnership agreement, any advances to the partnership are to be treated as loans to the partnership. The advance makes the partner a creditor of the firm who is entitled to interest from the date of the loan.

A PARTNER'S RIGHTS UPON DISSOLUTION

Upon dissolution of the partnership, a partner is entitled to be repaid her contribution whether consisting of advances, capital contributions, or unpaid profits and losses. This right is, however, second to the rights of the firm's creditors who must be paid their claims first.

EXAMPLE Oleg Yang and Nina Manley form a partnership. Yang contributed $10,000 while Manley contributed only services. The partnership agreement stated that they were to be equal partners. A year later, the partners agreed to dissolve. At the time of dissolution, partnership creditors are owed $8,000. Assuming that there is $23,000 in the partnership at the date of dissolution, the creditors will first be paid their $8,000, Yang is entitled to the return of his capital contribution of $10,000, and the partners will equally divide the remaining $5,000.

A PARTNER'S RIGHTS TO INSPECT THE PARTNERSHIP'S BOOKS AND RECORDS

Every partner has a right to receive information concerning the operation of the partnership. Failure to provide each partner with any required information acquired in the course of the firm's business can be treated as a breach of the partner's fiduciary duty. The partnership's books and records, including copies of its tax returns, must be kept at the partnership's principal place of business so as to give any interested partner the right to inspect or copy any important information. Partners are also free to select another place of business for keeping the firm's books and records should the principal place prove inconvenient.

LEGAL ACTIONS BETWEEN PARTNERS

General Rule: No Action at Law

As a general rule, no partner has the right to sue the partnership at law, nor may one partner sue another on matters relating to the partnership. This rule exists because a partner suing a partnership would, in effect, be suing himself.

EXAMPLE Jed Colson, Kent Jeeves, and Vera Stanton are partners in the CJS partnership, which sells fruits and vegetables. Stanton maintains a separate computer equipment and servicing company. Stanton sells CJS $10,000 in equipment but is not paid. Stanton cannot maintain an action for payment because, in effect, she would be suing herself.

There is one exception to the rule that one partner cannot sue another in matters pertaining to the partnership's business. One partner can sue another if the issue involves a single simple matter, such as the repayment of a single sum of money loaned by one partner to another.

Proceeding With an Action for an Accounting

A formal (meaning standard) accounting, whereby the partnership's assets are used to pay outside creditors and the remaining amounts are distributed to the partners, is both costly and inconvenient. Therefore, a formal accounting is not granted by the courts prior to the dissolution of the partnership. Dissolution may be required for a variety of reasons that will be discussed in Chap. 7. A partner can obtain an accounting *without* a formal accounting where she has been wrongfully excluded from participation in the management of the partnership, when the partnership agreement so provides, when the partner has obtained secret profits from her participation in the firm's business, or where there are just and reasonable circumstances requiring that an accounting be made.

THE PARTNER'S RIGHT TO WORKERS' COMPENSATION

A partner is an employer and not an employee. Therefore, a partner is not permitted to claim workers' compensation for injuries received within the scope of the partnership's business.

CHAPTER 6 Relations of Partners to Third Parties

IN GENERAL: HOW THE PARTNERS BIND THE PARTNERSHIP

Every partner is an agent of every other partner and for the partnership when acting within the scope of the firm's business. This means that not only are the acts of the partners binding on all of the partners when actually performed, but also those acts executed within the apparent (obvious) scope of the firm's business, even those not necessarily authorized. Thus, agreements among the partners fixing their duties and liabilities, and imposing limitations on their authority to deal with outside third parties are not binding on outside third parties unless the parties are aware of such limitations and have agreed to them.

EXAMPLE Joe Dingle, Hanna Burns, and Gina Hobby were partners in DBH, a retail clothing partnership. The partners agreed among themselves that only Dingle, who has the best experience as to how to buy quality clothing at reduced prices, would deal with all clothing manufacturers. Unaware of this partnership agreement, Kay Dickenson, a clothing manufacturer, signed a contract with Gina Hobby to manufacture a special line of women's clothing at a special price. While Dingle and Burns might object, the limitation of Hobby's authority is not binding on the manufacturer because she had no knowledge of the limitation. Of course, both Dingle and Burns can hold Hobby liable for possible damages and may even seek to dissolve the partnership should Hobby's continuous unauthorized acts prove damaging to the profitability of the firm.

Generally speaking, unless otherwise agreed, authority to conduct a transaction also includes the authority to do acts that are implied, incidental, or are reasonably necessary to accomplish a partnership objective.

EXAMPLE Norris Yelzin, a partner in a real estate partnership, with the authority of his other three partners, attempted to sell a vacant piece of land to a client. Yelzin has the implied authority to clean up the lot so as to make it more attractive to prospective purchasers.

Whether a partner has the express, actual or apparent authority to enter into a contract also depends on whether the partnership is a *trading* or *nontrading* partnership. A trading partnership is one that is in the business of selling goods from inventory. In this type of partnership, a partner has the apparent authority to borrow money on behalf of the partnership. The theory is that broader authority is required to finance the purchase and sale of inventory, borrow money, and to sign checks and notes.

In a nontrading partnership (one providing professional services such as law and accounting) a partner does not have the apparent authority to borrow money but may be expressly authorized to do so in the partnership agreement.

Note that as more nontrading partnerships expand their commercial activities into other areas, the difference between trading and nontrading partnerships has become less important.

Not only are partners liable for debts and other legal obligations incurred within the actual or apparent scope of the partnership's business, they are also liable for all negligent acts committed during the partnership's normal business. Each partner can be held both individually and jointly liable with all of the other partners for all of these acts.

EXAMPLE 1 Phil Sparks and Doreen Winter operated an investment firm. Ken Tone, a client of the firm, wanted to borrow $100,000 from a bank. He, therefore, asked Sparks to give him a statement that Tone had $100,000 in stocks and bonds on deposit with the partnership that Tone could show to the bank in order to obtain the loan. In actuality, Tone only had $10,000 on deposit. However, in order to please Tone and without telling Winters, Sparks gave Tone a statement saying that he had on deposit the $100,000 amount. Tone obtained but subsequently failed to repay the loan. Upon discovering the facts, the bank may hold the partnership liable for the fraud committed by Sparks while acting as a partner.

EXAMPLE 2 Dean Salmon, Joe Cadence, and Tina Moore operated the SCM Retail Office Supply Store as a partnership. One day, Salmon mopped the floor leaving a wet spot behind as he worked. Mary Quatro, a customer, slipped on the wet spot and broke a leg. She sued the partnership claiming personal injuries and won. Salmon's negligence, committed within the normal course of the partnership's business, caused Quatro's injuries.

Partners are not, however, liable for crimes committed within the scope of the partnership's business unless they aided and participated in such illegal acts.

EXAMPLE The accounting partnership of Anita Bradley and Olivia Johns was one that specialized in tax law. Without the knowledge of Bradley, Johns prepared a fraudulent tax return for a client. Upon subsequent examination by the Internal Revenue Service, the fraud was detected and Johns was accused of participating in the scheme. Bradley would not be held liable since she was unaware of the fraudulent scheme and did not aid in the preparation of the tax return.

ACTUAL AUTHORITY

Authorized in Agreement
The specific duties and responsibilities of each partner generally are fixed by partnership agreement.

EXAMPLE Three partners, Ray Marks, Stacy Duke, and Roger Candy, form a partnership to operate a restaurant. The partners agree that Candy will hire all employees. Thus, any third parties hired by Candy are entitled to assume that the partner is authorized to hire them and are entitled to hold the partnership liable for the compensation promised.

Majority Vote
In the event that the partnership agreement does not specifically authorize any individual to do a particular act or acts, then the majority vote of all of the partners governs.

EXAMPLE Susan Benis, Henry Calhoun, and Herbert Rice operate a retail lighting fixture store. Both Benis and Calhoun feel that the store is in need of modernization, but Rice objects claiming that it will cost too much. Benis and Calhoun claim that majority rules and proceed to remodel the store. Can they do so? **HELD:** Yes. This is an ordinary matter of partnership business and absent any specific provision in the partnership agreement, majority vote governs.

If a vote is tied, the action being considered generally is considered to be defeated. A great danger to a working partnership is the operating deadlock. In this dangerous situation, an equal number of partners are involved in a tie vote that cannot be broken despite several attempts to do so. This situation may prevent the partnership from functioning.

· ·

What This Means to You *To avoid a deadlock among the partners regarding ordinary business decisions, the partnership agreement should contain a statement to the effect that "......................(name of partner) shall have the sole discretion to .... [hire and fire employees, make purchases up to $............... (amount)] on behalf of the partnership."*

· ·

Unanimous Vote

The UPA states that unless otherwise agreed to or unless all of the other partners have abandoned the business, a unanimous vote is required to do the following:

1. **Assign partnership property for the benefit of creditors.** An assignment for the benefit of creditors (called an "ABC") is a voluntary transfer of all the debtor's assets to another person in trust who liquidates the assets and distributes the proceeds to the creditors. Generally, the debtor, or partnership, is not fully discharged if outstanding debts remain after the distribution of the partnership's assets.
2. **Dispose of the goodwill of the firm.**
3. **Do any other act that would make it impossible to carry on the ordinary business of the partnership.**

EXAMPLE The Greenwald family partnership, consisting of the parents and a son, operated a motel. The parents made a contract to sell the motel but the son objected. In a subsequent lawsuit the son prevailed because selling the motel would make it impossible to continue in the partnership business.

4. **Confess a judgment.** A confession of judgment is a sworn statement found in a contract that permits a creditor to enter a judgment in a court without instituting a lawsuit.
5. **Submit a partnership claim or liability to arbitration.**

In addition to specific actions forbidden by the UPA, certain extraordinary business matters require the unanimous vote of all of the partners. They include the following:

1. **Bind the firm in a suretyship or guaranty arrangement.**

EXAMPLE Harry Marple, a partner in Marple, Craig, and Henry, borrowed $50,000 from a bank for his personal use. Marple signed a note promising to repay signing both his own name and the name of the partnership as a guarantor of collection. This meant that if Marple did not pay, the partnership would make the payment. When the note became due, Marple could not pay so the bank demanded that the partnership make payment. The partnership did not have to pay because the contract was outside the scope of the partnership's business. Without the express or actual authority of all of the partners, no partner has the authority to bind a partnership to a contract of suretyship or guaranty.

2. **Do any act not allowed in the partnership agreement.**

EXAMPLE Alan Fentis, Paul Hoe, and Mary Worth practiced law as partners sharing profits equally. Hoe became ill, and Fentis and Worth had to assume Hoe's workload. They then demanded that Hoe accept a reduced share of the partnership's profits. Hoe objected and ultimately won. Any change in the distribution of the partnership's profits requires the unanimous consent of all of the partners unless the partnership agreement stated otherwise.

3. **Admit a new partner to the firm.** No person can become a partner in a firm without the consent of all of the partners.

EXAMPLE Won, Too, Three, Fore, and Five formed a medical partnership. Unless the partnership agreement provides otherwise, a new member cannot be admitted without the unanimous consent of all of the partners. Of course, if the partnership agreement allowed admission of a new partner by majority vote, then such provision would govern.

OBSERVATION *Partners may agree to change the unanimity and majority rules. For example, partners may agree to create an executive committee to manage the firm. In other partnership agreements, some partners may receive more than one vote based upon their capital contribution, profit and loss ratio, or seniority in the partnership. They may also vote to create different classes of partners with unequal voting power, such as junior and senior partners.*

EXAMPLE The partnership agreement of Essex, Manning, Norton, Holt, and Truax stated that because of his seniority and capital contribution, Essex was to have five votes, and the remaining, or junior partners, would have one vote each. Normal operating decisions were to be managed by an executive committee consisting of all the partners with one vote each. However, decisions involving payments or amounts in excess of $100,000 would require a minimum of six votes. In addition, any change of the partnership agreement would require a minimum of eight votes consisting of the vote of Essex and at least three junior partners.

4. **Change the place of the firm's business.**

EXAMPLE Rita Gross and Harry Helm, a partnership doing business as the RH Communications Service, are in the business of selling radio and television time by phone. Their main place of business is in New York City, but Rita wants to move to Jersey City because the cost of office rental space is much lower. The partnership cannot move its main place of business without the consent of both partners.

5. **Change the capital of the firm.** Assuming that each partner has contributed to the partnership the amount required by the partnership agreement, any change in the amount of the required capital contribution must be by a unanimous vote of all of the partners.

6. **Change the scope or main operations of the partnership's operations.**

EXAMPLE Fred Bartles and Joan Rios ran a taxi service as the BR partnership. Joan suggested that they also get involved in buying and selling used automobiles. Since the act of buying and selling taxis is not part of the normal course of the partnership's business, both partners would have to agree to the change in operations.

APPARENT (OBVIOUS) AUTHORITY

Whether or not a partner has express authority, a partner has the apparent authority to bind the partnership in business matters that are the usual ways that a partnership does business. Thus, partners have the apparent authority to make sales, buy goods and supplies, buy on credit, issue commercial paper, such as notes and checks, hire and fire employees, and receive payments from outside third parties.

With or without actual or apparent authority, a partner cannot do anything to bind a partnership for any act that is totally outside the business operations of the partnership or clearly violates company policy.

EXAMPLE Rex Kean and Andy Terranova were partners in a law firm. The firm's hiring practices required that all starting lawyers fresh out of business school would start at $25,000 and that no relatives, such as sons and daughters, could be hired by the firm. Kean hired his son, who had just graduated from law school and who had no experience, at a starting salary of $50,000. Kean had no authority, either express or apparent, to hire his son. Not only was the partnership's hiring policy violated, but his son's starting salary was totally unreasonable.

OBSERVATION *A partnership can make gifts. Partners may unanimously agree to make gifts of partnership assets so long as the partnership's creditors are not in danger of not being paid. Partners must be just before they are generous. However, no single partner alone has the implied authority to make a gift of any of the partnership's assets.*

AMENDING THE PARTNERSHIP AGREEMENT

Generally, the partnership agreement can only be amended by the unanimous vote of all of the partners. The clause in the partnership agreement might read as follows:

"This agreement cannot be amended without the written consent of all of the partners given at a meeting specifically called for such purpose."

The partnership agreement can also state that the agreement can be amended by a majority vote of all of the partners who must be present at a meeting specifically called for such purpose. The clause in the partnership agreement might read as follows:

"This agreement cannot be amended without the written consent of a majority of all of the partners given at a meeting specifically called for such purpose."

The partners agreement, for the sake of simplicity, may disregard the unanimity and majority rules and instead create an executive committee to either authorize amendments or to examine a potential person for admission. This provision can be extremely useful where there are a large number of partners spread over many locations that might make attendance at a meeting inconvenient or even difficult. The clause in the partnership agreement might read as follows:

"The partners, by written consent mailed to (a designated partner), will vote to appoint three partners to an executive committee who will determine whether to........(either to amend the partnership agreement or to interview a prospective candidate to be admitted). The members of the executive committee shall be appointed by a plurality of votes (meaning the three individuals receiving the most votes) at a meeting specifically called for such purpose."

EXAMPLE A trading partnership consists of fifty partners who are voting for three members to be on the executive committee to consider the admission of two new partners. At a meeting called for such purposes, Partner A received 19 votes, Partner B 14 votes, and Partner C 10 votes. The other partners either received one vote, no votes, or were not interested in being on the committee. The executive committee will consist of Partners A, B, and C.

LIABILITY OF AN INCOMING OR RETIRING PARTNER

Liability of an Incoming Partner

A person admitted into a partnership is liable for all debts existing at the time of her admission. However, payment of the existing debts can only be made to the extent of her interest in the firm's assets.

EXAMPLE Clara Colby was admitted as a one-third partner in the Sykes Crawford Real Estate Partnership. At the time of her admission, the partnership owed $300,000 to banks and other creditors. At her entry, Colby contributed $50,000. Should the partnership fail to make payment on the $300,000 in liabilities existing at her admission, Colby would not be liable for more than $50,000, her interest in the firm's assets.

....

OBSERVATION *Suppose that in the prior example, Colby does not wish to expose her $50,000 capital contribution to the claims of the preexisting creditors. She could demand that all of the claims be paid prior to her admission.*

....

Note that if a potential partner is anxious to enter the partnership, he may agree by contract to become personally liable for all existing partnership debts, including those in excess of his partnership interest.

Sample Partnership Agreement to Admit a New Partner

The Agreement to Admit New Partner, in Appendix B, can be used when admitting a new partner.

Liability of a Retiring Partner

A retiring partner remains liable for all debts existing at the time of his leaving unless the remaining partners agree to release him from all partnership debts or payment of the debts has been made prior to his departure. Not only is the departing partner liable for debts existing at the time he leaves but for all debts that are incurred after his having left unless he has given notice to all required creditors, i.e., those who have extended credit to the partnership before he left.

Sample Partnership Agreement for Withdrawing Partner

The Agreement Giving Notice to Withdraw, in Appendix B, can be used when a partner withdraws.

OBSERVATION *A retiring partner is not liable for firm debts incurred after her retirement provided she has given proper notice of her retirement to all required outside parties. Such notice must be actual to all parties who have extended credit to the partnership and constructively (notice by advertisement) to all others. This requirement is discussed in detail in the next chapter.*

CHAPTER 7

Dissolution and Termination of a Partnership

WHAT IS DISSOLUTION?

Many people do not understand the meaning of the term "dissolution" when attempting to terminate an operating partnership. A partnership dissolution does not mean the termination of the business. The UPA defines a dissolution of a partnership as "the change in relationship of the partners caused by any partner ceasing to be associated in the carrying on as distinguished from the winding up of a business." What this actually means is that the partnership continues until the winding up of partnership affairs is completed. Thus, the process starts with dissolution, followed by the winding up and termination of the partnership's legal existence.

HOW IS DISSOLUTION BROUGHT ABOUT?

Dissolution may be caused in three ways: (1) by act of the parties; (2) by operation of law; or (3) by court order.

By Act of the Parties

The partnership agreement may state that a partnership will have a definite life or operate for the attainment of a specific purpose only and then automatically terminate. When the life is over or the goal has been accomplished, the partnership will terminate and dissolve.

By a Partner's Act Contrary to the Partnership Agreement

Even if the partnership agreement states that the firm shall operate for a fixed period of time, any partner may bring about a termination by her express intent to withdraw *unless the partnership agreement states otherwise.* A partner cannot be compelled to remain in a firm longer than she wishes to. However, a partner's early intentional withdrawal is not without legal problems and may make the terminating partner liable for damages for breach of contract.

EXAMPLE Tom Veblen was one of five partners operating as the ABCDV Partnership. The partnership agreement stated that the firm was to operate for five years and then terminate. In the third year, Veblen, tiring of the relationship, left the firm to form a sole proprietorship. His action of leaving, in violation of the partnership agreement, will subject him to possible liability for damages for breaching the agreement.

OBSERVATION *In computing damages and the net interest due the departing partner, the firm's goodwill is excluded.*

Mutual Assent

Whether or not the partnership agreement has a definite term or purpose, partners may agree to terminate by express agreement of all of the partners. This frequently happens when a partner expresses a desire to retire and the remaining partners unanimously consent to the admission of a new partner to take the retiring partner's place.

EXAMPLE Tina Lugo was one of four partners operating as the MNOL Partnership. The partnership agreement stated that the firm was to operate for five years and then terminate. In the fourth year, Lugo advised the partnership that she wanted to retire for health reasons. The remaining partners agreed to permit Grant Rice, a younger person who could bring a fresh approach and additional capital into the partnership, to take Lugo's place.

The admission of an incoming partner dissolves the old partnership and creates a new one.

Expulsion of Partner

The expulsion of a partner in accordance with the terms of the partnership agreement will result in a dissolution *unless the partnership agreement, or a separate agreement, states otherwise* (see page 36 for a discussion of the continuation agreement). A partnership agreement is not unchangeable and a partnership may be dissolved at any time by the wrongful acts and expulsion of a partner at any time. The expelled partner is also liable for immediate and consequential damages.

Involuntary dismissal, in the form of an expulsion, must be done in good faith, and in accordance with the terms of the partnership agreement.

EXAMPLE Rufus Young was a partner in an architectural partnership operating as Old, Bold, New, and Young. An independent audit of the firm's books and records by the firm's accountant uncovered the fact that Young had been stealing thousands of dollars from the firm and charging them to fictitious accounts. The partnership agreement stated that the unauthorized or illegal acts of any partner shall constitute grounds for expulsion. Such expulsion shall be warranted after calling a meeting at which all partners, including the partner to be expelled, is to be called, evidence of the alleged acts presented, and a vote to expel taken. The expulsion must follow the guidelines set forth in the partnership agreement.

OBSERVATION *Expulsion of a partner generally, but not in all cases, causes a partnership to dissolve, and the remaining partners must draw up a new partnership agreement. If the partnership agreement makes no provision for expulsion or if the expulsion is made in bad faith, the expelled partner will be allowed to recover damages.*

WARNING *When a partnership terminates, its tax year is closed, thereby requiring the partners to include their share of the partnership's earnings for the short-period partnership tax year in their personal tax return. If the termination is not properly timed or is unforeseen, it may lead to having a partner including his share of the partnership income for the regular twelve-month period, as well as the income for the short tax year. This will cause a bunching up of the partner's income in one year thereby making the income subject to a tax rate higher than normal. Thus, unplanned tax problems could result from the expulsion of a partner.*

EXAMPLE Roy Mulligan is a partner in a partnership whose natural tax year ends on April 30, 19XX. For the partnership tax year ending on April 30, 19XX, Roy's share of the partnership's taxable income is $40,000. On November 30, 19XX, the partnership expels John Seacroft, another partner. This causes the partnership's tax year to end on this date. As of November 30, 19XX, Roy's share of the partnership's income is $25,000. Thus, for the tax year ending December 31, 19XX, Roy must include the $40,000 from the partnership tax year ending April 30, 19XX, plus his share of the partnership's income ($25,000) for the short tax year from May 1, 19XX through November 30, 19XX. Roy's total reportable income for 19XX will be $65,000.

OBSERVATION *As we will see later on in this chapter, a continuation agreement can be used to allow the partnership to continue after a partner leaves, thus avoiding the unforeseen tax consequences just discussed.*

What happens when the partnership agreement makes no provision for expelling a partner? In a recent 1996 New York State case, a law firm's partnership agreement surprisingly enough made no provision for expelling a partner. Unhappy with the work of one of its active partners, the firm voted to dissolve and reform itself without the old partner. The expelled partner brought an action for damages based on the firms' bad faith and for failure to include the value of goodwill in their distribution to him. Not only was the expelled partner awarded his interest plus damages but also his share of the suggested goodwill of the partnership despite the fact that the partnership agreement stated that the goodwill of the partnership shall have no value. The best way to avoid this problem is to have the partnership agreement specifically state that goodwill is to be excluded when distributing assets. Failure to insert such a provision will require that the remaining partners each come up with cash to pay the departing partner.

HOW TO GIVE NOTICE OF EXPULSION *After a duly called meeting of all of the partners who have voted to expel, the expelled partner should be given a written notice of the decision to expel that includes the date of the withdrawal and a statement that the expelled partner will not have the right after this date to participate in future partnership profits. This provision is always found in the partnership agreement.*

WHAT THIS MEANS TO YOU *It would be wise to insert into the partnership agreement a statement indicating that "any decision to expel a partner in accordance with the terms of this partnership agreement is final and shall not be reviewable by any court of law or arbitrator." This clause in the partnership agreement will minimize the possibility of a lawsuit by the expelled partner thereby keeping possible litigation costs to a minimum.*

Partnership at Will
A partner may terminate without incurring liability to the other partners if no time or particular undertaking is specified in the partnership agreement.

EXAMPLE Ralph Howell and Linda Everest formed a dental partnership and orally agreed to continue the business for an indefinite period of time to see "how things work out." After six months, Linda expressed her intention to dissolve the partnership as soon as reasonably possible. The partnership is treated as one at will and may be dissolved at any time without subjecting either party to liability.

The most effective way of notifying the other partners in a partnership at will of a partner's intent to withdraw is by a written statement to each partner signed by the terminating partner giving notice that he is withdrawing either immediately upon receipt of the notice of termination or at a certain date.

As noted previously, an assignment by a partner of her interest in the firm does not of itself dissolve the partnership, nor does it entitle the assignee to interfere in the management of the firm. In case of dissolution, the assignee is only entitled to receive the assignor's interest.

By Operation of Law

When the Partnership Activity Is Unlawful
A partnership is dissolved by operation of law when it becomes illegal to continue with the partnership business.

EXAMPLE Rona Nugent, Lex Botel, and Yuri Harding operated a gambling casino in a state allowing such enterprises. A newly elected state government was able to pass a new law prohibiting gambling within the state. The partnership would automatically be dissolved by the law prohibiting gambling within the state.

When a Partner Dies
The death of a partner automatically dissolves a partnership *unless the partnership agreement states otherwise*. The UPA specifically lists death as one of the causes of partnership dissolution. Upon the death of a partner, her personal legal representative (an executor or administrator) stands in the deceased partner's place. The representative has the right to require that the surviving partner or partners wind up the affairs of the partnership within a reasonable period of time and to pay over to the

estate the deceased partner's share of the firm's assets after payment of all firm debts.

OBSERVATION *When a partnership is dissolved by the death of a partner, the estate of the deceased partner is liable to the same extent as the deceased partner.*

Bankruptcy of a Partner

The bankruptcy of any partner will dissolve the partnership. Upon dissolution, the bankruptcy court appoints a trustee to take the bankrupt partner's place. This rule is similar to what happens when a partner dies.

OBSERVATION *It is the bankruptcy of a partner and not his insolvency (inability to meet his personal debts as they come due) that requires dissolution. Thus, a lawsuit against the partner individually because he has not paid his personal debts does not by itself constitute bankruptcy and is therefore not grounds for automatically dissolving the partnership.*

Decree of Dissolution by a Court of Equity

A court of equity (a court that can grant a person a legal remedy besides money) has the power to dissolve a partnership for a proper cause. A court will not, however, listen to minor or temporary complaints that will not result in serious or permanent damage to the partnership.

Breach of the Partnership Agreement

Where one partner has breached her fiduciary duty, or is guilty of misconduct, rather than expel the partner, the remaining partners can seek a dissolution by applying to a court that has the legal authority to do so.

Inability to Earn a Profit

If the partnership is operating at an excessive loss or it becomes evident that there is no possibility of realizing future profits, a court order of dissolution may be obtained by the partners to prevent further operating losses.

Misconduct of a Partner

The partners may apply for a dissolution when the conduct of a partner seriously interferes with the carrying on of the partnership. Examples include a serious neglect of the firm's business, abandonment of the partner's obligations to the firm, persistent violations of the partnership agreement, dishonesty, and habitual drunkenness on the job.

EXAMPLE Val Lawford was a partner in the newly formed LMNO Partnership. During the first year of the partnership's operations, he consistently violated the partnership agreement by failing to attend all required partnership meetings, could not account for monies given to him for partnership purposes, and began drinking heavily, causing a steady loss of customers. The partners may apply for a dissolution.

Incompetence of a Partner

The UPA states that upon application by or for a partner, a court of law can dissolve the partnership where a partner has been declared either a lunatic or of unsound mind and can no longer carry out his partnership duties.

EXAMPLE A personal tragedy caused serious emotional problems and an eventual breakdown of one of the general partners in a retail store. Upon application to a court, a court order can be obtained to dissolve the partnership.

Incapacity of a Partner

If the disability of the partner is relatively permanent and not temporary, a motion can be made to a court that the partner does not have the necessary health and physical strength to carry our her duties as a general partner.

EXAMPLE The permanent disability of an aging partner preventing him from carrying out his daily activities as a managing partner would be grounds for applying to a court for dissolution.

Any Other Circumstances

The partners may seek relief from possible lawsuit from the other partners under certain circumstances under which they want to dissolve but fear possible lawsuit from other dissenting partners.

EXAMPLE The partnership of Bea Ellen, Joe Norton, and Sue Tolliver has been operating for ten years. Norton joined the partnership in the ninth year of the partnership's operations by mere oral agreement with the understanding that the partnership would operate indefinitely. He was, therefore, not prepared when both Ellen and Tolliver gave him written notice that they intended to retire. Rather than risk a possible expensive lawsuit, both partners may apply to a court for a court ordered dissolution thereby avoiding a costly lawsuit.

SAFEGUARDING THE GOING CONCERN VALUE OF THE PARTNERSHIP BY USE OF A CONTINUATION AGREEMENT

The major disadvantage of a liquidation is the hardships that may be faced by the partners. For example, they may have experience in only one field of work, such as car repairs, and fear not being able to be get employment elsewhere under working conditions similar to those that existed under the current partnership. In addition, the partnership may be worth more as a continuing business rather than the total cash that might be obtained from the likely piecemeal sale of the firm's assets. To avoid these problems, the UPA provides that the liquidation right is granted only "unless otherwise agreed." Thus, the partners may, by use of a *continuation agreement*, limit or reject the liquidation right generally arising upon dissolution.

A continuation agreement is a safeguard measure that enables a profitable but troubled partnership to expel one or more difficult partners without forcing the partnership into a liquidation. The agreement may be part of the original partnership agreement or it can be drawn up at the time of the dissolution. Matters that should be covered include the causes of dissolution, the method of computing the value of the departing partner's interest, the method of payment (such as a lump-sum cash payment or cash plus a series of notes payable over a period of time, or simply notes payable with interest) for the partner's interest, the method of funding the buyout (such as firm assets or the partners' individual assets), a restrictive understanding (e.g., that the expelled partner will not set up a competing business for a period of three years within a radius of twenty-five miles of the partnership's principal office), and the method of protecting the departing partner against firm debts. Thus, the rights of all of the parties are defined in the continuation agreement as a precaution against future harmful lawsuits by all parties concerned.

The continuation clause inserted in the partnership agreement might read as follows:

> "In the case of a partner leaving the partnership for any reason whatsoever, including death, disability, retirement, withdrawal, or expulsion, the partnership shall not dissolve or terminate but shall continue to operate. Under such circumstances, the remaining partners shall continue to operate the partnership according to the terms of this partnership agreement."

NOTICE OF DISSOLUTION (TERMINATION OF APPARENT AUTHORITY)

Dissolution operates to terminate the authority of the partners to act on behalf of the partnership insofar as new business is concerned except to the extent necessary in order to wind up the partnership affairs.

Proper Notice to Third Parties

When the time comes for dissolving the partnership, it is very important that all third parties that have done business with the partnership, except those individuals and companies that have extended credit, be notified that the partnership is dissolving. Notice must be published in a newspaper of general circulation and preferably in a second newspaper that the clientele of the partnership would most likely read. For example, a dress manufacturer might put an announcement in *The Women's Wear Daily* that "as of a certain date, the XYZ partnership will cease operations and dissolve." It might also be prudent to run the announcement for several days or every other day for a week.

When dissolution is caused by operation of law, notice to third parties is not required.

Actual Notice to Creditors Who Have Extended Credit

Under the UPA, actual notice is required only as to creditors who have extended credit to the partnership prior to its intended dissolution date. The amount of the transaction is immaterial, and the same notice must be given whether the credit extended to the partnership was $10 or $10,000.

OBSERVATION *Proper notice and not actual notice may be given to outside third parties who have dealt with the partnership only on a cash basis.*

Liability of Nonparticipating or Silent Partners for Transactions Entered Into After Dissolution

If a partner is so inactive in partnership affairs that his participation is negligible, liability for transactions incurred after dissolution where notification is *not* given will be limited to his share of partnership assets. The presumption is that credit was not extended to the partnership based on the business expertise, credit standing, and integrity of a partner who was actually unknown to the general public.

AUTHORITY OF PARTNERS TO TRANSACT BUSINESS AFTER DISSOLUTION

Immediately upon dissolution, the power of the partners to enter into new business ceases at once while the authority of the partners to wind up partnership affairs continues. If new business is entered into by a partner who has notice of the dissolution but chooses to disregard it, such new business becomes the sole liability of the partner entering into the transaction and payment cannot be made from the firm's assets. However, if the partnership failed to give either actual or proper notice to the third party who entered into the transaction, the entire partnership remains liable.

Without the continuation agreement, dissolution gives each partner the right to have the partnership liquidated and his share of any surplus, after payment to all creditors, paid back to her in cash or property. During liquidation, "old business" must be wound up. This includes selling partnership assets, completing any unfulfilled contracts, collecting accounts receivable and any other debts due, paying off creditors, and distributing the remaining assets to the partners.

"New business" includes entering into new contracts and extending the time for payment of any partnership debts.

EXAMPLE The FGH Machine Tool partnership agrees to dissolve effective December 31, 19XX. At year-end there were $100,000 of notes and accounts receivable owed to the partnership. The partners agreed to extend the time for payment for $50,000 of the accounts receivable. For the year 19X1, the partners entered into transactions necessary to terminate operations, such as hiring a contractor to remove the machinery for eventual sale, paying off creditors, and hiring a lawyer to help liquidate the partnership. Only the extension of time given to the partnership's creditors in which to pay the partnership is treated as new business.

WHO HAS THE AUTHORITY TO WIND UP A PARTNERSHIP'S AFFAIRS?

If all of the partners have agreed to dissolution or to terminate when the partnership term expires, then all of them have the right to participate in winding up the affairs of the partnership. If the partnership is dissolving due to the bankruptcy of a partner, then the remaining nonbankrupt partners have the authority to wind up the partnership affairs.

OBSERVATION *Where the liquidating partners are at odds over the matters affecting the dissolving firm and are hopelessly deadlocked, an application may be made to a court requesting that it appoint a receiver to wind up the affairs of the firm. The appointment of a receiver requires that the issues be genuine and not trifling, and the request must be made by a partner acting in good faith and not by one who is a reluctant or difficult complainer.*

EXAMPLE The Telly Telephone Service Company, which has four partners, decides that it is not in their best interests to continue operating. The halt to operations is due to Wiley Secord, a partner who constantly disagrees with the majority's decisions because "he knows the business better than anyone else." After the unanimous vote to dissolve, he remains uncooperative, refuses to assist in the sale of the firm's assets, and does not attend to matters vital to the liquidation process. The remaining partners, acting in good faith, may request that a court appoint a receiver to wind up the firm's affairs thereby avoiding further difficulties.

If the dissolution was caused by the death of a partner, then the surviving partners are authorized by law to wind up the affairs of the firm. Finally, if the partnership's affairs have not been wound up by the time the last partner dies, then her legal representative, whether an executor or administrator, has the right to wind up the firm's affairs.

A partner whose wrongful actions caused the dissolution has no right to participate in the winding up the firm's affairs.

EXAMPLE Mona Allen and Donald Tree were partners in a supermarket. When Tree died, Allen claimed that the partnership did not exist and that Tree was only a manager and not a partner. Allen, therefore, refused to account to Tree's executor for any partnership assets due Tree upon liquidation. When the executor sued and proved the existence of the partnership, Allen demanded that she be paid extra for work done as the surviving partner. Her argument is deceitful, obnoxious, and unfair, and she will not recover any additional money.

A partner cannot purchase any of the partnership's property without the consent of the other partners.

Finally, a surviving partner is entitled to reasonable compensation for her services and reimbursement for any costs incurred in the winding up of the partnership's affairs.

The accounting concepts of dissolution will be discussed in greater detail in Chap. 9.

PARTNERSHIP BUY-SELL AGREEMENTS

While individuals usually enter into a partnership arrangement with the intent of getting along with one another, it is always possible that the situation may change requiring that one or more partners buy out the other. The best way to handle this type of situation is through a buy-sell agreement whereby a partner or partners who wish to leave are bought out by one or more of the other partners. The agree-

ment usually stipulates that the partner wanting to leave give a 30-day notice (or other time period) stating that he wishes to leave at the end of a particular period, such as the end of a month or at year-end. It is then required that some outside third party, such as the firm's independent accountant, compute the value of the firm at that date so that the remaining partners can purchase the departing partner's interest at that price. Alternately, the partners may agree that all or a majority of the partners shall have the right to determine the price at a particular date.

Alternatively, similar agreement can be made whereby the partnership purchase a life insurance policy on the life of each partner. Upon death, the proceeds of the policy are payable to the partnership to be used to pay the deceased partner's estate the value of the partner's interest at her death.

A typical buy-sell clause inserted in the partnership agreement might read as follows:

> "Upon prior written notice ..... days prior to the end of any (calendar, fiscal) year, a partner may retire. The remaining partner(s) may terminate or elect to continue the business, in which case the remaining partner(s) can, at their option, purchase the interest of the retiring partner.
>
> Valuation of the retiring partner's interest shall be at ....(description of the method used, such as fair market value at a particular date) as determined by the partnership's independent accountant at the end of the month in which such written notice is given."

For other acceptable methods of valuation for buy-out purposes, see Chap. 12.

INSOLVENCY: CONFLICT BETWEEN PARTNERSHIP CREDITORS AND INDIVIDUAL CREDITORS

Under the Federal Bankruptcy Act, partnership creditors are given priority with respect to payment out of partnership assets. Should the partnership's creditors remain unpaid, they will share equally with the partner's personal creditors in the personal assets of the partner. Federal law controls all bankruptcy proceedings, including those of partnerships.

CHECKLIST FOR DISSOLVING A GENERAL PARTNERSHIP

The following checklist highlights factors that must be considered when dissolving a partnership.

1. Does the partnership agreement specifically state that the withdrawal, death, or termination of a partner does not dissolve the partnership? This provision avoids time-consuming and costly legal fees as to the disposition of a partner's interest.
2. What are the procedures for termination of the partnership?
3. In case of dissolution for any reason, the following items must be considered:
   - All notes and accounts receivable due the firm must be collected.
   - How are net assets to be distributed among the partners?
   - How will machinery and equipment be distributed?
   - Must inventory in partial production be completed?
   - Method of disposition of the firm's name must be decided on.
   - Does the firm owe any taxes?
   - How much cash will be required to pay off all liabilities?
   - How will leases and other contractual obligations be disposed of?
   - What will be the effect of a dissolution upon the reputations, professional and otherwise, of the partners?

From a practical viewpoint when liquidating, the partners must also consider whether they have the experience, education, and health to enter into another business with minimum disruption to their personal lives.

CHAPTER 8

Limited Partnerships

INTRODUCTION

A limited (or special) partnership is one formed according to a special state law and consisting of one or more general partners and one or more limited partners. This type of partnership requires that limited partners be silent or inactive thereby allowing them to limit their liability to the amounts of their investments. Thus, in organizing the limited partnership, it is important that the limited partners be given no rights or powers over partnership affairs because their involvement in the operation of the limited partnership may cause them to be treated as a general partner subject to unlimited liability.

EXAMPLE A limited partnership was formed according to state law. Bob Endicott and Roberta Small each invested $25,000 and as general partners, were to manage the partnership. Allen Dozen, Phoebe Cowls, and Juanita Denmark, as limited partners, each agreed to invest $50,000, but are to have no voice in management. All five partners have formed a limited partnership.

....
OBSERVATION *A limited partnership can be used to bring family members into a business without giving them a voice in management.*
....

The Uniform Limited Partnership Act (ULPA) was used by most states until 1976 when virtually all states and the District of Columbia adopted the Revised Uniform Limited Partnership Act (RULPA). Thus, RULPA is the dominant law and will serve as the main basis for discussing when to use the limited partnership form.

FORMATION OF THE LIMITED PARTNERSHIP

The formation of a limited partnership requires the drafting of a limited partnership agreement, sometimes called the certificate of limited partnership. The certificate of limited partnership must be recorded locally in the office of the official in charge of public records. Ordinarily, this will be the office of the county clerk or recorder of deeds of the county in which the principal place of business of the limited partnership is located. Under RULPA, the limited partnership is formed when the certificate of limited partnership is filed. State law may limit the activities of the limited partnership. This information is usually supplied by the county clerk or recorder of deeds.

Checklist for Forming a Limited Partnership

The following matters must be covered to complete an effective limited partnership agreement:

1. Name;
2. Principal place of business;
3. Agent for service of process;
4. Character or purpose of the limited partnership;
5. Term of the limited partnership;
6. Identity of the general partner or partners;
7. Number, identity, and manner of admitting a limited partner;
8. Whether a limited partner may assign her interest, and if so, the procedures for doing so;
9. Manner of terminating the limited partnership;
10. Tax year-end;
11. Method of accounting to be used (i.e., cash or accrual);
12. Contribution in the way of capital (a description of the cash, property, or services);
13. Determined factors as to whether additional capital contributions are required, and if so, in what form (i.e., cash, property, or services);
14. Allocation of profits and losses;
15. Whether any general partner is to be paid compensation, and for what services;
16. Review applicable tax problems and tax elections;
17. Review local statutes for possible problems.

Sample Limited Partnership Agreement

The Sample Limited Partnership Agreement, in Appendix B, can be used when forming your partnership.

SELECTING A NAME FOR THE LIMITED PARTNERSHIP

The name of the limited partnership cannot contain the name of a limited partner unless it is also the name of a general partner or the name of the partnership business has been carried on under that name before the admission of that limited partner.

EXAMPLE The limited partnership composed of Howard Sherlock, Betty Holmes, and Winston Varga, who are the general partners, and twenty limited partners plans to admit William Sherlock, the son of Howard, as a limited partner. The name of the limited partnership does not have to be changed.

If a limited partner's name is used in the name of the limited partnership, he may be held personally liable to partnership creditors.

EXAMPLE A limited partnership was composed of Dina Wong, Harold Too, and Woodrow Yee, who were general partners, and Benson Hamada, the sole limited partner. All of their names appeared on the firm's stationery, which made it appear that Hamada was a general partner. Upon a subsequent lawsuit brought against the firm for nonpayment of bills, the creditors sought to hold him personally liable for all debts even though he was only a limited partner.

NATURE OF THE LIMITED PARTNER'S CONTRIBUTION

A limited partner is one who makes a capital contribution in the form of cash or property to the limited partnership and thus obtains a part ownership.

A partner can be, at the same time, both a general and limited partner.

EXAMPLE Patricia Lombard was a general partner in the AVOL Limited Partnership, which was in the process of selling 100 additional limited partnership interests at $10,000 each. If Lombard purchased a limited partner interest, she will be both a general and limited partner.

A limited partner has virtually all of the rights of a general partner except that the limited partner has no right to manage the partnership. Thus, a partner who takes control of the partnership becomes personally liable to the firm's creditors.

The Revised Uniform Limited Partnership Act (RULPA) attempts to ease this tough rule by listing partnership activities that by themselves do not amount to control. They include the following:

1. Being an employee of the limited partnership or of a general partner; or
2. Consulting with a general partner with regard to limited partnership matters; or
3. Acting as a surety for the limited partnership. A surety is one who promises to pay a creditor if another party, called a debtor, does not; or
4. Attending a meeting of the partners; or
5. Voting on important partnership matters, such as dissolution and winding up.

In addition, unlike the old ULPA, RULPA provides that a limited partner who participates in control of the partnership business is only liable to the persons who had actual knowledge that the limited partner was involved in the partnership's management.

WHAT ARE THE RIGHTS OF A LIMITED PARTNER?

A limited partner has the right to vote on specific matters, so long as there is only limited participation, as listed above, in the affairs of the firm. A limited partner also has a right to share in the profits and earnings according to the limited partnership agreement. The limited partners can agree that some of them may have priority in the distribution of profits and losses or return of capital. However, without such an agreement, all limited partners stand on an equal footing.

EXAMPLE The limited partnership of Luella Grayson and Steven Bock has ten limited partners. The limited partnership agreement states that, upon dissolution and winding up, limited partners whose capital contributions exceed $10,000 at the date dissolution is voted upon shall receive their distributions first, in the order of payment of the highest balances first until all capital accounts of the limited partners are equal. Sally Hornsby, Boyd Camper, and Rick Hooten, who are limited partners, each have balances in their capital accounts as shown below.

Limited partners have the same rights as general partners to examine and copy the books and records of the firm, and access to all information regarding the affairs of the partnership.

A limited partner may assign her partnership interest but only if the limited partnership agreement permits. The assignee (the person who receives the limited partnership interest) does not, however, get the same rights as the original limited partner. If the agreement is missing this provision, then the other partners must consent to the assignment. Another way would be to amend the limited partnership agreement to allow such assignment.

Finally, upon dissolution, a limited partner is entitled to return of her contribution as set forth in the limited partnership agreement.

RIGHTS AND LIABILITIES OF A GENERAL PARTNER IN A LIMITED PARTNERSHIP

A general partner in a limited partnership has all the rights and powers that a general partner would have in a general partnership. This means that, absent any restriction in the limited partnership agreement, a general partner may manage the affairs of the firm, hire and fire employees, and is subject to unlimited liability in case a lawsuit is brought against the business.

A general partner in a limited partnership cannot do anything that is prohibited in the partnership agreement, nor can he admit another general partner, confess a judgment (admit that the partnership is automatically liable in a lawsuit) against the firm, or do anything that would make it impossible for the limited partnership to continue to carry out its daily business. These are basically the same legal limitations that are applicable to a general partnership.

	Hornsby	Camper	Hooten	Total
Capital Contributions at Date of Dissolution	$11,000	$12,000	$15,000	$38,000
First Distribution			3,000	3,000
Balance	$11,000	$12,000	$12,000	$35,000
Second Distribution		1,000	1,000	2,000
Balance	$11,000	$11,000	$11,000	$33,000
Third Distribution	1,000	1,000	1,000	3,000
Account Balance Equal to That of All Other Limited Partners	$10,000	$10,000	$10,000	$30,000

WHAT HAPPENS WHEN A PERSON ERRONEOUSLY BELIEVES HIMSELF TO BE A LIMITED PARTNER?

Sometimes a person makes a contribution to the limited partnership with the mistaken belief that he is a limited partner subject to the limited liability protection. To avoid liability upon learning the true facts, the person must give up all interests in the business and any other form of payment. If necessary, the limited partnership agreement may have to be changed to indicate that he is a limited partner. Of course, the partner will still remain personally liable to the firm's creditors for any business previously transacted under the mistaken belief that the person, now a limited partner, was a general partner.

DISSOLUTION AND DISTRIBUTION OF THE ASSETS OF A LIMITED PARTNERSHIP: THE FINAL ACCOUNTING

Where a limited partnership is dissolved and the assets reduced to cash, the assets are distributed in the following order:

1. To creditors, including partners who are creditors;
2. Unpaid distributions owed to partners. Unpaid distributions are any distributions a partner is entitled to upon withdrawal from the firm;
3. To all partners, both general and limited, to the extent of their capital contributions; and
4. To all partners, both general and limited, as to profits.

EXAMPLE The XY Limited Partnership includes two general partners, X and Y, and A, a limited partner. Each general partner originally agreed to contribute $10,000 while A, a limited partner, contributed $25,000. At December 31, 19XX, the end of the year in which they unanimously vote to dissolve, the partnership's cash balance was $95,000. Creditors are owed $40,000, partner A loaned the partnership $4,000, and the balances in the capital accounts of X, Y, and A are $10,000, $11,000 and $30,000, respectively. Payments to the creditors, for the partner's loan, and for the remaining balances in the partner's respective capital accounts would be as shown below.

If the individuals forming the limited partnership wish to do so, they may design a partnership agreement to make distributions in another way once all outside creditors' claims are satisfied.

EXAMPLE Using the information in the prior example, assume that the limited partnership agreement stated that the limited partners must first be repaid

Payables to Outside Creditors	Loans Owed to Ltd. Partner A	Capital Account Balance X	Capital Account Balance Y	Ltd. Partner Capital Account Balance A	Total
$40,000	$4,000	$10,000	$11,000	$30,000	$95,000
(40,000)					(40,000)[1]
$ –0–	4,000	10,000	11,000	30,000	$55,000
	(4,000)				(4,000)[2]
$ –0–	–0–	10,000	11,000	30,000	$51,000
		10,000	10,000	25,000	45,000[3]
$ –0–	–0–	–0–	1,000	5,000	$ 6,000
			1,000	5,000	6,000[4]
$ –0–	–0–	–0–	–0–	–0–	$ –0–

[1] Payment to the firm's creditors.
[2] Payment to partner A, the limited partner, in repayment for his loan to the limited partnership.
[3] Repayment for each partner's original capital contribution.
[4] Repayment for profits.

all of their advances, capital contributions, and profits, before any distributions can be made to the general partners. Assuming a cash balance of $95,000, payments to the creditors, for the limited partner's loan, and for the remaining payments to each general partner would be as follows:

Payables to Outside Creditors	Loans Owed to Ltd. Partner A	Capital Account Balance X	Capital Account Balance Y	Ltd. Partner Capital Account Balance A	Total
$40,000	$4,000	$10,000	$11,000	$30,000	$95,000
(40,000)					(40,000)[1]
$ –0–	4,000	10,000	11,000	30,000	$55,000
	(4,000)			30,000	(34,000)[2]
$ –0–	–0–	10,000	11,000	–0–	$21,000
		10,000	11,000	–0–	21,000[3]
$ –0–	–0–	–0–	–0–	–0–	$ –0–

[1]Payment to the firm's creditors.
[2]Payment to partner A, the limited partner, in repayment for his loan to the limited partnership, his share of his initial capital contribution, and any remaining profits.
[3]Repayment for each general partner's original capital contribution and any remaining profits.

CHAPTER 9

How to Deal With Partnership Accounting

GENERAL CONSIDERATIONS: HOW TO GET STARTED

Accounting records for partnerships are similar to those of other businesses. The firm must account for all assets, liabilities, revenues, and expenses. Although the partnership is not a separate legal person, it is, nevertheless, an economic or business unit. The books of the partnership must show the equity (amount invested in the business plus any profits not yet withdrawn from the partnership) of each individual partner. The initial investment is usually stated in the partnership's agreement. It consists of cash, property, or nothing at all if the partners agree that the partner contributing nothing has valuable services to offer in the future.

Note that the basic accounting equation is as follows:

Assets = Liabilities + Capital (Partners' Total Equity or Capital Accounts)

To record the initial investment on the books of the partnership, a journal entry showing the cash or property contribution of each partner must be recorded on the books of account.

EXAMPLE 1 On January 1, 19XX, Randolph Gee and Candyce Ulan form a general partnership, called the Geelan Company, with each agreeing to contribute $10,000. The journal entry (an entry on the partnership books showing what each partner has invested) would be made as follows to record the cash contribution of each partner:

Cash	20,000	
Randolph Gee: Capital		10,000
Candyce Ulan: Capital		10,000

The partnership's balance sheet, which is a listing of a firm's assets, liabilities, and capital (also called owners' or partners' equity) would appear as follows after the receipt of the $20,000:

The Geelan Company
Balance Sheet
January 1, 19XX

Assets		
Cash		$20,000

Partners' Capital		
Randolph Gee: Capital	$10,000	
Candyce Ulan: Capital	10,000	$20,000

EXAMPLE 2 Assume the same facts as in EXAMPLE 1 except that Gee will invest $10,000 and Ulan $5,000. The journal entry would be made as follows to record the cash contribution of each partner:

Cash	15,000	
Randolph Gee: Capital		10,000
Candyce Ulan: Capital		5,000

The partnership's balance sheet, after receipt of the $15,000, would appear as follows:

The Geelan Company
Balance Sheet
January 1, 19XX

Assets

Cash		$15,000

Partners' Capital

Randolph Gee: Capital	$10,000	
Candyce Ulan: Capital	5,000	$15,000

EXAMPLE 3 On January 1, 19XX, Wyona O'Connor, Charles Drake, and Harrison Pitt form a general partnership called the ODP Partnership. O'Connor will contribute $10,000, and Drake will donate land costing $30,000. Pitt is to invest nothing but will devote his full time to the partnership. The journal entry would be made as follows to record the contribution of each partner:

Cash	40,000	
Wyona O'Connor: Capital		10,000
Charles Drake: Capital		30,000
Harrison Pitt: Capital		–0–

The partnership's balance sheet, after it is formed, would appear as follows:

The ODP Partnership
Balance Sheet
January 1, 19XX

Assets

Cash	$10,000	
Land	30,000	
Total	$40,000	

Partners' Capital

Wyona O'Connor: Capital	$10,000	
Charles Drake: Capital	30,000	
Harrison Pitt: Capital	–0–	$40,000

Partnership contributions are generally made based upon their agreed upon share of profits and losses, *but this in not always the case.* For example, each of three partners may agree to equally invest $10,000 for a total of $30,000 but may agree to share profits and losses in a ratio of 50%, 25%, and 25%. Thus, there may be no relationship between the amount invested by each partner and their agreed upon share of future profits and losses.

The formation of a limited partnership results in the same journal entries used to record the investments of each partner, except that the capital accounts must indicate who is a general and who is a limited partner.

EXAMPLE On July 1, 19XX, Phil Snow, Lana Cotter, and Martina Babson form a limited partnership to be called the Snow-Cotter Company. Snow and Cotter will act as the general partners with each investing $10,000 while Babson will invest $25,000 as a limited partner. The journal entry to record the original capital investments of each partner will be as follows:

Cash	45,000	
Phil Snow, General Partner: Capital		10,000
Lana Cotter, General Partner: Capital		10,000
Martina Babson, Limited Partner: Capital		25,000

The partnership's balance sheet, after receipt of the $45,000, will appear as follows:

The Snow-Cotter Company
Balance Sheet
July 1, 19XX

Assets		
Cash		$45,000

Capital		
Phil Snow, General Partner:		
Capital	$10,000	
Lana Cotter, General		
Partner: Capital	10,000	
Martina Babson, Limited		
Partner: Capital	25,000	$45,000

HOW TO HANDLE A PARTNER'S DRAWING ACCOUNT

For bookkeeping purposes, amounts drawn from the firm for an accounting period are charged to an account called "Drawings." Balances in the drawing account of each partner are transferred, usually at the end of an accounting period, to the corresponding partners' capital account and reduces that account.

EXAMPLE A limited partnership consisting of Glen Hotchkiss, Paul Verry, and Barbara Fry was started on July 1, 19XX. Both Hotchkiss and Verry were to act as the general partners while Fry was listed as a limited partner. Each partner initially invested $10,000 and each withdrew $1,000 for the six-month period ending December 31. Prior to the recording and distribution of each partner's share of partnership profits, the balances in each partner's account will be $9,000 calculated as follows:

	Hotchkiss General Partner Capital	Verry General Partner Capital	Fry Limited Partner Capital	Total
7/1/XX	$10,000	$10,000	$10,000	$30,000
Withdrawals	(1,000)	(1,000)	(1,000)	(3,000)
Balance 12/31/XX	$ 9,000	$ 9,000	$ 9,000	$27,000

HOW TO DIVIDE PROFITS AND LOSSES

The word "profits" is a flexible term. The most commonly used methods of dividing profits are as follows:
1. Equally; or
2. In the ratio of the average capital balance; or
3. In an agreed ratio after allowing interest on partners' capital or salaries to the partners or both; or
4. In some other ratio.

Therefore, it is important that the partnership agreement draw up an exact definition of the term "profits."

EXAMPLE 1 The general partnership of Aldo Gary, Ellen Moore, and Paula Kent was started on January 1, 19XX. Each partner initially invested $10,000. Profits, if any, were to be distributed in the ratio of 3, 3, and 2. Gary and Moore each withdrew $15,000 while Kent withdrew $7,000 for the year. Assuming a profit of $80,000 for the year, the balances in each partner's account on December 31, 19XX would be calculated as follows:

	Gary General Partner Capital	Moore General Partner Capital	Kent General Partner Capital	Total
1/1/XX	$10,000	$10,000	$10,000	$ 30,000
Profits	30,000(3)	30,000(3)	20,000(2)	80,000
	$40,000	$40,000	$30,000	$110,000
Withdrawals	(15,000)	(15,000)	(7,000)	(37,000)
Balance 12/31/XX	$25,000	$25,000	$23,000	$ 73,000

EXAMPLE 2 On January 1, 19XX, Wayne Holtz, Sheldon Swing, and Ella Alson form a partnership called Beauty Cosmetics. Holtz contributed an initial capital of $10,000 while Swing and Alson each invested $20,000. Interest shall be paid to each partner at a rate of 10 percent annually on beginning capital balances. Each partner is to receive a salary of $5,000 in addition to an equal share of profits after deducting interest and each partner's salary. If the partnership net income on December 31, 19XX before deducting each partner's interest and salary is $50,000, Holtz will receive $16,000 while Swing and Alson would each get $17,000 calculated as follows:

	Holtz	Swing	Alson	Total
Interest on beginning capital				
Holtz				
$10,000 × 10%	$1,000			$1,000
Swing				
$20,000 × 10%		$2,000		2,000
Alson				
$20,000 × 10%			$ 2,000	2,000
Salaries	5,000	5,000	5,000	15,000
Subtotal	6,000	7,000	7,000	20,000
Balance	10,000	10,000	10,000	30,000
Total	$16,000	$17,000	$17,000	$50,000

Generally, the partnership agreement also contains a provision stating that "partners who leave profits in the firm shall not be entitled to interest on such profits."

Where profits distribution is unequal, losses are shared in the same ratio unless the partners agree otherwise.

EXAMPLE Three partners, Moe Zarn, Bella Gina Foley, and Sam Rizzo, form a partnership that requires both Zarn and Foley contribute at least forty hours a week to the partnership while Rizzo will work only one day a week. The partners agree to share profits equally while losses shall be absorbed solely by Rizzo because he is the least active partner.

ADMISSION OF A PARTNER

The partners may, upon unanimous consent, admit a new partner at any time. This act, however, causes a dissolution of the old partnership and the formation of a new one. Unless a new arrangement for the sharing of profits is made, the profits and losses will continue to be shared equally among all of the partners.

Although the admission of a new partner requires a new set of books and records, as a practical matter, the accounting records of the old firm are continued but with the additional capital account for the new partner. Prior to the admission of a new partner, the books and records of the old partnership must brought up to date, the profit or loss determined, and a distribution made to each partner for any profits or losses.

There are several ways of admitting a new partner. One way is for the new partner to buy out the interest of a member who wishes to leave the partnership, and the second way is to simply admit a new partner upon her making an initial investment in the partnership.

EXAMPLE 1 The VBNM General Partnership of V, B, N, and M consists of four equal partners who have capital balances of $25,000 each at September 30, 19XX, the date that M has decided to leave the partnership. On that date, he sells his interest for $50,000 to Y who is to be admitted, by unanimous consent, to the partnership. Y's interest in the new VBNY Partnership continues to be $25,000 because the $50,000 payment price is strictly a private matter between M and Y. It may be said that M has sold his $25,000 interest in the partnership to Y for $50,000.

EXAMPLE 2 The general partnership of FGH and M consists of four equal partners who have capital balances of $25,000 each on September 30, 19XX. On October 1, 19XX, the partners agree to admit Q who has agreed to make a $50,000 investment. M has agreed to leave the partnership on that date after being paid his $25,000 capital balance. The new partnership consists of FGH and Q and has a total capital of $125,000 ($25,000 for each partner × 3 = $75,000 + $50,000 from Q).

DISSOLUTION AND LIQUIDATION OF THE PARTNERSHIP: THE FINAL ACCOUNTING

Handling a Simple Dissolution

Where a solvent general partnership is dissolved and the assets reduced to cash, the assets are distributed in the following order:
1. To creditors other than partners;
2. To partners for advances other than for capital and profits;
3. To partners in repayment for their agreed upon capital contributions;
4. To partners for any surplus remaining after the above payments are made.

EXAMPLE The XYZ Partnership is composed of three equal partners. Each partner originally contributed $10,000. On December 31, 19XX, the end of the year in which they unanimously vote to dissolve, the partnership's cash balance was $94,000. Liabilities to creditors, loans made by partners, and balances in their respective capital accounts were as follows:

Payables to outside creditors	$40,000
Loans by Partner X (advances)	18,000
Balance in each partner's capital account:	
Partner X	12,000
Partner Y	12,000
Partner Z	12,000
	$94,000

The outside creditors would be paid $40,000; partner X would receive repayment of his $18,000, and the remaining $42,000 would be distributed equally to each partner as payment for their original capital contributions of $10,000 each plus their share of undistributed profits.

What Happens When There Are Losses Upon Dissolution?

Where profits are shared equally, losses must be handled in the same way unless there is an agreement stipulating otherwise.

EXAMPLE 1 The MNC Partnership is composed of three equal partners. M contributed $20,000, N $10,000, and C her skills. On December 31, 19XX, the end of the year in which they unanimously voted to dissolve, the partnership's cash balance, after paying all of the partnership's creditors, was $6,000. In the absence of an agreement, the combined loss of $24,000 (M's $20,000 + N's $10,000 – $6,000) must be divided equally and each partner will be liable for one third of such loss. The sharing of the loss will be as follows:

Partner	Capital Contribution	Equal Share of Loss	Payment to Each Partner
M	$20,000	$8,000	$12,000
N	10,000	8,000	2,000
C	–0–	8,000	(8,000)

In the above situation, partner C would owe the firm $8,000, which when added to the $6,000 will make up the $14,000 owed to partners M and N.

EXAMPLE 2 Assume the same facts as in EXAMPLE 1 except that partner C is bankrupt and unable to pay. The distribution would then be as follows:

Partner	Capital Contribution	Equal Share of Loss	Payment to Each Partner
M	$20,000	$12,000	$8,000
N	10,000	12,000	(2,000)

Partner N would be forced to contribute $2,000 to the partnership.

CHAPTER 10

Getting Started With the Day-to-Day Operations of the Partnership

HOW TO SELECT AN ACCOUNTANT

Now that you and your partners have decided to go into business, it becomes necessary to hire an accountant. A Certified Public Accountant (CPA) is a person who has the required number of years of experience (usually a minimum of two) necessary to sit for and pass a rigid state accountancy examination to practice as a CPA. However, the fact that the individual is a CPA should not be the only qualification that the partners should look for. Other questions should involve her fees, her expertise in your specific field of operations, and her knowledge and experience with the tax laws. When interviewing a prospective accountant, inquire about her experience with businesses similar to yours, the number of years that she has been in practice, and whether she returns a client's calls promptly. When the business commences, will the accountant be able to review the partnership's books on a weekly, monthly, or quarterly basis? Can the accountant work with all of the partners or should the partnership designate just one partner, presumably someone with an accounting background, to deal with all accounting and tax matters. Ask her whether she has connections with a bank or other type of financial institution in case your business requires additional financing. Are you comfortable with this person and do you feel that she has the ability to handle confidential information?

All of the partners should be in agreement as to whether you want to hire this particular CPA. Before hiring this individual, you can call up either the American Institute of Certified Public Accountants (AICPA) or the state society of CPA's in your state to find out whether the accountant has been or is currently subject to any disciplinary proceedings, censures, or reprimands based upon her professional work.

Remember that her recommendations on both accounting and tax matters will have potentially serious consequences on the financial lives of all of the partners.

SETTING UP THE PARTNERSHIP'S BOOKS AND RECORDS

When starting up a new partnership, the Internal Revenue Code requires that a system of record keeping must be set up suitable for the business. The failure to keep proper business records can lead to tax audits, additional taxes, and in extreme cases, even criminal charges.

CHOOSING THE RIGHT ACCOUNTING METHOD

When starting to operate, the partnership should set up books using an accounting method that clearly shows income for the accounting period that is the partnership's tax year. The firm must also decide whether to use a single-entry or a double-entry bookkeeping system. The single-entry system is simple and easy to maintain but may not be suitable for every corporation. Partnerships may find the double-entry system better because it has built-in procedures to assure accuracy and control.

Single-Entry

The single-entry bookkeeping system is based on the profit or loss statement and includes only the partnership's business income and expense accounts. It can be a simple and very practical system if a small partnership is just starting out. For tax purposes, this system records all income and expenses through the use of a daily summary of cash receipts and a monthly summary of cash receipts and cash payments.

Double-Entry

The double-entry bookkeeping system uses books, called journals, and is based on both the income statement and the balance sheet. Transactions are first entered in a journal and then monthly totals of the journal transactions are entered in ledger accounts. Ledger accounts include income, expense, asset, liability, and net worth (the difference between what the firm owns and what it owes). These accounts are used to prepare a partnership's financial statements.

ACCRUAL VERSUS THE CASH BASIS OF ACCOUNTING

Accrual Accounting

Accrual accounting is based on the fundamental principle that all income earned for a period be matched with the expenses assignable to that period. This process "matches" the revenue earned for the period with the expenses for the same period irrespective of when the income has been received or the expenses paid. All companies listed on the various exchanges (i.e., New York, American) use the accrual basis of accounting. Small businesses, particularly professional and service type organizations, tend to use the "cash basis" of accounting.

Cash Basis

Under the cash basis, income is recorded when received, and expenses are recorded when paid. This method is simple but does not match income and costs for a given period.

EXAMPLE Zodiac Contractors, a partnership, performed work billed at $7,300 during the month of September, 19XX. The firm received payments of $4,000 on September 16 and $3,300 on October 12. Wages of $2,600, the only expense, was paid on September 30. The difference in net income for the months of September and October, would be as follows:

	Cash Basis		Accrual Basis	
	September	October	September	October
Revenue	$4,000	$3,300	$7,300	None
Expense	2,600	None	2,600	None
Net Income	$1,400	$3,300	$4,700	None

It is evident from the above illustration that the accrual basis gives more accurate results because it reflects the correct net income earned in each period.

....

OBSERVATION *The cash receipts and disbursements method of accounting can be used by most partnerships that do not have inventories. The accrual method must be used where the sale of inventory is the most important part of the business. The hybrid method, which is really a combination of the cash and accrual methods, can be used only with approval from the IRS.*[3]

....

HOW TO SUPPORT ALL THE ENTRIES MADE IN THE PARTNERSHIP'S BOOKS AND RECORDS

Sales slips, invoices, canceled checks, paid bills, duplicate deposit slips, and any other documents that explain and support entries made in your books should be filed in an orderly manner and stored in a safe place. Memorandums or sketchy records that

---

[3]IRC Regulation §1.446-1(c) (2) (ii).

approximate income, deductions, or other items may not be allowed by the Internal Revenue Service (IRS) and may result in additional taxes and other charges.

HOW TO GET AN EMPLOYER IDENTIFICATION NUMBER (EIN)

A partnership must obtain an employer's identification number (EIN) for tax purposes by obtaining and filing Form SS-4 with its local IRS office. This form is available from the IRS and Social Security Administration offices. The EIN is used on filed tax returns and correspondence with the IRS. Form SS-4 can be obtained at all IRS or Social Security offices or by calling 1-800-829-1040 and requesting that the form be mailed to you. There is no charge for an EIN, and it will probably take several weeks to process your application. If tax filings are required during the period before you receive your number, write "applied" in the box that asks for the EIN.

A partnership converting into a corporation needs a new EIN.

The state where you operate may also require a separate identification number for your business.

....

NOTE *Other IRS forms and publications can also be obtained by dialing 1-800-829-FORM. When you call, it is suggested that you also pick up two publications: Publication 15 entitled* Circular E—Employer's Tax Guide, *and Publication 541 entitled* Tax Information on Partnerships. *Other helpful IRS tax publications that are free, include the following:*

Publication

334	Tax Guide for Small Business
463	Travel, Entertainment, and Gift Taxes
509	Tax Calendars for 199X
538	Accounting Periods and Methods
551	Basis of Assets
583	Starting a Business and Keeping Records
587	Business Use of Your Home
917	Business Use of a Car
946	How to Depreciate Property

....

PAYROLL RECORDS

An employer, regardless of the number of employees, must maintain all records pertaining to payroll taxes (income tax withholding, social security, unemployment tax) for at least four years after the tax becomes due or is paid, whichever is later.

Employers must withhold taxes from all employees except partners who are required to pay self-employment tax on their partnership earnings. In order to withhold properly, a new employee must fill out Form W-4 (Employee's Withholding Allowance Certificate) listing her appropriate exemptions and then sign it. The partnership will then withhold income tax based on the IRS's withholding tables. If the employee for some reason does not prepare a W-4, the partnership must treat her as a single person with no withholding exemptions. The firm must advise its employees to prepare a new certificate if their status changes (e.g., there is an decrease in the number of their dependents). This new certificate must be filed within ten days of the change in status. However, if an employee knows during the current year that his number of dependents will decrease next year, he must file a new W-4 by December 1 of the current year to report the change.

On or before January 31, the partnership must provide employees, the IRS, and state and local tax agencies with copies of Form W-2 (Wage and Tax Statement) listing the salary earned and taxes withheld for the last calendar year.

....

OBSERVATION *Employees who expect to have no tax liability can be exempt from income tax withholding by certifying on Form W-4 to his employer that he had no federal income tax liability in the preceding year and expects to have no tax liability for the current year as well.*

....

If an employee receives tips of $20 or more in a month, the partnership must report these tips for tax purposes on or before the tenth of the following month.

The partnership must deduct social security taxes from the employee's salary and must also match the employee's contribution. Form 941 is used to remit withholding taxes and social security deductions to the IRS. A completed Form 941 is found in back of this book. Form 941 must be filed by the last day of the month following the end of the quarter (i.e., April 30, June 30, September 30, and January 31 of the following year). For example, Form 941 for the first quarter of the year (January 1 to March 31) must be filed by April 30. The partnership must also deposit the withholding and social security deductions in a separate account. This is accomplished with Form 501 (Federal Tax Deposits, Withheld Income, and FICA taxes). This form, along with the remittances, is sent to a bank authorized to accept tax deposits.

Unemployment tax is paid to both the state and the federal government. The IRS gives a partial credit for unemployment taxes paid to the state. The partnership must first register with the state Bureau of Labor; it will then receive an identification number so that its deposits will be credited to its account. The partnership's employment experience rate will partly determine how much unemployment tax it must pay; the rate will change depending on how many employees are hired and fired. For example, if the partnership terminates a large number of employees, its unemployment tax rate will increase because of the higher demand placed on the state's unemployment fund.

The federal unemployment tax (FUTA) is less than the state rate. Because wages are calculated on a December 31 basis rather than the partnership's fiscal year-end, Form 940 (and the simpler Form 940-EZ) is due no later than the following January 31. The partnership must then file Form 940 (or Form 940-EZ) with the IRS to show how the firm computed the unemployment tax. If the amount exceeds $100, the firm should use a Special Deposit Card 508 (Federal Unemployment Tax Deposit) and pay the tax to an authorized bank before January 31. If the tax is under $100, it may remit the amount directly with Form 940 (or Form 940-EZ). A completed Form 940-EZ is found in back of this book.

Usually, the partnership must have at least two full-time employees before the unemployment tax will exceed $100.

If the partnership hires individuals to perform services as independent contractors, it must file an annual information return (Form 1099) to report payments totaling $600 or more made to any indi-

vidual in the course of trade or business during the calendar year. The records in support of Form 1099 must list the name, address, and social security number of every independent contractor employed, along with pertinent dates and the amounts paid each person. The reports do not have to be mailed with copies of Form 1099 but must be available for examination by the IRS if required. Each payment must be supported by an invoice submitted by the contractor.

PAYROLL TAXES

The most common types of payroll deductions are Social Security taxes, federal, state, and city withholding taxes, and miscellaneous items, such as insurance premiums, employee savings, and union dues.

Social Security Taxes

All employers covered are required to collect the employee's share of Social Security tax by deducting it from the employee's gross pay and to remit it to the government along with the employer's share. Both the employer and the employee are taxed at the same rate. For 1997, the Social Security tax is 6.2% of the first $65,400 of gross wages. The Medicare tax is 1.45% of all wages with no ceiling. This gives a total of 7.65% on the first $65,400 of wages and 1.45% on the wages above $65,400. The partnership employer is required to remit to the government its share of Social Security tax along with the amount of Social Security tax deducted from each employee's gross salary.

Income Tax Withholding

Federal and some state income tax laws require employers to withhold from the pay of each employee the applicable income tax due on those wages. The amount of income tax withheld is computed by the employer according to a government-prescribed formula or withholding tax table. The amount to be withheld for the pay period depends on each employee's taxable wages, marital status, and claimed dependents.

If the income tax withheld plus the employee and the employer social security taxes exceeds specified amounts per month, the employer is required to make payments to the Internal Revenue Service at given intervals during the month. Monthly deposits are not required if the employer's liability for the calendar quarter is less than $500. Instead, the tax liability is paid with the employer's quarterly payroll tax return.

EXAMPLE Assume a weekly payroll of $10,000, entirely subject to Social Security and Medicare (7.65%), income tax withholding of $1,500, and a deduction of $100 in union dues.

The salaries paid and the employee payroll deductions would be:

Wages and Salaries		$10,000
Less:		
Social Security Taxes Payable	765	
Withholding Taxes Payable	$1,500	
Union Dues	100	2,365
Net Payroll Payable		$7,635

Unemployment Taxes

Another payroll tax levied by the federal government in cooperation with state governments provides a system of unemployment insurance. All employers who (1) paid wages of $1,500 or more during any calendar quarter in the year or preceding year or (2) employed at least one individual on at least one day in each of 20 weeks during the current or preceding calendar year are subject to the Federal Unemployment Tax Act (FUTA). This tax is levied *only on the employer* at a rate of 6.2% (1997) on the first $7,000 of compensation paid to each employee during the calendar year. However, a credit is granted for up to 5.4% of wages paid to the state government so that the amount paid to the federal government may be as low as 0.8%.

State unemployment compensation laws differ from the federal law and differ among various states. Therefore, employers must be familiar with the unemployment tax laws in each state in which they pay wages and salaries. Although the normal state tax may range from 3% to 7% or higher, all states provide for some form of merit rating under which a reduction in the state contribution rate is allowed.

In order not to penalize an employer who has earned a reduction in the state contribution rate, the federal law allows a credit of 5.4% even though the effective state contribution rate is less than 5.4%.

EXAMPLE The XYZ Partnership, which has a taxable payroll of $100,000, is subject to a federal rate of 6.2% and a state contribution rate of 5.7%. But because of stable employment experience, the company's state rate is 1%. The computation of the federal and state unemployment taxes for XYZ is as follows:

State unemployment tax payment	
(1%)($100,000)	$1,000
Federal unemployment tax	
(6.2% – 5.4%)($100,000)	800
Total federal and state	
unemployment tax	$1,800

The federal unemployment tax is paid annually on or before January 31 following the taxable calendar year. State contributions generally are required to be paid quarterly.

The IRS has established an electronic funds transfer (EFT) system for federal tax deposits by which employer-withheld taxes may be transferred to a financial institution authorized to collect such funds on behalf of the government.

ESTABLISHING EMPLOYEE BENEFIT PACKAGES

While employee compensation is taxable, the tax law encourages certain types of fringe benefits by allowing the partnership to deduct the cost of the benefit while permitting the employee to exclude the value of the benefits from her income.

H.R. 10 (Keogh Plans)

Partners in a business are not classified as employees and are subject to special retirement plan rules known as H.R. 10 plans (also called Keogh plans). Generally, a partner may contribute the smaller of $30,000 and 25% of earned income. Earned income means net earnings from the partnership. An H.R. 10 plan must be established before the end of the tax year, but contributions may be made up to the due date for filing the partner's personal tax return. One major disadvantage of establishing an H.R. 10 plan is that in addition to covering all partners, the plan must also include all eligible full-time employees thereby making it very costly to the partnership.

Life Insurance Arrangements

The partnership can make the following programs available to its employees:

1. **Group-term.** Under this arrangement, the partnership provides group insurance coverage for its employees. The firm gets a deduction for the premium payment, and the premiums attributable to the first $50,000 of coverage are excluded from the employee's gross income.

2. **Split-dollar.** Split-dollar insurance is an arrangement in which the firm purchases life insurance on certain key employees. The firm pays that part of the premium equal to the annual increase in the cash value of the policy, and the employee pays the balance of the premium.

Health Insurance Arrangements

These plans may include the following:

1. **Accident and health insurance.** A partnership may provide accident and health insurance coverage for its employees. Under the Internal Revenue Code, the employer's premium payments are deductible by the firm and are not included in the employee's income. Moreover, the actual payment of the insurance benefit is not included in the employee's income.

2. **Medical reimbursement plans.** This type of plan allows employees to exclude from income amounts received as reimbursement for medical expenses they incur for their medical care and those of their spouses and dependents.

Cafeteria Plans

These are plans that offer employees the option of choosing cash or certain nontaxable fringe benefits (such as group term life insurance, accident and health benefits). If the employee chooses cash, the cash is taxable. However, if the employee instead chooses a nontaxable fringe benefit, the value of the benefit is excluded from gross income. The fact that the employee could have chosen cash will not cause the fringe benefit to be taxed. The plan cannot discriminate in favor of highly compensated employees or their dependents or spouses. Employer plans may specify what benefits are offered and may limit the amount of benefits that individual employees may receive.

"Flextime" Programs

In order to allow employees to spend more time with their families, some firms offer "flextime" where employees can arrange their work schedules in different ways, such as four 10-hour days with three days off or work from home part of the day.

The Family and Medical Leave Act of 1993

Under the Family and Medical Leave Act (FMLA), covered employers must provide access to up to twelve weeks' unpaid leave per calendar or fiscal year for the employee's own illness, the illness of a close family member, or the birth or adoption of a child. This act applies to employers with fifty or more employees in each day of twenty or more workweeks in a year in which an employee seeks to take leave.

Other Miscellaneous Benefits

Partnerships may also establish such nontaxable fringe benefit programs as employee discounts on the purchase of the employer's products and services, free parking subject to a monthly statutory limit, employer-provided educational assistance, and the nontaxable use of athletic facilities.

ACCOUNTING FOR THE COSTS OF DOING BUSINESS

Deductible business expenses, such as salaries and wages of employees, are the costs of carrying on a trade, business, or profession. These expenses are usually deductible if they are part of the partnership's operations.

Keep in mind that it is important for you to distinguish costs that are capital expenses, such as the purchase of a car or machinery, from costs that are deductible expenses in the current year.

What Is Inventory?

In general, tangible personal property that has any of the following characteristics is defined as inventory:

1. The items are held for resale in the ordinary course of business.
2. The items are "work-in-process" of a manufacturer.
3. The items are the "raw materials" of the manufacturing process and will be consumed in the production of the finished product.

How to Treat Inventories for Tax Purposes

If the partnership earns most of its income from either buying and selling or manufacturing merchandise, it must take into account its inventory at the beginning and end of tax year in order to determine its cost of goods sold, gross profit, and final taxable income. To calculate the cost of goods sold, the firm must start with its beginning inventory, add its purchases for the year, and then subtract its ending inventory. Cost of goods sold is then subtracted from total sales to get gross profit. After determining gross profit, the firm will subtract all operating expenses (i.e., rent, travel and entertainment, repairs, salaries, interest, and depreciation) to arrive at taxable income for the year.

EXAMPLE 1 A partnership's beginning inventory is $1,000. The partnership purchases merchandise for $10,000 and has inventory at the end of the year of $2,500. Cost of goods sold is $8,500 calculated as follows:

Beginning Inventory	$ 1,000
Add: Purchases	10,000
Goods Available for Sale	$11,000
Less: Ending Inventory	2,500
Cost of Goods Sold	$ 8,500

EXAMPLE 2 Using the figures from EXAMPLE 1, assume that partnership sales for the year were $25,000, and that operating expenses (rent, travel and entertainment, repairs, salaries, interest, and depreciation) were $6,700. Partnership net income is $9,800 calculated as follows:

Sales	$25,000
Less: Cost of Goods Sold	8,500
Gross Profit	$16,500
Less: Operating Expenses	6,700
Partnership Net Income	$ 9,800

Items That Must Be Included in Ending Inventory

A company is usually faced with determining what goods are to be included in their ending inventory. Ordinarily, the rules of ownership are governed by the passage of title. For example, if the goods in transit are shipped f.o.b. (free on board) shipping point, title passes when the goods are put aboard the common carrier. In effect, the carrier is acting as the agent of the buyer. If the goods are shipped f.o.b. destination, title does not pass until the goods are received by the purchaser.

Goods held on consignment for others are not to be included in ending inventory because they are owned by a third party and not by the partnership.

Perpetual Versus Periodic Inventory Methods

In a periodic system, the inventory is determined periodically by actual count at the end of a monthly, quarterly, semiannual, or annual accounting period. Enterprises such as supermarkets and hardware stores that sell a large variety of low-cost items rely on the periodic inventory system. At that time, the inventory is priced out in accordance with some cost flow assumption. Cost of goods sold is determined by adding the cost of the beginning inventory to the net purchases and subtracting the ending inventory as determined by the periodic count.

In general, the perpetual system is used when the individual inventory items are either relatively expensive or the number of items in inventory is relatively small. An automobile dealership and a jewelry company would be examples that would satisfy both criteria. The proper application of a perpetual system requires detailed paperwork that is best handled in a computerized accounting system. An actual count of the inventory (commonly referred to as "taking inventory") is conducted at least annually to establish the correctness of the perpetual records and to satisfy IRS tax rules.

Office Expenses

Office expenses include stationery, office supplies, telephone, and postage.

Rent or Lease Expenses

Rental costs incurred in the course of your business include the rental of office space or the leasing of cars or equipment.

Repairs and Maintenance

Machinery repairs, the cost of replacing light bulbs and adding new electrical wiring, the cost of painting your office or equipment, and such other costs as polishing a display case are deductible repairs and maintenance costs.

Supplies

The costs of such items as shipping tags and tape, packaging supplies, and marking pens are treated as the cost of supplies.

Taxes and Licenses

You can deduct various taxes imposed by federal, state local, and foreign governments if you incur them in the ordinary course of your partnership business and if they are directly related to that trade or business. If you use the cash method of accounting, you can deduct taxes only in the year paid. If you use an accrual method, you can deduct them only in the year they are properly accrued.

Real Estate Taxes

Real estate (real property) taxes are the taxes that the partnership pays on land and buildings that the partnership owns. Assessments for local benefits that tend to increase the value of the partnership property, such as assessments for construction of streets, sidewalks, and water and sewerage systems, or to provide public parking facilities, generally are not deductible. If the local benefit increases the value of the partnership's property, you must capitalize the cost (add the value of the assessment to the cost of the property).

Local assessments for maintenance, repairs, or interest charges for benefits, such as streets, sidewalks, and water and sewerage systems, are tax deductible. If only part of the assessment is for

maintenance, repairs, or interest, the partnership must be able to show the amount allocated to the different purposes. If the partnership cannot show what part of the assessment is for maintenance, repairs, or interest, none of it is deductible.

Water bills, sewerage, and other service charges assessed against your business property are deductible as business expenses.

State and Local Income Taxes

State income taxes imposed on the partnership are deductible.

Travel Expenses

There are two basic types of business travel: local travel and expenses incurred while away-from-home, which includes meals and lodging. Commuting expenses between a taxpayer's residence and a business location within the area of the taxpayer's tax home are never deductible. If the taxpayer's work requires the transportation of heavy or bulk tools or instruments, and the taxpayer can prove that transportation costs were incurred in addition to the ordinary nondeductible commuting expenses, a deduction for these expenses will be allowed.

Ordinary and necessary expenses incurred in the pursuit of business while away from home are deductions as business expenses. These business "away-from-home" expenses include travel and other costs incurred by a self-employed person away from home at least overnight. Under these rules, the person does not have to be away for an entire 24-hour period so long as the period is longer than the normal working day. Away-from-home travel expenses include transportation costs, airplane, bus and travel fares, meals and lodging to the extent that they are not lavish or extravagant, taxicabs, tips, phone calls, and the costs of transporting display cases and similar equipment.

Meals and Entertainment Expenses

A partnership can deduct meals and entertainment expenses, including the cost of tickets, incurred in partnership's business provided that the expenses are directly related to its trade or business. The partners must be able to prove the amount spent and the business nature of the expense. Even if they meet these requirements, the amount deductible may be limited.

The amount allowable as a deduction for meals and entertainment is limited to 50 percent of such expenses. This 50-percent rule is taken into account only after determining what part of the expense is allowable. For example, if any portion of the meal is considered to be lavish or extravagant, it is not tax deductible.

EXAMPLE You take a client to dinner that you can prove is related to your business. The cost of the dinner is $100. If $40 of the dinner is considered to be lavish and extravagant you can only deduct $60. Of this amount, only $30 is deductible ($60 × 50%).

The allowable cost of any entertainment ticket is limited to the face value of the ticket. That means that if the ticket cost $100 while its face value was $25, the additional "scalping fee" of $75 in nondeductible.

Good tax planning in the entertainment and travel area requires that detailed records be kept, including dates, amounts, places, and the business relationship of the person or persons involved.

If a company pays for the meals of its owners and employees, they are fully deductible by the partnership and tax-free to the employee if furnished "for the convenience of the employer." This is an extremely valuable benefit to employees working late or for those required to work through their lunch or supper hour.

Business Gifts

Deductions for business gifts are limited to $25 per person. A husband and wife are treated as one person for this purpose. Thus, if the partnership gives a gift worth $30 to a customer and a bottle of perfume to his wife worth $40, the total deductible amount is not $50 ($25 plus $25) but one amount of $25. An exception is made for an item such as a pen imprinted with your company's name or logo if it costs no more than $4.

Utilities

The costs of heat, hot water, and electricity required to run the office and any business equipment that is part of the operation of the business are deductible.

Wages

Wages paid only to full and part-time employees, but not to the self-employed owner, are included in this account.

Other Expenses

Miscellaneous expenses that cannot be classified into any of the other categories can be included in this account. They might include settlement of a lawsuit or the costs of education and training classes.

The partnership then calculates net income by subtracting the total of all operating expenses from gross income to arrive at tentative net income or loss from the business.

Office in the Home

Employees and self-employed individuals are not allowed a deduction for office in the home expenses unless a portion of the residence is used exclusively on a regular basis as either:

- The principal place of business for any trade or business of the taxpayer, or
- A place of business used by clients or customers.

Because of strict tax rules, this deduction is generally restricted to professionals, such as attorneys, doctors, accountants, and so on, who do not maintain a permanent place of business elsewhere and employees who conduct a separate trade or business on a part-time basis exclusively in a portion of their personal residence.

Depreciation Methods Available to a Partnership

When a partnership buys property with a useful life of more than one year, it can recover the cost over several years by taking annual deductions from gross income. These annual deductions, called depreciation expense, represent the portion of the property's cost written off each year because of wear and tear deterioration and normal obsolescence. How quickly taxpayers depreciate business property depends on (1) whether the property is real property or tangible personal property and (2) when they placed the property in service.

Taxpayers recover the cost of tangible personal property more quickly than the cost of real property. In addition, a partnership can use more accelerated methods to depreciate the cost of tangible personal property. Real property includes all real estate, such as office buildings, physical plants, and warehouses. Tangible personal property includes tangible property other than real estate, such as furniture and fixtures, machinery and equipment, and cars.

Depreciation and Cost Recovery Systems

Although there are four basic methods for depreciating property, a new partnership should be aware of two basic methods, the Modified Accelerated Cost Recovery System (MACRS) and the Alternative Depreciation System (ADS), both used for assets bought after 1986.

Modified Accelerated Cost Recovery System (MACRS)

MACRS assigns tangible personal property to one of six recovery periods. The IRS publishes depreciation tables with lives of 3, 5, 7, 10, 15, 20, 27.5, 31.5, and 39 years. MACRS assigns the more common business properties a 5-year or 7-year life. The 5-year class life includes automobiles, office equipment (copiers, typewriters, fax machines, computers, and printers), and cellular phones. The 7-year class life includes furniture and fixtures, machinery, and equipment.

A partnership will use the property's cost basis to compute annual depreciation under MACRS. To make the calculation of depreciation easier, the Internal Revenue Code uses rules called half-year and mid-quarter conventions when making up depreciation tables under MACRS.

For example, a MACRS Table for 3-, 5-, 7-, and 10-Year Classes Using a Half-Year Convention would appear as follows:

	Recovery Period			
Year	3-Year	5-Year	7-Year	10-Year
1	33.33%	20.00%	14.29%	10.00%
2	44.45	32.00	24.49	18.00
3	14.81	19.20	17.49	14.40
4	7.41	11.52	12.49	11.52
5		11.52	8.93	9.22
6		5.76	8.92	7.37
7			8.93	6.55
8			4.46	6.55
9				6.56
10				6.55
11				3.28

EXAMPLE In 19XX, The VBN Partnership bought five-year property for $10,000. Using the above table, deprecation applicable to the property would be as follows:

Year		MACRS
19XX	$10,000 × 20%	$2,000
19X1	10,000 × 32%	3,200
19X2	10,000 × 19.2%	1,920
19X3	10,000 × 11.52%	1,152
19X4	10,000 × 11.52%	1,152
19X5	10,000 × 5.76	576

Alternative Depreciation System (ADS)

ADS differs from MACRS in that most properties have longer depreciation periods. For example, the following table compares the recovery periods under MACRS and ADS.

	MACRS	ADS
Furniture, fixtures and equipment	7 yrs.	10 yrs.
Automobiles and computers	5 yrs.	5 yrs.
Copiers, calculators, typewriters	5 yrs.	6 yrs.
Heavy general purpose trucks	5 yrs.	6 yrs.

EXAMPLE In 19XX, the partnership of Brett Harvey and Tony Bean bought office equipment. They can choose either the MACRS or ADS methods of depreciation.

How to Depreciate (Write Off) up to $18,000 Per Year

Beginning in 1997, the total business cost you can elect to write off for personal property deducted under Section 179 for a tax year has been increased from $17,500 to $18,000. This $18,000 maximum dollar limit applies to each taxpayer, *not* to each business.

EXAMPLE In 1997, the partnership bought a used automobile for $10,000 and office equipment for $8,000. Both items will be used in the business. The partnership can elect to deduct the full $10,000 for the car and the entire $8,000 for the office equipment for a total of $18,000. This is the maximum dollar limit you can deduct in 1997.

In addition, the amount of write-off increases over the years until it reaches $25,000 according to the following schedule:

1998	$18,500
1999	19,000
2000	20,000
2001	24,000
2002	24,000
2003 and thereafter	25,000

....

NOTE *In the case of a partnership, the partnership and each partner are individually subject to the annual $18,000 limitation and higher amounts in later years.*

....

The section 179 deduction is not automatic. If the partnership wants to take the deduction, it must elect to do so on its tax return.

Nondeductible Expenses

Remember that traffic tickets, bribes, kickbacks, and tax penalties are never tax deductible by any business, including a partnership, because they are contrary to public policy.

CHAPTER 11

How a Partnership Is Taxed

INTRODUCTION

F or federal income tax purposes, the term "partnership" includes a syndicate, group, pool, joint venture, or similar organization that is carrying on a trade or business. A joint undertaking simply to share expenses is not a partnership. Mere co-ownership of property maintained and leased or rented is not a partnership. However, if the co-owners provide services to the tenants, a partnership exists.

LIMITED LIABILITY COMPANY (LLC)

An LLC is an entity formed under state law by filing articles of organization as an LLC. Unlike the partners in a partnership, none of the members of an LLC are personally liable for its debts. An LLC may be classified as either a partnership or a corporation for federal income tax purposes. It is classified as a partnership if it has no more than two of the following corporate characteristics:

1. Limited liability of the owners;
2. Free transferability of interests;
3. Continuity of life;
4. Centralization of management.

If the LLC has no more than one of the last three corporate characteristics (items 2 through 4),

then the rules applicable to a partnership prevails. LLCs file Form 1065, U.S. Partnership Return of Income. An LLC must distribute Form 1065 K-1 at the end of each tax year to each member showing her proportionate share of income and losses.

....

OBSERVATION *CONVERSION OF PARTNERSHIP INTO AN LLC. The conversion of a partnership into an LLC classified as a partnership for federal tax purposes does not terminate the partnership. The conversion is not a sale, exchange, or liquidation of any partnership interest, the partnership's tax year does not close, and the LLC can continue to use the partnership's taxpayer identification number. The same rules apply if an LLC classified as a partnership is converted into a partnership.*
....

Note that some states may tax LLCs even though the IRS does not do so.

LIMITED LIABILITY PARTNERSHIP (LLP)

A limited liability partnership (LLP) is similar to an LLC but is formed under a separate state law that generally applies to professional service organizations, such as law and accounting firms. Under this type of arrangement, no partner in an LLP is liable or accountable for any debts or liabilities chargeable to the LLP or to any other partner whether arising by tort or contract. This rule of limited liability does not apply to any negligent or wrongful act or misconduct committed by any partner or by any person under the partner's supervision or control while rendering professional services on behalf of the LLP.

In an LLP, each partner must be a professional authorized to perform that particular professional service. That means that in an LLP formed to render public accounting services, all partners must be Certified Public Accountants authorized to practice in the state where the LLP does business.

Like a general or limited partnership, the business form is like that of a partnership for tax purposes and all partnership tax rules apply to this form of doing business just as they would for any other partnership.

THE FAMILY LIMITED PARTNERSHIP (FLP)

Family limited partnerships (FLP) are used as a way to pass on the family business and other assets at minimal tax cost. Here is how it works. The owner of real estate, a business, or a stock portfolio puts that property in a family limited partnership. She keeps an ownership interest, often only 1% or 2%, and becomes a general partner. The rest of the ownership interest can then be given as a gift to the limited partners—typically the children or grandchildren—either all at once or in steps to take advantage of the $10,000 per person annual gift tax exclusion.

Under the partnership form, the general partner has management control and may even draw a management fee for compensation. The limited partners—here, the children or grandchildren—have no say in day-to-day operations. But any income, if distributions are made by the general partner, passes directly to them proportionately.

EXAMPLE Dorothy Deux, a wealthy grandparent, transfers a business and real estate to a FLP, retaining a 1% general partnership interest, and gifts away the remaining 99% limited partnership interest. After this transaction, she still effectively controls the partnership and its underlying assets.

However, there is even a greater tax-saving advantage. Because the limited partners have no control over the partnership assets, the value of the assets is decreased. This translates into significant tax savings because estate and gift taxes are based upon the fair market value of these interests. Limited control gives rise to big discounts.

EXAMPLE With a 25% discount, for example, a $800,000 stock portfolio would be valued at only $600,000, the amount that can pass free of federal estate taxes imposed at death. And if the value of the family limited partnership interest is discounted just 30%, you can give away $14,000 instead of $10,000 (the maximum amount that an annual gift can be valued at before a federal gift tax is imposed) to each of your children and grandchildren without triggering gift taxes.

For older family members who worry that their children will be unable to manage large sums of money, the FLP is an excellent way to retain control over any funds distributed to the children.

THE FAMILY PARTNERSHIP

Members of a family can be partners. However, family members will be recognized as partners only if one of the following requirements is met:

1. **Where capital is a material income-producing factor.** If capital is a material income-producing factor, a partner acquired his capital interest in a bona fide transaction (even if by gift or purchase from another family member), and actually owns and controls the partnership interest; or

2. **Where capital is not a material income-producing factor.** If capital is not a material income-producing factor, partners must have joined together in good faith to conduct a business. In addition, they must have agreed that contributions of each entitle them to a share in the profits. Some capital or service must be provided by each partner.

OBSERVATION *Capital means that the operation of the business requires substantial inventories or investments in plant, machinery, or equipment.*

THE HUSBAND AND WIFE PARTNERSHIP

If spouses carry on a business together and share in the profits and losses, they may be partners whether or not they have a formal partnership agreement. If so, they should report income or loss from the business on Form 1065 (U.S. Partnership Return of Income). They should not report the income on a Schedule C (Form 1040) in the name of one spouse as a sole proprietor.

Each spouse should carry his or her share of the partnership income or loss from Schedule K-1 (Form 1065) to their joint or separate Form(s) 1040. Each spouse should include his or her respective share of self-employment income on a separate Schedule SE (Form 1040), Self-Employment Tax. Usually this will not increase their total tax but it will give each spouse credit for social security earnings on which retirement benefits are based.

SELECTING THE PARTNERSHIP'S TAX YEAR

Taxable income is figured on the basis of a tax year. A "tax year" is the accounting period used for keeping records and reporting income and expenses.

A partnership generally must conform its tax year to its partners' tax years as follows:

1. **Majority interest tax year.** If one or more partners having the same tax year own an interest in partnership profits and capital of more than 50% (a majority interest), the partnership must use the tax year of those partners.
2. **Principal partner.** If there is no majority interest, the partnership must use the tax year of all its principal partners. A principal partner is one who has a 5% or more interest in the profits or capital of the partnership.

If a partnership establishes an acceptable business purpose for having a tax year that is different from its required tax year, it may use that different tax year. For example, a partnership, if it shows an acceptable business purpose, can use a regular fiscal year of twelve consecutive months ending on the last day of any month except December. A partnership may elect to use a fiscal tax year that varies from 52 to 53 weeks if such a period always ends on the same day of the week (Monday, Tuesday, etc.), either on the last such day in a calendar month or the closest such day to the last day of a calendar month.

PARTNERS' TAX ELECTIONS (TO LOWER THEIR PERSONAL TAXES)

The costs of organizing a partnership are treated as capital expenditures (meaning they cannot be deducted at once but must be written off over a predetermined number of years). Eligible expenditures include legal fees for negotiating and preparing partnership agreements, accounting fees for establishing the initial accounting system, and filing fees. The partnership can choose to amortize these expenses over a period of not less than 60 months beginning with the month that the partnership begins doing business.

Making the Election

The election to amortize (meaning to write off as an expense thereby lowering their taxable income) organization expenses is made by attaching a statement to the partnership's tax return for the tax year the partnership begins doing business. The statement must provide the following information:

1. A description of each organization expense incurred (whether or not paid);
2. The amount of each expense;
3. The date each expense was incurred;
4. The month the partnership began its business;
5. The number of months (not less than 60) over which the expenses are to be amortized.

REPORTING OF PARTNERSHIP INCOME AND EXPENSE ITEMS BY EACH PARTNER

Partners must take into account their shares of partnership taxable income and any separately stated partnership items in computing their taxable income. The net income or loss and all separately stated items attributable to each partner must be reported on Schedule K-1 (Form 1065). These partnership items include the following:

1. Long-term capital gains and losses;
2. Short-term capital gains and losses;

3. Gains and losses from the sale of certain business property;

4. Charitable contributions;

5. Dividend income;

6. Taxable interest;

7. Tax-exempt interest;

8. Foreign taxes paid;

9. Income or loss from rental activities;

10. Miscellaneous taxable income or losses.

EXAMPLE The income statement on December 31, 19XX of the A & B Partnership, consisting of two equal partners, showed the following items that resulted in net income of $63,000 for the year:

Partnership Item	Income Statement	Net Income	Separately Stated
Sales	$230,000	$230,000	
Cost of Goods Sold	(120,000)	(120,000)	
Operating Expenses	(50,000)	(50,000)	
State and Local Taxes	(4,000)	(4,000)	
Foreign Taxes	(1,000)		(1,000)
Dividends	2,400		2,400
Taxable Interest	2,000		2,000
Tax-exempt Interest	1,500		1,500
Charitable Contributions	(2,300)		(2,300)
Short-Term Capital Gains	5,000		5,000
Long-Term Capital Losses	(600)		(600)
	$63,000	$56,000	$7,000

The partners will list their shares of the income as follows:

Partnership Item	Income Statement	Partner A	Partner B
Ordinary Net Income	$ 56,000	$ 28,000	$ 28,000
Foreign Taxes	(1,000)	(500)	(500)
Dividends	2,400	1,200	1,200
Taxable Interest	2,000	1,000	1,000
Tax-exempt Interest	1,500	750	750
Charitable Contributions	(2,300)	(1,150)	(1,150)
Short-Term Capital Gains	5,000	2,500	2,500
Long-Term Capital Losses	(600)	(300)	(300)
	$63,000	$31,500	$31,500

A Partner's Share of Income and the Self-Employment Tax

Individual partners must report their share of partnership taxable income as self-employment income subject to self-employment tax. A self-employment tax is in addition to the regular income tax that a partner must pay annually.

Estimated Taxes

Estimated tax is the method used to pay tax on income that is not subject to withholding, such as partnership income. Individuals use Form 1040-ES to pay both the income and the self-employment tax. Individuals must make estimated tax payments if they expect to owe at least $500 for the tax year. Payments are usually made on April 15, June 15, September 15, and January 15 of the following tax year.

EXAMPLE Joe Jordan expects to owe $4,000 in both income and self-employment taxes for the tax year 19XX. He is required to make the following payments for 19XX:

April 15, 19XX	$1,000
June 15, 19XX	1,000
September 15, 19XX	1,000
January 15, 19X1	1,000
	$4,000

TERMINATION OF THE PARTNERSHIP

A partnership terminates when:

1. All of its operations are discontinued and no part of any business, financial operation, or venture is continued by any of its partners in a partnership or an LLC classified as a partnership; or

2. At least 50% of the total interest in partnership capital and profits is sold or exchanged within a twelve-month period, including a sale or exchange to another partner.

When a partnership terminates, its tax year is closed, requiring the partners to include their share of partnership earnings for the short-period partnership year in their tax returns. If the termination is not properly timed, partnership income for the regular twelve-month tax year may already be included in the same personal tax return that must include the short-tax year.

COMPUTING THE BASIS OF YOUR INTEREST IN THE PARTNERSHIP

A partner who contributes property in exchange for a partnership interest does not recognize gain or loss on the transaction. The contributing partner's basis is the amount of money contributed, plus her adjusted basis of any property contributed, plus any taxable income realized on acquisition of the interest.

EXAMPLE Valerie Hopp, Ted Skip, and David Jump form an equal partnership. Valerie contributes $1,000 in cash, Ted contributes property Y (basis $600, fair market value $1,500), and David contributes property Z (basis $800, Fair market value $1,400.) No gain or loss is recognized on the transaction. The partnership's basis for each property is the same as the contributing partner's basis. Thus, Valerie's basis is $1,000, Ted's basis is $600, and David's basis is $800.

The value of a partnership's interest in *capital* acquired for services rendered is ordinary income to the partner. The interest is valued (1) when received, if given for past services, or (2) when the services are rendered if the interest depends on future services.

INCORPORATING YOUR PARTNERSHIP

Under the Internal Revenue Code, gains and losses earned by partners who eventually decide to incorporate will not be taxable if the following three requirements are met:

1. The partners making the transfer to the corporation must together control the corporation immediately after the exchange;

2. Each of the partners must receive back stock in the new corporation;

3. The corporation does not assume any liabilities of any of the partners.

EXAMPLE Alex Troy owns a special machine with a cost basis of $2,000 and a fair market value of $20,000. Baron Lowe owns land with a cost basis of $40,000 and a fair market value of $20,000. They both transfer their property to a newly organized corporation in exchange for equal shares of stock. Under the Internal Revenue Code, Alex's $18,000 gain and Baron's $20,000 loss are not recognized.

In order to meet the requirements for not having taxable gains or deductible losses, all of the transferring partners must meet a "control" test. "Control" means at least 80% of the combined voting power of all classes of both voting and nonvoting stock of the new corporation.

USING AN S CORPORATION TO AVOID DOUBLE TAXATION

S Corporations can avoid paying corporate income taxes if all the shareholders consent to taxation of corporate income at the shareholder level. Although there are exceptions, most often the corporation itself is not a tax-paying entity. This is in sharp contrast to the separate taxpayer status held by regular corporations who are subject to double taxation. In effect, the election makes the S Corporation a tax-reporting rather than a tax-paying entity. The income of the corporation flows through to the individuals as if the reporting entity was a partnership. Simplified, the S election treats the corporation as if it was a partnership. S Corporations file Form 1120S annually.

In order to qualify under Subchapter S, a corporation must be a small business corporation. The following additional requirements must be met in order to be a small business corporation:

1. Must be a domestic corporation (meaning a corporation formed in the United States);
2. Must not have more than 35 (75 shareholders for tax years beginning after 1996) shareholders;
3. Must include only eligible shareholders;
4. Must have only one class of stock;
5. Must not be an ineligible corporation.

....

OBSERVATION *The corporation may not have more than 35 shareholders (75 shareholders for tax years beginning after 1996). Thus, if a husband and wife own shares as joint owners, they are considered as one shareholder for this purpose. However, should the couple later divorce, then each would count as a separate shareholder even if the stock is still held jointly. If one spouse dies while the couple is married, there is only one shareholder as long as the stock remains in the deceased shareholder's estate.[4]*
....

Shareholders elect S corporation status by filing Form 2553. All shareholders must consent to the election.

WHAT IS A "TAX SHELTER"?

A tax shelter is a general term that refers to publicly or privately distributed offerings of *limited partnership* interests, which offer significant tax benefits. Popular examples, at least in the past, included oil and gas drilling programs, real estate deals, and equipment leasing partnerships. Tax shelters have, as their tax features, a deferral (postponement of income), immediate deductions against a partner's other income, and capital gains treatment when the partner's interest is later sold at a gain.

In order to prevent what Congress deemed the harmful and excessive use of tax shelters, Congress changed the Internal Revenue Code and placed far-reaching restrictions[5] on how deductions, losses, and certain tax credits from a tax shelter can be used to offset any other income earned by a limited partner.

....

[4] IRC §1361 (b) (10) (A).
[5] Section 469.

CHAPTER 12

How to Buy and/or Sell an Ongoing Partnership

INTRODUCTION

There is no absolute value that can be put on an operating partnership, although value, when determined, must be translated into terms of money. A valuation is a means of justifying the asking price of a business. While net worth (assets less liabilities) is a primary factor in valuing most privately owned businesses, you cannot rely entirely on balance sheet figures because they are based upon original cost and, therefore, may not reflect the current value of assets.

Another issue is goodwill. Goodwill (meaning the positive reputation of the partnership in the business community) may not be shown on the balance sheet, but it may be material in amount. The common practice of ignoring goodwill on the partnership balance sheet might lead to a serious undervaluation of a company's assets.

CHECKLIST OF DIFFERENCES BETWEEN A LARGE AND SMALL PARTNERSHIP AS A DETERMINANT FACTOR IN SELECTING A VALUATION TECHNIQUE

1. If a partnership is small, a key partner may play a greater role in the success of it. This situation may call for the partner to continue her role as manager after the purchase of the business.
2. Larger partnerships usually pay their managers the market rate in salaries while smaller partnerships tend to pay their managers only what they can afford.
3. Large businesses tend to be sold for cash, stock of the purchasing entity, and installment notes while small enterprises are usually sold for a cash down payment plus monthly payments for a fixed number of years.
4. Larger businesses have usually been in business for longer than smaller entities, thus, making it easier to study and evaluate their financial history and potential future value.
5. Most larger partnerships use the accrual basis of accounting while smaller businesses tend to use the cash basis unless inventory is a material income producing factor.
6. Larger partnerships usually have audited financial statements while smaller partnerships tend to have compiled statements (financial statements where the CPA compiles the accounting data according to generally accepted accounting principles but does not express an opinion as to the accuracy of the financial statements).
7. Larger partnerships generally have better accounting records than smaller entities.
8. Larger partnerships tend to have more union problems than smaller ones.

Some of the more important and useful methods of valuation are discussed below.

HOW TO VALUE AN ONGOING BUSINESS

Suppose that you decide to purchase an ongoing business. It does have its advantages. First, there is a recognized product with established sales outlets. Second, you have experienced employees working for you. Third, there is no start-up or break-in period where costly mistakes are made in order to "learn the ropes." Of course, purchasing an ongoing business can be costly, and there is always the risk that you, as a buyer, may overpay. The other side of the coin is that you, as a seller, may risk undervaluation of perhaps your most valuable asset, your business. What follows is a basic discussion regarding the use of certain methods for accurately valuing an ongoing partnership.

Tangible Book Value

This value is determined by the partnership's last balance sheet. Basically the computation involves subtracting the entity's total liabilities from its total assets.

DANGER *Because balance sheet assets are reflected at cost, which ignores fair market value, and because goodwill may not be recorded on the balance sheet, a business with high resale value assets or unrecorded goodwill should avoid this method.*

Adjusted Tangible Book Value

This method takes the book value of all assets and liabilities and adjusts them to fair market value.

EXAMPLE Bantam Sales Company, a general partnership, presents the following financial data:

	Reported Net Book Value	Fair Market Value
Inventory	$ 20,000	$ 25,000
Land and plant	45,000	60,000
Equipment	50,000	100,000
	$115,000	$185,000
Liabilities	20,000	

Assuming that there is unrecorded goodwill of $40,000, the fair market value of the company would be $205,000 ($185,000 + $40,000 − $20,000).

Liquidation Value

This method assumes that the partnership ceases operations, sells its assets, pays off all of its liabilities, and distributes the remaining cash to its partners in proportion to their ownership.

EXAMPLE Sundial Paper Products, a partnership consisting of five general partners, plans to liquidate by selling all of its assets, paying its liabilities, and making a liquidating distribution to its partners. Assuming assets with a net realizable value of $200,000, and liabilities of $50,000, each partner would be expected to get $30,000 each calculated as follows:

Estimated fair market value of assets	$200,000
Less: Liabilities	50,000
Net liquidation value	$150,000
Number of equal partners	5
Liquidation value per partner	$30,000

Replacement Value

Where there is a strong possibility that many assets are undervalued, an independent appraiser or a panel of appraisers may be called in by the partners or potential buyers.

HOW TO GET THE BEST TAX BREAK *Once the buyer and the seller have decided to structure the transaction as a taxable purchase of assets, they must then decide whether to allocate the total sales price among the individual assets sold or whether to merely agree on and set forth in a single lump-sum price.*

OBSERVATION *Note that in allocating the purchase price of a business to the newly acquired assets, the capitalized cost of goodwill and most other intangibles such as licenses, patents, and covenants not to compete are ratably amortized (written off) over a 15-year period beginning in the month of acquisition.*

EXAMPLE On January 2, 19XX, Tiger Supermarkets Ltd. purchased all of the net assets of Iris Flowers, a partnership, for $200,000. Among the acquired assets were the following intangible assets:

Goodwill	$20,000
Patents	10,000
Licenses	5,000
A covenant not to compete for 5 years	30,000
	$65,000

All of the above assets are amortizable ratably over a period of 15 years beginning with the first month of the acquisition.

SETTING THE TERMS OF VALUATION FOR A PARTNER'S INTEREST

Sample Partnership Agreement to Value a Partner's Interest Prior to Admitting or Buying Out a Departing or Deceased Partner's Interest

The Agreement as to Valuation of a Partner's Interest, in Appendix B, can be used when valuing a partner's interest.

NOTE *The agreement may also contain any other provisions that the partners deem necessary, such as a new revaluation within one month (or six months for federal estate tax purposes) after the partner dies so that a more accurate appraisal of the deceased partner's interest can be ascertained.*

WARNING *In order to avoid questions from the IRS, the partners should keep records, use an attorney to draw up any supporting documents, allocate asset values fairly, and keep all records pertaining to the sale. Normally, after three years, persons no longer have to worry about an audit. IRS Publication 544, Sales & Other Dispositions of Assets is also useful and is available free from the IRS.*

GLOSSARY

ACCOUNTING EQUATION Assets = Liabilities + Capital (Partners' Total Equity or Capital Accounts)

ACCRUAL ACCOUNTING Principle that all income earned for a period be matched with the expenses assignable to that period.

AGENT One who is authorized to act for another. Every partner in a partnership is an agent of every other partner when dealing with third parties.

APPARENT AUTHORITY The unauthorized acts of a partner that are similar to those made by a real partner that would cause an innocent third person who deals with the partner in good faith to enter into a contract with the partnership.

ARTICLES OF COPARTNERSHIP Also called the partnership agreement. The articles contain the rules and conditions under which all of the partners agree to operate.

"ASSUMED" OR "TRADE" NAME A partnership usually has the opportunity to operate under an "assumed" or "trade" name, such as "Acme Printing" or "Marvelous Home Decorators." Most states have laws regarding the use of an assumed name.

BASIS In tax law, it is roughly the equivalent of the cost of the property by the taxpayer. To compute gain or loss on the sale or exchange of property, the basis of property is generally subtracted from the amount realized from the sale or exchange.

CAFETERIA PLANS Employee benefit plans that offer workers the option of choosing cash or certain nontaxable fringe benefits (such as group term life insurance, and accident and health benefits).

CAPITAL GAINS AND LOSSES Under the Internal Revenue Code, property (such as stock) that is sold and results in either a short-term or long-term gain or loss.

CASH BASIS ACCOUNTING Income is recorded when received, and expenses are recorded when paid.

CONTINUATION AGREEMENT This type of agreement denies to a partner the liquidation right generally available upon dissolution. The agreement gives the partnership the right to continue in existence by compensating a partner who leaves the business and only allowing for liquidation in specific circumstances.

CORPORATION A fictitious entity validly formed under state statutes applicable to corporations. Being an artificial person, it can only act through its directors, officers, employees, and agents. Corporations can become partners in most states.

DEADLOCK Occurs when there are an equal number of partners, and there is a tie vote that cannot be broken despite several attempts to do so, which may prevent the partnership from functioning.

DISSOLUTION A change in the relation of the partners caused by any partner ceasing to be associated in the carrying on of the partnership's business.

DORMANT PARTNER A dormant or sleeping partner is one who is both secret and inactive. Upon discovery of his connection with the firm, his liability to third parties is the same as that of a general partner.

DOUBLE-ENTRY BOOKKEEPING Under this system, debits and credits reflecting business transactions are entered into both journals and ledgers. The total amounts in the ledger are then added and adjusted at the end of the accounting period to create the financial statements.

DUTY TO INFORM A duty that each partner in a partnership owes to the other copartners regarding all information that she possesses or obtains that is relevant to the partnership's business.

EMPLOYER IDENTIFICATION NUMBER (EIN) A partnership must obtain an employer's identification number (EIN) for tax purposes by obtaining and filing Form SS-4 with its local IRS office. The EIN is used on filed tax returns and correspondence with the IRS.

FAMILY AND MEDICAL LEAVE ACT (FMLA) OF 1993 Under this federal act, covered employers must provide access to up to 12 weeks' leave per calendar or fiscal year for the employee's own illness, the illness of a close family member, or the birth or adoption of a child.

FAMILY LIMITED PARTNERSHIP (FLP) A term that has informally developed for a limited partnership under state law in which there is a family relationship among the general and limited partners.

FAMILY PARTNERSHIP A partnership consisting of members who are related to one another by either birth or through marriage. It is not required that all partners in a family partnership be related to another.

FIDUCIARY An individual who is in a trust relationship. Partners have a fiduciary duty to both the partnership and to one another. This means that they are not permitted to work on behalf of the partnership if their acts are motivated by self-interest.

FISCAL TAX YEAR A regular fiscal year is twelve consecutive months ending on the last day of any month except December. A 52–53 week year is a fiscal tax year that varies from 52 to 53 weeks.

GENERAL PARTNER A general (or active) partner is one who takes an active part in the management of the partnership and is subject to unlimited liability to partnership creditors. General partners may also have membership in a special or limited partnership.

GENERAL PARTNERSHIP Composed of two or more individuals who contribute their capital and skills toward ongoing profit-directed activities. In a partnership, every partner is an agent of the partnership in dealing with third parties. Each partner is jointly (meaning that each copromisor is liable for the entire debt) and/or severally liable (meaning that each party is liable alone or individually) for the debts of the partnership.

GOODWILL The positive reputation of the partnership in the business community. Goodwill may be based upon the management skills of the partners, effective advertising, good labor relations, an excellent location, and an outstanding credit rating.

JOINT VENTURE An undertaking by two or more persons or other entities, usually to accomplish a single objective. Aside from the single-objective feature, it is identical to a general partnership.

LIMITED LIABILITY COMPANY (LLC) A recent form of organization that may offer greater business and tax advantages than a regular corporation. Profits and losses flow through to each individual owner on the personal level (called a "member" for LLC purposes). An LLC has the advantages of a partnership's nontaxable flow-through tax treatment, a corporate shareholder's limited liability, and a general partner's control of management (called a "manager" for LLC purposes).

LIMITED LIABILITY PARTNERSHIP (LLP) A limited liability partnership (LLP) is similar to an LLC but is formed under a separate state statute that generally applies to professional service organizations, such as law and accounting firms.

LIMITED PARTNERSHIP The limited partnership form of doing business can only be created according to the formalities stated in the Uniform Limited Partnership Act (ULPA), which has been adopted in virtually all states. Every limited partnership must have at least one general and one limited partner.

MAJORITY More than half the votes cast.

NATURAL BUSINESS YEAR Exists when a business has a peak period and a non-peak period.

NOMINAL PARTNER A nominal partner is one who appears to the world as a partner and who may be charged with the liabilities of a partner whether or not he has an actual interest in the firm. A nominal partner is sometimes known as a *partner by estoppel.*

NONTRADING PARTNERSHIP Partners in a nontrading partnership may have the implied authority by necessity or by custom and usage applicable to other similar partnerships to buy property for use in the partnership's business.

PARTNER BY ESTOPPEL A nominal partner is one who appears to the world as a partner and who may be charged with the liabilities of a partner whether or not he has an actual interest in the firm.

PARTNERSHIP AGREEMENT Also called the articles of copartnership. Contains the rules and conditions under which all of the partners agree to operate.

REVISED UNIFORM LIMITED PARTNERSHIP ACT (RULPA) Both the Uniform Limited Partnership Act (ULPA) and RULPA form the basis for the governing of the limited partnership. RULPA is the partnership law in virtually all states today.

S CORPORATION Under the Internal Revenue Code, a corporation that avoids double taxation, once at the corporate level and again at the shareholder level, by electing to be taxed as if it was a partnership. S corporations cannot have more than 75 shareholders as of 1997.

SECRET (OR UNDISCLOSED) PARTNER A secret partner is one who actually participates in the management of the partnership but whose connection with the firm is not publicly disclosed. A secret partner is liable like any other general partner.

SINGLE-ENTRY ACCOUNTING SYSTEM A single-entry bookkeeping system is based on the company's profit or loss statement and includes only the partnership's business income and expense accounts.

SOLE OR INDIVIDUAL PROPRIETORSHIP This a natural form of doing business at lowest initial cost. The sole proprietor is the owner and "boss."

TAX-FREE INCORPORATION Where the incorporators contribute property, but not services, to the corporation and take back control of the corporation. Control under the Internal Revenue Code means at least 80 percent of the combined voting power of all classes of voting stock and, in addition, at least 80 percent of all other classes of stock of the corporation.

TAX SHELTER A general term that refers to publicly or privately distributed offerings of limited partnership interests, which offer significant tax benefits. Tax shelters have as their tax features a deferral (meaning the postponement) of income, immediate deductions against the partner's other income, and beneficial long-term capital gains treatment when the partner's interest is later sold at a gain.

TAX YEAR A partnership must calculate its net income on the basis of a tax year. The "tax year" is the annual accounting period the partnership uses for maintaining its records and reporting income and expenses. A partnership can use either a calendar or a fiscal year.

TENANCY IN PARTNERSHIP Partners hold title to specific partnership property under a special form of co-ownership known as tenancy in partnership. This means that each partner has an equal right with his partners to possess and use specific partnership property solely for partnership purposes.

TERMINATION Occurs when the process of winding up the partnership is completed and marks the end of the partnership.

UNIFORM LIMITED PARTNERSHIP ACT (ULPA) Both this act and RULPA (Revised Uniform Limited Partnership Act) form the basis for governing of the limited partnership.

WINDING UP The process of liquidating the partnership's assets and distributing the proceeds to satisfy the claims against the partnership.

Fifty Commonly Asked Questions Regarding Partnerships

Q: CAN A FRIEND OR FAMILY MEMBER FORCE ME INTO AN UNINTENDED PARTNERSHIP?

A: No. Although the UPA does not require a specific intent to enter into a partnership, it is required that the parties voluntarily intend to enter into a partnership.

Q: IS THERE A DEFINITE LIMITATION ON THE NUMBER OF INDIVIDUALS WHO CAN BECOME PARTNERS?

A: No. There is no limitation on the number of individuals who can become partners in a partnership.

Q: IF I SHARE PROFITS WITH ANOTHER PERSON WHO IS ENGAGED IN A BUSINESS, DOES THIS ARRANGEMENT REPRESENT CONCLUSIVE PROOF THAT I AM A PARTNER WITH THIS PERSON?

A: No. Although not *conclusive* evidence that a partnership exists, an agreement to share net profits continues to be an essential element in determining whether a partnership arrangement exists.

Q: WHAT IS A JOINT VENTURE?

A: A joint venture is merely co-ownership for a limited purpose, without the usual powers and duties, and responsibilities that go with a partnership.

Q: I INTEND TO BE A SILENT PARTNER IN A PARTNERSHIP TO BE FORMED. WOULD THIS STATUS MAKE ME PERSONALLY LIABLE AS IF I WAS A GENERAL PARTNER?

A: A silent partner, or one who has no voice in management, has the same liability as that of any other partner.

Q: I AM THE SOLE STOCKHOLDER IN A CORPORATION. CAN MY CORPORATION BECOME A GENERAL PARTNER IN A PARTNERSHIP?

A: Yes. In the absence of a particular prohibition in the state law where your corporation was formed, a corporation can assume the role of a general partner in a partnership.

Q: I LOAN A FRIEND $1,000 TO GO INTO HIS OWN BUSINESS. DOES THE LOAN MAKE ME A PARTNER?

A: The mere lending of money to an individual, without the intent to enter into a continuous business arrangement, does not make a person a partner.

Q: CAN PERSONS FORM A PARTNER OF PARTNERSHIPS?

A: Yes. A partnership may enter into a partnership with other firms provided that all of the other members consent. For example, the VO Partnership, consisting of Vax and Oliver can become a partner with the XYZ Company, consisting of Xerses, Yolanda, and Zues, with the consent of all five individuals. In dividing profits and liabilities, each of the two entities will be treated as separate partners. As to outside creditors, Vax, Oliver, Xerses, Yolanda, and Zues will be personally liable as single members in the firm.

Q: I ENTER INTO A PARTNERSHIP WITH ANOTHER PERSON WHEREBY I WILL CONTRIBUTE MY SERVICES AND EXPERTISE AND THE OTHER PARTY WILL CONTRIBUTE $10,000 IN CASH. WE BOTH AGREE TO SHARE PROFITS AND LOSSES EQUALLY. IS SUCH AN ARRANGEMENT PERMISSIBLE?

A: Yes. Such arrangement, if agreed to by all of the parties, is recognized under the UPA.

Q: I PLAN TO HIRE AN INDIVIDUAL AT A FIXED SALARY PLUS TWENTY PERCENT OF THE NET PROFITS. WOULD THESE FACTS MAKE US PARTNERS?

A: No. Employees who share profits in the form of wages or a bonus are not considered to be partners.

Q: A NEWLY HIRED EMPLOYEE OF A PARTNERSHIP MAY BE REQUIRED TO CONDUCT HERSELF IN SUCH A MANNER THAT THIRD PARTIES WHO DEAL WITH THE EMPLOYEE MIGHT HAVE REASON TO BELIEVE THAT SHE IS A PARTNER. HOW CAN THE EMPLOYEE PROTECT HERSELF AGAINST SUCH LIABILITY?

A: An employee, before signing an employment contract, would be advised to stipulate the following in her employment contract: (1) she has been hired as an employee and is not assuming the role of a partner; (2) any compensation is to be treated as salary and not as a share of net profits; (3) the employee will not share in any profits or losses; (4) the employee is not required to contribute any capital as a condition of her employ-

ment; and (5) the name of the employee will not appear on the stationery of the firm in such a way as to appear to be that of a partner.

Q: IF TWO PEOPLE DECIDE TO ENTER INTO A PARTNERSHIP AND LATER FIND THAT THE PARTNERSHIP IS NOT WORKING OUT SATISFACTORILY, CAN THEY MUTUALLY AGREE TO DISSOLVE?

A: Yes. A partnership can be dissolved by mutual consent of all of the partners with minimum difficulty.

Q: AN INDIVIDUAL IS CONSIDERING ENTERING INTO A PARTNERSHIP WITH CERTAIN OTHER PEOPLE. WHAT PERSONAL CHARACTERISTICS SHOULD AN INDIVIDUAL LOOK FOR WHEN CHOOSING A PARTNER?

A: The individual should answer the following questions: (1) Can the person in question withstand the financial risks involved? (2) Does the potential partner have additional financial resources? (3) Does the person appear to be an individual of integrity? (4) What is the business background of this person? Does she have the required skill and experience to successfully function in the operation of the partnership? (5) Can the potential partner get along with the other members of the partnership?

Q: TWO PERSONS PLAN TO ENTER INTO A PARTNERSHIP. PARTNER A WILL CONTRIBUTE $20,000 WHILE PARTNER B WILL LOAN THE PARTNERSHIP $15,000. IN CASE OF DISSOLUTION, WHICH OBLIGATION MUST BE PAID FIRST?

A: The $15,000 loan. When a partner loans a partnership money, the advance is not regarded as capital but as an obligation to be repaid ahead of capital.

Q: THREE PERSONS AGREE TO FORM A PARTNERSHIP. PARTNER X WILL CONTRIBUTE $40,000, PARTNER B WILL CONTRIBUTE LAND WORTH $35,000, AND PARTNER C WILL CONTRIBUTE $20,000 IN INVENTORY. WHAT IS THE TOTAL VALUE OF THE PROPERTY OWNED BY THE PARTNERSHIP?

A: $95,000. All cash, inventory, and real estate contributed become the property of the partnership.

Q: AXEL AND BAKER JOINTLY OWN SHARES IN SEVERAL DIFFERENT CORPORATIONS. THEY SHARE DIVIDENDS EQUALLY AND HAVE MONTHLY MEETINGS TO DISCUSS HOW TO MANAGE THEIR INVESTMENTS. ARE THEY PARTNERS IN THEIR VENTURES?

A: No. Co-ownership of property does not, by itself, establish the existence of a partnership.

Q: SANDERS BORROWED $20,000 FOR CAULFIELD TO ESTABLISH A COMPUTER SUPPLY BUSINESS. SANDERS AGREED TO REPAY THE LOAN AT A RATE OF 20 PERCENT OF THE ANNUAL GROSS PROFITS FOR THREE YEARS. ARE SANDERS AND CAULFIELD PARTNERS?

A: No. The repayment of a loan to an individual without any other provisions, such as a sharing of net profits, does not constitute a partnership.

Q: WALTON, IZAACS, AND REED OWNED A 900-ACRE FARM FREE OF ANY MORTGAGES. WHEN REED DIED, HIS WIFE DEMANDED A DEED TO 300 ACRES. IS SHE ENTITLED TO SUCH A DEED?

A: No. Reed's widow is not entitled to any particular partnership asset. A partnership's assets pass to the surviving partners. So that all Reed's widow is entitled to is her husband's interest in the partnership itself.

Q: RANDALL AND ZORN, DOING BUSINESS AS THE RZ PARTNERSHIP, BOUGHT LAND WITH PARTNERSHIP FUNDS. CAN A PARTNERSHIP TAKE TITLE TO REAL ESTATE?

A: Yes. The UPA expressly allows a partnership to own land.

Q: THE PARTNERSHIP OF DOUGHBOY AND TOLL OPERATED A STATIONERY SUPPLY STORE EMPLOYING THREE EMPLOYEES. MUST THE FIRM WITHHOLD INCOME AND SOCIAL SECURITY TAXES FROM ITS EMPLOYEES?

A: Yes. For Internal Revenue Code purposes, a partnership is treated as a tax paying entity.

Q: THE REPAIR SHOP OF ANDERS AND BLAKE OPERATED AS A PARTNERSHIP. IN 19XX, IT EARNED A NET INCOME OF $50,000. IS THE PARTNERSHIP REQUIRED TO PAY FEDERAL INCOME TAXES?

A: No. A partnership does not pay income taxes. Instead, it files Form 1065 (US Partnership Return of Income) which is merely an informational tax return showing the partnership's net income and each partner's taxable share of net income (or deductible loss).

Q: BAILEY AND FINE OPERATED A PARTNERSHIP DEALING IN LEATHER GOODS. FOR THE YEAR 19XX, EACH PARTNER'S SHARE OF PROFITS WAS $50,000. BOTH PARTNERS ELECTED NOT TO WITHDRAW THIS AMOUNT AS PROFITS. MUST EACH PARTNER PAY PERSONAL INCOME TAXES ON THEIR SHARE OF THE PARTNERSHIP'S PROFITS, EVEN IF NOT DISTRIBUTED TO THEM?

A: Yes. For Internal Revenue Code purposes, income is taxable to a partner, whether or not it is actually distributed.

Q: WHEN IS THE FEDERAL PARTNERSHIP TAX RETURN (FORM 1065) DUE?

A: The Federal partnership tax return (Form 1065) must be filed by the fifteenth day of the fourth month following the close of the partnership tax year. This means that if the year end is December 31, 19XX, the return is due April 15, 19X1.

Q: CAN A PARTNERSHIP AGREEMENT STATE THAT A DEPARTING PARTNER WILL BE ENTITLED TO AN UP-FRONT LUMP-SUM PAYMENT WITH THE BALANCE OF THE BUY-OUT PRICE PAID OVER SEVERAL YEARS?

A: Yes. Many partnership agreements contain a provision that the buy-out price shall be an initial lump-sum payment with the balance paid over several years on a monthly basis.

Q: CAN A PARTNERSHIP AGREEMENT STATE THAT ONLY ONE PARTNER CAN BE IN CHARGE OF THE BOOKS AND RECORDS OF THE PARTNERSHIP?

A: Yes. Generally, the partner with the most experience in accounting and financial matters will be designated to take charge of the partnership's books and records.

Q: THE PARTNERSHIP OF QUINCY, THOMAS, AND SELBY WAS FORMED IN 19XX. QUINCY AND SELBY WERE TO BE GENERAL PARTNERS CONTRIBUTING ONLY THEIR MANAGERIAL SKILLS. THOMAS WAS CLASSIFIED AS A LIMITED PARTNER REQUIRING THAT SHE CONTRIBUTE ONLY CAPITAL. WHAT KIND OF PARTNERSHIP ARE THEY OPERATING AS?

A: They are operating as a limited partnership. If one or more partners is/are designated as limited, the partnership is treated as a limited partnership.

Q: ARE PAYMENTS MADE TO A RETIRING PARTNER IN PAYMENT OF HER INTEREST TAX DEDUCTIBLE BY THE PARTNERSHIP?

A: No. Payments made to a retiring partner are treated as distributions of profits and are therefore not tax deductible by the partnership. Such distributions are composed of both taxable and nontaxable items.

Q: CAN PARTNERS AGREE TO ADVANCE WITHDRAWALS FROM PROFITS?

A: Yes. Partners can agree to advance withdrawals especially where one or more partners are actively engaged in the daily operations of the partnership.

Q: CAN A PARTNERSHIP AGREEMENT PROHIBIT CASH WITHDRAWALS IN ADVANCE?

A: Yes. Although this prohibition is risky because a partner may need cash advances during the year, such restriction is permissible. One flexible solution is to allow for a minimal advance, such as not more than $300 per week.

Q: TO AVOID ANY CONFLICTS AS TO HOW MUCH TIME IS TO BE CONTRIBUTED TO THE DAILY OPERATION OF THE PARTNERSHIP, CAN THE PARTNERS AGREE TO A MINIMUM NUMBER OF HOURS THAT EACH MUST WORK EACH WEEK?

A: Yes. Although it is presumed that each partner knows the working idiosyncrasies of each partner, it may be wise to state in the partnership agreement how many hours each partner must contribute each week to the partnership.

Q: MUST PARTNERS CONTRIBUTE EQUAL CAPITAL AND HOURS PER WEEK TO THE PARTNERSHIP?

A: Absolutely not. The partners may agree to any proportion of both hours and capital to be contributed to the partnership. Thus, some partners may agree to contribute more hours in return for a lower required capital contribution.

Q: WHAT IS THE BEST WAY FOR ALL PARTNERS, BOTH ACTIVE AND PASSIVE, TO KEEP UP WITH THE OPERATIONS AND PROFITABILITY OF THE PARTNERSHIP?

A: An independent CPA should audit the books on a monthly basis so that quarterly financial statements can be prepared. The CPA should then inform the partner(s), who is (are) in charge of the books, of any developing problems. The partners should also hold weekly or monthly meetings to discuss any emerging problems.

Q: WHAT ARE THE TAX RULES FOR EXPENSES INCURRED BY A PARTNERSHIP?

A: The tax rules for a partnership are the same as the tax rules for any other type of business. Any expenses incurred in a trade or business may be deductible for tax purposes if they are ordinary and necessary.

Q: HOW DOES A NEWLY FORMED PARTNERSHIP GET AN EMPLOYEE IDENTIFICATION NUMBER (EIN)?

A: To get an EIN, the partnership must file Form SS-4 (Application for Employer Identification Number) with the nearest IRS center listed in the instructions that accompany the form. In addition, you can call 1-800-829-1040 and request that Form SS-4 be sent to a partner. There is no charge for this service.

Q: THREE PARTNERS, HOUGHTON, ROYAL, AND BOX, EACH INVEST $10,000 IN THE HRB PARTNERSHIP. PROFITS ARE TO BE SHARED EQUALLY. IF THE PARTNERSHIP, IN ITS FIRST YEAR OF OPERATIONS, LOST $45,000 (OR $15,000 PER PARTNER), WHAT CAN EACH PARTNER DEDUCT ON HIS PERSONAL TAX RETURN FOR THE YEAR?

A: Each partner can deduct $10,000, or the amount of his capital contribution. The balance of the loss, or $5,000 ($15,000 – $10,000), is required to be carried forward and offset against the profits of future years.

Q: MONEY, PENN, AND SALT OPERATE AN ANTIQUE SHOP IN COLUMBUS, OHIO. MONEY AND PENN WANT TO MOVE THE BUSINESS TO NEWARK, NEW JERSEY. CAN THEY DO SO IF SALT OBJECTS?

A: No. A change in the location of the partnership is a fundamental change requiring the unanimous consent of all of the partners.

Q: COLT, RUIZ, AND ESTEVEZ OPERATE A PICTURE FRAMING STORE. THE PARTNERSHIP AGREEMENT DIRECTS THAT PROFITS AND LOSSES ARE TO BE SHARED EQUALLY. COLT AND RUIZ WANT TO CHANGE THE METHOD OF DISTRIBUTING PROFITS. CAN THEY DO SO?

A: No. Unless the partnership agreement calls for a majority vote for changing the ratio of sharing profits, the profit sharing arrangement cannot be altered without the unanimous consent of all of the partners.

Q: CAN A FIRM OF FOUR PARTNERS AGREE TO SHARE PROFITS EQUALLY AND LOSSES IN THE RESPECTIVE RATIOS OF 4, 3, 2, AND 1?

A: Yes. Partners may agree to share profits and losses according to any ratio, even if the ratios are not uniform.

Q: DONALD, ROSS, AND KENNER OPERATE A WHOLESALE MEAT DISTRIBUTING COMPANY AS A PARTNERSHIP. KENNER WISHES TO SELL FALK $5,000 WORTH OF MEAT ON CREDIT. DONALD AND ROSS OBJECT CLAIMING THAT FALK IS A BAD CREDIT RISK AND DEMAND THAT A LOWER AMOUNT OF CREDIT BE EXTENDED. DOES MAJORITY RULE GOVERN IN THIS CASE?

A: Yes. This is a typical day-to-day business decision and requires only majority rule.

Q: ABBOT OWED $1,000 TO THE PARTNERSHIP OF WONG, REED, AND HUNTLEY. ABBOT PAID REED WHO POCKETED THE MONEY AND NEVER INFORMED THE REMAINING PARTNERS OF THE PAYMENT. WHEN WONG SENT ABBOT A STATEMENT INFORMING ABBOT THAT HE STILL OWED THE PARTNERSHIP THE $1,000, ABBOT REFUSED TO MAKE PAYMENT STATING THAT HE HAD ALREADY PAID THE PARTNERSHIP. MUST ABBOT PAY A SECOND TIME?

A: No. Reed, as a partner, had the apparent authority to collect the firm's debts. When Abbot paid Reed, he satisfied his debt, even though Reed misappropriated the money. The remaining partners' sole recourse is against Reed, and not against Abbot.

Q: SAM, BEA, AND ROLL OPERATED A DRUGSTORE AS A PARTNERSHIP. CAN BEA AND ROLL PREVENT SAM FROM EXAMINING THE PARTNERSHIP'S BOOKS AND RECORDS?

A: No. All partners have the right to examine a firm's books and records, unless the partnership agreement states otherwise.

Q: DO MOST STATES HAVE THE SAME TAX REPORTING REQUIREMENTS AS THE IRS DOES WHEN IT COMES TO PARTNERSHIPS?

A: Yes. Most states require that a partnership file a state informational return similar to Form 1065, the informational tax return required by the IRS.

Q: ARE PARTNERS JOINTLY LIABLE FOR FIRM CONTRACTS?

A: Yes. Partners are jointly liable for firm contracts. This means that the creditors must look primarily to the joint property of the firm for satisfaction of their claims. If such property proves insufficient, then any of the partners are individually liable to pay all of the firm's debts out of their personal property.

Q: IF A PARTNER RETIRES, IS SHE LIABLE FOR THE PARTNERSHIP'S DEBTS INCURRED AFTER HER RETIREMENT?

A: No. A retiring partner is not liable for firm debts incurred after her retirement provided proper notice is given of her retirement. Such notice must be actual as to those creditors who previously extended credit to the firm, and constructive notice, meaning notice by advertising in a trade publication as to all other creditors.

Q: WHAT HAPPENS WHEN A PARTNERSHIP IS INVOLVED IN A BANKRUPTCY?

A: When a partnership is declared bankrupt, the separate assets of all the partners, as well as the partnership's assets, are drawn into the bankruptcy, regardless of whether or not the individual partners have declared bankruptcy.

Q: HOW CAN AN EXPERIENCED PERSON, WELL SUITED TO BE AN ACTIVE PARTNER, JOIN AN EXISTING PARTNERSHIP?

A: An individual can become a partner in an existing firm by either acquiring the interest of an existing partner, or by negotiating to make a capital contribution to the firm. However, even with the performance of these acts, the individual does not become a partner until the unanimous consent of all of the other partners is given.

Q: THAXTER AND TROUT OPERATED A DELIVERY SERVICE AS PARTNERS. WHILE MAKING A DELIVERY, TROUT WAS NEGLIGENTLY INVOLVED IN AN ACCIDENT IN WHICH SEVERAL PEOPLE WERE INJURED. THE INJURED PARTIES SUED THE FIRM. IS THAXTER INDIVIDUALLY LIABLE EVEN THOUGH IT WAS HIS PARTNER WHO WAS INVOLVED IN THE ACCIDENT?

A: Yes. Since the accident was committed during the performance of the partnership's business, the partnership, and all of its members, are individually liable for the firm's obligations.

Q: IF A PARTNER'S WIFE INHERITS ALL OF THE PROPERTY OF A PARTNER WHO HAS JUST DIED, DOES IT MAKE HER A PARTNER?

A: No. Although the wife may have inherited the deceased partner's interest, the receipt of the interest does not make her a partner, unless the surviving partners unanimously agree to make her a partner.

Q: SUPPOSE THAT A HUSBAND INHERITS THE PARTNERSHIP INTEREST OF HIS DECEASED WIFE. CAN HE COMPEL A LIQUIDATION OF THE PARTNERSHIP?

A: Yes. The husband could compel liquidation if he so chooses. Or, the surviving spouse could permit the partnership to continue and claim his interest in the continuing firm as a creditor.

Q: THE PARTNERSHIP OF CECIL, BROWN, AND FORGER WAS FOUND TO OWN A HAZARDOUS WASTE SIGHT LOCATED ON ONE OF ITS PROPERTIES. UNDER CURRENT FEDERAL ENVIRONMENTAL LAWS, WHAT IS THE LEGAL OBLIGATION OF THE FIRM AS TO WHETHER THEY ARE REQUIRED TO CLEAN UP THE WASTE SITE?

A: The Environmental Protection Agency (EPA) has the authority to order the cleanup of a hazardous waste sight by the following parties: (1) the persons or persons who created the waste; (2) the person who transported the waste to the site; (3) the owner of the site at the time of disposal; and (4) the current owner of the property. Needless to say, a partnership contemplating the purchase of land and buildings should hire an environmental engineer to inspect the site for possible environmental contaminants and hazards.

Sample Federal Tax Forms

T he forms in this appendix (accompanied by their respective instructions) represent some of the information needed to be prepared by a partnership for income tax purposes. They have been filled in with information from a fictional partnership in order to help you understand how they need to be prepared. You will, of course, need to determine which forms you will need and supply your own partnership's personal information on current tax forms, which can be obtained from your local IRS office.

Form **1065**		**U.S. Partnership Return of Income**		OMB No. 1545-0099

Department of the Treasury
Internal Revenue Service

For calendar year 1996, or tax year beginning ...., 1996, and ending ...., 19 ....

▶ **See separate instructions.**

1996

A Principal business activity
RETAIL

B Principal product or service
BOOKS

C Business code number
5942

Use the IRS label. Otherwise, please print or type.

Name of partnership
ABLEBAKER BOOK STORE

Number, street, and room or suite no. If a P.O. box, see page 10 of the instructions.
334 WEST MAIN STREET

City or town, state, and ZIP code
ORANGE, MD 20904

D Employer identification number

E Date business started
10-1-79

F Total assets (see page 10 of the instructions)
$ *45,391*

G Check applicable boxes: **(1)** ☐ Initial return **(2)** ☐ Final return **(3)** ☐ Change in address **(4)** ☐ Amended return

H Check accounting method: **(1)** ☐ Cash **(2)** ☑ Accrual **(3)** ☐ Other (specify) ▶ *2*

I Number of Schedules K-1. Attach one for each person who was a partner at any time during the tax year ▶ *2*

Caution: *Include only trade or business income and expenses on lines 1a through 22 below. See the instructions for more information.*

Income

1a Gross receipts or sales	1a *409,465*		
b Less returns and allowances	1b *3,365*	1c	*406,100*
2 Cost of goods sold (Schedule A, line 8)		2	*267,641*
3 Gross profit. Subtract line 2 from line 1c		3	*138,459*
4 Ordinary income (loss) from other partnerships, estates, and trusts (attach schedule)		4	
5 Net farm profit (loss) (attach Schedule F (Form 1040))		5	
6 Net gain (loss) from Form 4797, Part II, line 20		6	
7 Other income (loss) (attach schedule)		7	*559*
8 **Total income (loss).** Combine lines 3 through 7		8	*139,018*

Deductions (see page 11 of the instructions for limitations)

9 Salaries and wages (other than to partners) (less employment credits)		9	*29,350*
10 Guaranteed payments to partners		10	*25,000*
11 Repairs and maintenance		11	*1,125*
12 Bad debts		12	*250*
13 Rent		13	*20,000*
14 Taxes and licenses		14	*3,295*
15 Interest		15	*1,451*
16a Depreciation (if required, attach Form 4562)	16a *1,174*		
b Less depreciation reported on Schedule A and elsewhere on return	16b *-0-*	16c	*1,174*
17 Depletion **(Do not deduct oil and gas depletion.)**		17	
18 Retirement plans, etc.		18	
19 Employee benefit programs		19	
20 Other deductions (attach schedule)		20	*8,003*
21 **Total deductions.** Add the amounts shown in the far right column for lines 9 through 20		21	*89,648*
22 Ordinary income (loss) from trade or business activities. Subtract line 21 from line 8		22	*49,370*

Please Sign Here

Under penalties of perjury, I declare that I have examined this return, including accompanying schedules and statements, and to the best of my knowledge and belief, it is true, correct, and complete. Declaration of preparer (other than general partner or limited liability company member) is based on all information of which preparer has any knowledge.

▶ *Frank Jr. Able*
Signature of general partner or limited liability company member

▶ *3/10/97*
Date

Paid Preparer's Use Only

Preparer's signature ▶		Date	Check if self-employed ▶ ☐	Preparer's social security no.
Firm's name (or yours if self-employed) and address ▶			EIN ▶	
			ZIP code ▶	

For Paperwork Reduction Act Notice, see page 1 of separate instructions.

Cat. No. 11390Z

Form **1065** (1996)

Form 1065 (1996)   Page **2**

	Schedule A	**Cost of Goods Sold** (see page 13 of the instructions)			

1	Inventory at beginning of year	**1**	18,125
2	Purchases less cost of items withdrawn for personal use	**2**	268,741
3	Cost of labor	**3**	-0-
4	Additional section 263A costs (attach schedule)	**4**	-0-
5	Other costs (attach schedule)	**5**	-0-
6	**Total.** Add lines 1 through 5	**6**	286,866
7	Inventory at end of year	**7**	19,225
8	**Cost of goods sold.** Subtract line 7 from line 6. Enter here and on page 1, line 2	**8**	267,641

9a Check all methods used for valuing closing inventory:
 (i) ☐ Cost as described in Regulations section 1.471-3
 (ii) ☑ Lower of cost or market as described in Regulations section 1.471-4
 (iii) ☐ Other (specify method used and attach explanation) ▶ ....
 b Check this box if there was a writedown of "subnormal" goods as described in Regulations section 1.471-2(c). . . . ▶ ☐
 c Check this box if the LIFO inventory method was adopted this tax year for any goods (if checked, attach Form 970) . . ▶ ☐
 d Do the rules of section 263A (for property produced or acquired for resale) apply to the partnership? . . ☐ Yes ☑ No
 e Was there any change in determining quantities, cost, or valuations between opening and closing inventory? ☐ Yes ☑ No
 If "Yes," attach explanation.

	Schedule B	**Other Information**		

		Yes	No
1	What type of entity is filing this return? Check the applicable box:		
a	☑ General partnership b ☐ Limited partnership c ☐ Limited liability company		
d	☐ Other (see page 14 of the instructions) ▶		
2	Are any partners in this partnership also partnerships?		✓
3	Is this partnership a partner in another partnership?		✓
4	Is this partnership subject to the consolidated audit procedures of sections 6221 through 6233? If "Yes," see **Designation of Tax Matters Partner** below		✓
5	Does this partnership meet **ALL THREE** of the following requirements?		
a	The partnership's total receipts for the tax year were less than $250,000;		
b	The partnership's total assets at the end of the tax year were less than $600,000; **AND**		
c	Schedules K-1 are filed with the return and furnished to the partners on or before the due date (including extensions) for the partnership return.		
	If "Yes," the partnership is not required to complete Schedules L, M-1, and M-2; Item F on page 1 of Form 1065; or Item J on Schedule K-1	✓	
6	Does this partnership have any foreign partners?	✓	
7	Is this partnership a publicly traded partnership as defined in section 469(k)(2)?	✓	
8	Has this partnership filed, or is it required to file, **Form 8264,** Application for Registration of a Tax Shelter? . .		✓
9	At any time during calendar year 1996, did the partnership have an interest in or a signature or other authority over a financial account in a foreign country (such as a bank account, securities account, or other financial account)? See page 14 of the instructions for exceptions and filing requirements for Form TD F 90-22.1. If "Yes," enter the name of the foreign country. ▶		✓
10	During the tax year, did the partnership receive a distribution from, or was it the grantor of, or transferor to, a foreign trust? If "Yes," see page 14 of the instructions for other forms the partnership may have to file . . .		✓
11	Was there a distribution of property or a transfer (e.g., by sale or death) of a partnership interest during the tax year? If "Yes," you may elect to adjust the basis of the partnership's assets under section 754 by attaching the statement described under **Elections Made By the Partnership** on page 5 of the instructions		✓

Designation of Tax Matters Partner (see page 15 of the instructions)

Enter below the general partner designated as the tax matters partner (TMP) for the tax year of this return:

Name of designated TMP ▶	Identifying number of TMP ▶
Address of designated TMP ▶	

Form 1065 (1996)   Page **3**

Schedule K — Partners' Shares of Income, Credits, Deductions, etc.

	(a) Distributive share items		(b) Total amount
Income (Loss)	**1** Ordinary income (loss) from trade or business activities (page 1, line 22)	1	49,370
	2 Net income (loss) from rental real estate activities (attach Form 8825)	2	
	3a Gross income from other rental activities · · · · 3a		
	b Expenses from other rental activities (attach schedule) · · · · 3b		
	c Net income (loss) from other rental activities. Subtract line 3b from line 3a	3c	
	4 Portfolio income (loss): **a** Interest income	4a	
	b Dividend income	4b	150
	c Royalty income	4c	
	d Net short-term capital gain (loss) (attach Schedule D (Form 1065))	4d	
	e Net long-term capital gain (loss) (attach Schedule D (Form 1065))	4e	
	f Other portfolio income (loss) (attach schedule)	4f	
	5 Guaranteed payments to partners	5	25,000
	6 Net gain (loss) under section 1231 (other than due to casualty or theft) (attach Form 4797)	6	
	7 Other income (loss) (attach schedule)	7	
Deductions	**8** Charitable contributions (attach schedule)	8	650
	9 Section 179 expense deduction (attach Form 4562)	9	
	10 Deductions related to portfolio income (itemize)	10	
	11 Other deductions (attach schedule)	11	
Investment Interest	**12a** Interest expense on investment debts	12a	
	b (1) Investment income included on lines 4a, 4b, 4c, and 4f above	12b(1)	150
	(2) Investment expenses included on line 10 above	12b(2)	
Credits	**13a** Low-income housing credit:		
	(1) From partnerships to which section 42(j)(5) applies for property placed in service before 1990	13a(1)	
	(2) Other than on line 13a(1) for property placed in service before 1990	13a(2)	
	(3) From partnerships to which section 42(j)(5) applies for property placed in service after 1989	13a(3)	
	(4) Other than on line 13a(3) for property placed in service after 1989	13a(4)	
	b Qualified rehabilitation expenditures related to rental real estate activities (attach Form 3468)	13b	
	c Credits (other than credits shown on lines 13a and 13b) related to rental real estate activities	13c	
	d Credits related to other rental activities	13d	
	14 Other credits	14	
Self-Employment	**15a** Net earnings (loss) from self-employment	15a	74,370
	b Gross farming or fishing income	15b	
	c Gross nonfarm income	15c	
Adjustments and Tax Preference Items	**16a** Depreciation adjustment on property placed in service after 1986	16a	
	b Adjusted gain or loss	16b	
	c Depletion (other than oil and gas)	16c	
	d (1) Gross income from oil, gas, and geothermal properties	16d(1)	
	(2) Deductions allocable to oil, gas, and geothermal properties	16d(2)	
	e Other adjustments and tax preference items (attach schedule)	16e	
Foreign Taxes	**17a** Type of income ▶ .... **b** Foreign country or U.S. possession ▶		
	c Total gross income from sources outside the United States (attach schedule)	17c	
	d Total applicable deductions and losses (attach schedule)	17d	
	e Total foreign taxes (check one): ▶ ☐ Paid ☐ Accrued	17e	
	f Reduction in taxes available for credit (attach schedule)	17f	
	g Other foreign tax information (attach schedule)	17g	
Other	**18** Section 59(e)(2) expenditures: **a** Type ▶ .... **b** Amount ▶	18b	
	19 Tax-exempt interest income	19	50
	20 Other tax-exempt income	20	
	21 Nondeductible expenses	21	
	22 Distributions of money (cash and marketable securities)	22	52,880
	23 Distributions of property other than money	23	
	24 Other items and amounts required to be reported separately to partners (attach schedule)		
Analysis	**25a** Income (loss). Combine lines 1 through 7 in column (b). From the result, subtract the sum of lines 8 through 12a, 17e, and 18b	25a	73,870

b Analysis by type of partner:	(a) Corporate	(b) Individual		(c) Partnership	(d) Exempt organization	(e) Nominee/Other
		i. Active	ii. Passive			
(1) General partners		73,870				
(2) Limited partners						

Form 1065 (1996) — Page **4**

Note: *If Question 5 of Schedule B is answered "Yes," the partnership is not required to complete Schedules L, M-1, and M-2.*

Schedule L — Balance Sheets per Books

Assets	Beginning of tax year		End of tax year	
	(a)	(b)	(c)	(d)
1 Cash		3,455		3,350
2a Trade notes and accounts receivable	7,150		10,990	
b Less allowance for bad debts		7,150		10,990
3 Inventories		18,125		19,225
4 U.S. government obligations				
5 Tax-exempt securities		1,000		1,000
6 Other current assets (attach schedule)				
7 Mortgage and real estate loans				
8 Other investments (attach schedule)		1,000		1,000
9a Buildings and other depreciable assets	15,000		15,000	
b Less accumulated depreciation	4,000	11,000	5,174	9,826
10a Depletable assets				
b Less accumulated depletion				
11 Land (net of any amortization)				
12a Intangible assets (amortizable only)				
b Less accumulated amortization				
13 Other assets (attach schedule)				
14 Total assets		41,730		45,391
Liabilities and Capital				
15 Accounts payable		10,180		10,462
16 Mortgages, notes, bonds payable in less than 1 year		4,000		3,600
17 Other current liabilities (attach schedule)				
18 All nonrecourse loans				
19 Mortgages, notes, bonds payable in 1 year or more				7,739
20 Other liabilities (attach schedule)				
21 Partners' capital accounts		27,550		23,590
22 Total liabilities and capital		41,730		45,391

Schedule M-1 — Reconciliation of Income (Loss) per Books With Income (Loss) per Return
(see page 23 of the instructions)

1 Net income (loss) per books	48,920	
2 Income included on Schedule K, lines 1 through 4, 6, and 7, not recorded on books this year (itemize):		
3 Guaranteed payments (other than health insurance)	25,000	
4 Expenses recorded on books this year not included on Schedule K, lines 1 through 12a, 17e, and 18b (itemize):		
a Depreciation $		
b Travel and entertainment $		
5 Add lines 1 through 4	73,920	

6 Income recorded on books this year not included on Schedule K, lines 1 through 7 (itemize):		
a Tax-exempt interest $		50
7 Deductions included on Schedule K, lines 1 through 12a, 17e, and 18b, not charged against book income this year (itemize):		
a Depreciation $		
8 Add lines 6 and 7		50
9 Income (loss) (Schedule K, line 25a). Subtract line 8 from line 5		73,870

Schedule M-2 — Analysis of Partners' Capital Accounts

1 Balance at beginning of year	27,550	
2 Capital contributed during year		
3 Net income (loss) per books	48,920	
4 Other increases (itemize):		
5 Add lines 1 through 4	76,470	

6 Distributions: a Cash		52,880
b Property		
7 Other decreases (itemize):		
8 Add lines 6 and 7		52,880
9 Balance at end of year. Subtract line 8 from line 5		23,590

Printed on recycled paper — *U.S. Government Printing Office: 1997 - 417-677/60137

1996

Department of the Treasury
Internal Revenue Service

Instructions for Form 1065

U.S. Partnership Return of Income

Section references are to the Internal Revenue Code unless otherwise noted.

Paperwork Reduction Act Notice

We ask for the information on this form to carry out the Internal Revenue laws of the United States. You are required to give us the information. We need it to ensure that you are complying with these laws and to allow us to figure and collect the right amount of tax.

You are not required to provide the information requested on a form that is subject to the Paperwork Reduction Act unless the form displays a valid OMB control number. Books or records relating to a form or its instructions must be retained as long as their contents may become material in the administration of any Internal Revenue law. Generally, tax returns and return information are confidential, as required by section 6103.

The time needed to complete and file this form and related schedules will vary depending on individual circumstances. The estimated average times are:

Form	Recordkeeping	Learning about the law or the form	Preparing the form	Copying, assembling, and sending the form to the IRS
1065	39 hr., 22 min.	20 hr., 58 min.	36 hr., 39 min.	4 hr., 1 min.
Schedule D (Form 1065)	5 hr., 30 min.	1 hr., 41 min.	1 hr., 51 min.	
Schedule K-1 (Form 1065)	25 hr., 7 min.	9 hr., 2 min.	9 hr., 51 min.	
Schedule L (Form 1065)	15 hr., 32 min.	6 min.		22 min.
Schedule M-1 (Form 1065)	3 hr., 21 min.	12 min.		16 min.
Schedule M-2 (Form 1065)	2 hr., 52 min.	6 min.		9 min.

If you have comments concerning the accuracy of these time estimates or suggestions for making these forms simpler, we would be happy to hear from you. You can write to the Tax Forms Committee, Western Area Distribution Center, Rancho Cordova, CA 95743-0001. **DO NOT** send the tax form to this address. Instead, see **Where To File** on page 3.

Contents

Changes To Note

The Small Business Job Protection Act of 1996 reinstated certain expired credits and also changed the rules for claiming certain credits. The affected credits include:

● The work opportunity credit (formerly the jobs credit), which covers qualified individuals who begin work after September 30, 1996, and before October 1, 1997. Get **Form 5884,** Work Opportunity Credit, for more details.

● The credit for increasing research activities, which is generally effective for amounts paid or incurred after June 30, 1996, and before June 1, 1997. Get **Form 6765,** Credit for Increasing Research Activities, for more details.

● The orphan drug credit, which is effective for amounts paid or incurred after June 30, 1996, and before June 1, 1997. Get **Form 8820,** Orphan Drug Credit, for more details.

● The credit for employer social security and Medicare taxes paid on certain employee tips. For tips received for services performed after 1996, this credit has been expanded to cover establishments that provide food and beverages for consumption off the premises (if tipping is customary). Get **Form 8846,** Credit for Employer Social Security and Medicare Taxes Paid on Certain Employee Tips, for more details.

Unresolved Tax Problems

The Problem Resolution Program is for taxpayers that have been unable to resolve their problems with the IRS. If the partnership has a tax problem it cannot clear up through normal channels, write to the partnership's local IRS District Director or call the partnership's local IRS office and ask for Problem Resolution assistance. Persons who have access to TTY/TDD equipment may call 1-800-829-4059 to ask for help from Problem Resolution. This office cannot change the tax law or technical decisions. But it can help the

Cat. No. 11392V

partnership clear up problems that resulted from previous contacts.

How To Get Forms and Publications

By Personal Computer

If you subscribe to an on-line service, ask if IRS information is available and, if so, how to access it. You can get information through IRIS, the Internal Revenue Information Services, on FedWorld, a government bulletin board. Tax forms, instructions, publications, and other IRS information are available through IRIS.

IRIS is accessible directly using your modem by calling 703-321-8020. On the Internet, telnet to iris.irs ustreas.gov or, for file transfer protocol services, connect to ftp.irs.ustreas.gov. If you are using the World Wide Web, connect to http://www.irs.ustreas.gov. FedWorld's help desk offers technical assistance on accessing IRIS (not tax help) during regular business hours at 703-487-4608. The IRIS menus offer information on available file formats and software needed to read and print files. You must print the forms to use them; they are not designed to be filled in on-screen.

Tax forms, instructions, and publications are also available on CD-ROM, including prior-year forms starting with the 1991 tax year. For ordering information and software requirements, contact the Government Printing Office's Superintendent of Documents (202-512-1800) or Federal Bulletin Board (202-512-1387).

By Phone and In Person

To order forms and publications, call 1-800-TAX-FORM (1-800-829-3676). You can also get most forms and publications at your local IRS office.

General Instructions

Purpose of Form

Form 1065 is an information return used to report the income, deductions, gains, losses, etc., from the operation of a partnership. A partnership does not pay tax on its income but "passes through" any profits or losses to its partners. Partners must include partnership items on their tax returns.

Definitions

Partnership

A partnership is the relationship between two or more persons who join to carry on a trade or business, with each person contributing money, property, labor, or skill and each expecting to share in the profits and losses of the business whether or not a formal partnership agreement is made.

The term "partnership" includes a limited partnership, syndicate, group, pool, joint venture, or other unincorporated organization, through or by which any business, financial operation, or venture is carried on, that is not, within the meaning of the Internal Revenue Code, a corporation, trust, estate, or sole proprietorship. If an organization more nearly resembles a corporation than a partnership or trust, it is considered to be a corporation.

A joint undertaking merely to share expenses is not a partnership. Mere co-ownership of property that is maintained and leased or rented is not a partnership.

However, if the co-owners provide services to the tenants, a partnership exists.

General Partner

A general partner is a partner who is personally liable for partnership debts.

General Partnership

A general partnership is composed only of general partners.

Limited Partner

A limited partner is a partner in a partnership formed under a state limited partnership law, whose personal liability for partnership debts is limited to the amount of money or other property that the partner contributed or is required to contribute to the partnership. Some members of other entities, such as domestic or foreign business trusts or limited liability companies that are classified as partnerships, may be treated as limited partners for certain purposes. See, for example, Temporary Regulations section 1.469-5T(e)(3), which treats all members with limited liability as limited partners for purposes of section 469(h)(2).

Limited Partnership

A limited partnership is formed under a state limited partnership law and composed of at least one general partner and one or more limited partners.

Limited Liability Company

A limited liability company (LLC) is an entity formed under state law by filing articles of organization as an LLC. Unlike a partnership, none of the members of an LLC are personally liable for its debts. An LLC may be classified for Federal income tax purposes either as a partnership or a corporation, depending on whether it has the corporate characteristics of centralization of management, continuity of life, free transferability of interests, and limited liability. To be classified as a partnership, it may have no more than two of these characteristics. Similar rules apply to a limited liability company formed under the laws of a foreign country.

Nonrecourse Loans

Nonrecourse loans are those liabilities of the partnership for which no partner bears the economic risk of loss.

Who Must File

Every partnership that engages in a trade or business or has income from sources in the United States must file Form 1065. A partnership must file even if its principal place of business is outside the United States or all its members are nonresident aliens.

A partnership is not considered to engage in a trade or business, and is therefore not required to file, for any tax year in which it neither receives income nor incurs any expenditures treated as deductions or credits for Federal income tax purposes.

Entities formed as limited liability companies and treated as partnerships for Federal income tax purposes must file Form 1065.

A religious or apostolic organization exempt from income tax under section 501(d) must file Form 1065 to report its taxable income, which must be allocated to its members as a dividend, whether distributed or not. Such an organization must figure its taxable income on

an attachment to Form 1065 in the same manner as a corporation. **Form 1120**, U.S. Corporation Income Tax Return, may be used for this purpose. Enter the organization's taxable income, if any, on line 4b of Schedule K and each member's pro rata share on line 4b of Schedule K-1. Net operating losses are not deductible by the members but may be carried back or forward by the organization under the rules of section 172.

A qualifying syndicate, pool, joint venture, or similar organization may elect under section 761(a) not to be treated as a partnership for Federal income tax purposes and will not be required to file Form 1065 except for the year of election. See section 761(a) and Regulations section 1.761-2 for more information.

Real estate mortgage investment conduits (REMICs) must file Form 1066.

Certain publicly traded partnerships treated as corporations under section 7704 must file Form 1120.

Termination of the Partnership

A partnership terminates when:

1. All its operations are discontinued and no part of any business, financial operation, or venture is continued by any of its partners in a partnership, OR

2. At least 50% of the total interest in partnership capital and profits is sold or exchanged within a 12-month period, including a sale or exchange to another partner. See Regulations section 1.708-1(b)(1) for more details.

The partnership's tax year ends on the date of termination. For purposes of 1 above, the date of termination is the date the partnership completes the winding up of its affairs. For purposes of 2 above, the date of termination is the date the partnership interest is sold or exchanged that, of itself or together with other sales or exchanges in the preceding 12 months, transfers an interest of 50% or more in both partnership capital and profits.

Special rules apply in the case of a merger, consolidation, or division of a partnership. See Regulations section 1.708-1(b)(2) for details.

Electronic and Magnetic Media Filing

Qualified partnerships or transmitters can file Form 1065 and related schedules electronically or on magnetic media. Tax return data may be filed electronically using a dial-up MITRON communications device or remote bulletin board system or on magnetic media using magnetic tape or floppy diskette.

If the partnership wishes to do this, **Form 9041**, Application for Electronic/Magnetic Media Filing of Business and Employee Benefit Plan Returns, must be filed. If the partnership return is filed electronically or on magnetic media, **Form 8453-P**, U.S. Partnership Declaration and Signature for Electronic and Magnetic Media Filing, must also be filed. For more details, get **Pub. 1524**, Procedures for Electronic and Magnetic Media Filing of Form 1065, U.S. Partnership Return of Income (Including the "Paper-Parent Option"), and **Pub. 1525**, File Specifications, Validation Criteria, and Record Layouts for Electronic and Magnetic Media Filing of Form 1065, U.S. Partnership Return of Income (Including the "Paper-Parent

Page 2

Option"). To order these forms and publications, or for more information on electronic and magnetic media filing of Form 1065, call the Electronic Filing Unit at the Andover Service Center at 508-474-9486 (not a toll-free number), or write to:

Internal Revenue Service Center
Electronic Filing Unit II, Stop 983
P.O. Box 4050
Woburn, MA 01888-4050

When To File

Generally, a domestic partnership must file Form 1065 by the 15th day of the 4th month following the date its tax year ended as shown at the top of Form 1065. A partnership whose partners are all nonresident aliens must file its return by the 15th day of the 6th month following the date its tax year ended. If the due date falls on a Saturday, Sunday, or legal holiday, file on the next business day. A business day is any day that is not a Saturday, Sunday, or legal holiday.

Extension

If you need more time to file a partnership return, file **Form 8736,** Application for Automatic Extension of Time To File U.S. Return for a Partnership, REMIC, or for Certain Trusts, for an automatic 3-month extension. File Form 8736 by the regular due date of the partnership return.

If, after you have filed Form 8736, you still need more time to file the partnership return, file **Form 8800,** Application for Additional Extension of Time To File U.S. Return for a Partnership, REMIC, or for Certain Trusts, for an additional extension of up to 3 months. The partnership must show reasonable cause to get this additional extension. Form 8800 must be filed by the extended due date of the partnership return.

Period Covered

Form 1065 is an information return for calendar year 1996 and fiscal years beginning in 1996 and ending in 1997. If the return is for a fiscal year or a short tax year, fill in the tax year space at the top of the form.

The 1996 Form 1065 may also be used if:

1. The partnership has a tax year of less than 12 months that begins and ends in 1997; and

2. The 1997 Form 1065 is not available by the time the partnership is required to file its return.

However, the partnership must show its 1997 tax year on the 1996 Form 1065 and incorporate any tax law changes that are effective for tax years beginning after 1996.

Where To File

File your return at the applicable IRS address listed below.

If the partnership's principal place of business or principal office or agency is located in	Use the following Internal Revenue Service Center address
New Jersey, New York (New York City and counties of Nassau, Rockland, Suffolk, and Westchester)	Holtsville, NY 00501-0011
New York (all other counties), Connecticut, Maine, Massachusetts, New Hampshire, Rhode Island, Vermont	Andover, MA 05501-0011
Florida, Georgia, South Carolina	Atlanta, GA 39901-0011
Indiana, Kentucky, Michigan, Ohio, West Virginia	Cincinnati, OH 45999-0011
Kansas, New Mexico, Oklahoma, Texas	Austin, TX 73301-0011
Alaska, Arizona, California (counties of Alpine, Amador, Butte, Calaveras, Colusa, Contra Costa, Del Norte, El Dorado, Glenn, Humboldt, Lake, Lassen, Marin, Mendocino, Modoc, Napa, Nevada, Placer, Plumas, Sacramento, San Joaquin, Shasta, Sierra, Siskiyou, Solano, Sonoma, Sutter, Tehama, Trinity, Yolo, and Yuba), Colorado, Idaho, Montana, Nebraska, Nevada, North Dakota, Oregon, South Dakota, Utah, Washington, Wyoming	Ogden, UT 84201-0011
California (all other counties), Hawaii	Fresno, CA 93888-0011
Illinois, Iowa, Minnesota, Missouri, Wisconsin	Kansas City, MO 64999-0011
Alabama, Arkansas, Louisiana, Mississippi, North Carolina, Tennessee	Memphis, TN 37501-0011
Delaware, District of Columbia, Maryland, Pennsylvania, Virginia	Philadelphia, PA 19255-0011

A partnership without a principal office or agency or principal place of business in the United States must file its return with the Internal Revenue Service Center, Philadelphia, PA 19255-0011.

Who Must Sign

General Partner or Limited Liability Company Member

Form 1065 is not considered to be a return unless it is signed. One general partner or limited liability company member must sign the return. If a receiver, trustee in bankruptcy, or assignee controls the organization's property or business, that person must sign the return.

Paid Preparer's Information

If someone prepares the return and does not charge the partnership, that person should not sign the partnership return.

Generally, anyone who is paid to prepare the partnership return must sign the return and fill in the other blanks in the **Paid Preparer's Use Only** area of the return.

The preparer required to sign the partnership return **must** complete the required preparer information and:

● Sign it, by hand, in the space provided for the preparer's signature. Signature stamps or labels are not acceptable.

● Give the partnership a copy of the return in addition to the copy to be filed with the IRS.

Penalties

Late Filing of Return

A penalty is assessed against the partnership if it is required to file a partnership return and it **(a)** fails to file the return by the due date, including extensions, or **(b)** files a return that fails to show all the information required, unless such failure is due to reasonable cause. If the failure is due to reasonable cause, attach an explanation to the partnership return. The penalty is $50 for each month or part of a month (for a maximum of 5 months) the failure continues, multiplied by the total number of persons who were partners in the partnership during any part of the partnership's tax year for which the return is due. This penalty will not be imposed on partnerships for which the answer to Question 4 on Schedule B of Form 1065 is **No,** provided all partners have timely filed income tax returns fully reporting their shares of the income, deductions, and credits of the partnership. See page 14 of the instructions for further information.

Failure To Furnish Information Timely

For each failure to furnish Schedule K-1 to a partner when due and each failure to include on Schedule K-1 all the information required to be shown (or the inclusion of incorrect information), a $50 penalty may be imposed with respect to each Schedule K-1 for which a failure occurs. The maximum penalty is $100,000 for all such failures during a calendar year. If the requirement to report correct information is intentionally disregarded, each $50 penalty is increased to $100 or, if greater, 10% of the aggregate amount of items required to be reported, and the $100,000 maximum does not apply.

Trust Fund Recovery Penalty

This penalty may apply if certain excise, income, social security, and Medicare taxes that must be collected or withheld are not collected or withheld, or these taxes are not paid to the IRS. These taxes are generally reported on Forms 720, 941, 943, or 945. The trust fund recovery penalty may be imposed on all persons who are determined by the IRS to have been **responsible** for collecting, accounting for, and paying over these taxes, and who acted willfully in not doing so. The penalty is equal to the unpaid trust fund tax. See the instructions for Form 720, **Pub. 15 (Circular E),** Employer's Tax Guide, or **Pub. 51 (Circular A),** Agricultural Employer's Tax Guide, for more details, including the definition of responsible person.

Accounting Methods

Figure ordinary income using the method of accounting regularly used in keeping the partnership's books and records. Generally, permissible methods include the cash method, the accrual method, or any other method authorized by the Internal Revenue Code. In all cases, the method used must clearly reflect income.

Generally, a partnership may not use the cash method of accounting if **(a)** it has at least one corporate partner, average annual gross receipts of more than $5 million, and it is not a farming business or **(b)** it is a tax shelter (as defined in section 448(d)(3)). See section 448 for details.

Under the accrual method, an amount is includible in income when all the events have occurred that fix the right to receive the income and the amount can be determined with reasonable accuracy.

Generally, an accrual basis taxpayer can deduct accrued expenses in the tax year in which all events that determine liability have occurred, the amount of the liability can be figured with reasonable accuracy, and economic performance takes place with

Page 3

respect to the expense. There are exceptions for recurring items.

Except for certain home construction contracts and other real property small construction contracts, long-term contracts must generally be accounted for using the percentage of completion method described in section 460.

Generally, the partnership may change its method of accounting used to report income (for income as a whole or for any material item) only by getting consent on **Form 3115,** Application for Change in Accounting Method. For more information, get **Pub. 538,** Accounting Periods and Methods.

Accounting Periods

A partnership is generally required to have one of the following tax years:

1. The tax year of a majority of its partners (majority tax year); or

2. If there is no majority tax year, then the tax year common to all of the partnership's principal partners (partners with an interest of 5% or more in the partnership profits or capital); or

3. If there is neither a majority tax year nor a tax year common to all principal partners, then the tax year that results in the least aggregate deferral of income; or

4. Some other tax year, if **(a)** the partnership can establish that there is a business purpose for the tax year (see Rev. Proc. 87-32, 1987-2 C.B. 396); or **(b)** the tax year is a "grandfathered" year (see Rev. Proc. 87-32); or **(c)** the partnership elects under section 444 to have a tax year other than a required tax year by filing **Form 8716,** Election to Have a Tax Year Other Than a Required Tax Year. For a partnership to have this election in effect, it must make the payments required by section 7519 and file **Form 8752,** Required Payment or Refund Under Section 7519. A section 444 election ends if a partnership changes its accounting period to its required tax year or some other permitted year or it is penalized for willfully failing to comply with the requirements of section 7519. If the termination results in a short tax year, type or legibly print at the top of the first page of Form 1065 for the short tax year, "SECTION 444 ELECTION TERMINATED."

To change an accounting period, see Pub. 538 and **Form 1128,** Application To Adopt, Change, or Retain a Tax Year (unless the partnership is making an election under section 444).

Note: *Under the provisions of section 584(h), the tax year of a common trust fund must be the calendar year.*

Rounding Off to Whole Dollars

You may round off cents to whole dollars on your return and accompanying schedules. To do so, drop amounts under 50 cents and increase amounts from 50 to 99 cents to the next higher dollar.

Recordkeeping

The partnership must keep its records as long as they may be needed for the administration of any provision of the Internal Revenue Code. If the consolidated audit procedures of sections 6221 through 6233 apply, the partnership usually must keep records that

Page 4

support an item of income, deduction, or credit on the partnership return for 3 years from the date the return is due or is filed, whichever is later. If the consolidated audit procedures do not apply, these records usually must be kept for 3 years from the date each partner's return is due or is filed, whichever is later. Keep records that verify the partnership's basis in property for as long as they are needed to figure the basis of the original or replacement property.

The partnership should also keep copies of any returns it has filed as part of its records. They help in preparing future returns and in making computations when filing an amended return.

Amended Return

To correct an error on a Form 1065 already filed, file an amended Form 1065 and check box G(4) on page 1. If the income, deductions, credits, or other information provided to any partner on Schedule K-1 are incorrect, file an amended Schedule K-1 (Form 1065) for that partner with the amended Form 1065. Also give a copy of the amended Schedule K-1 to that partner. Be sure to check box I(2) on the Schedule K-1 to indicate that it is an amended Schedule K-1.

Note: *If you are filing an amended partnership return and you answered "Yes" to Question 4 in Schedule B, the tax matters partner must file* **Form 8082,** *Notice of Inconsistent Treatment or Amended Return (Administrative Adjustment Request (AAR)).*

A change to the partnership's Federal return may affect its state return. This includes changes made as a result of an examination of the partnership return by the IRS. For more information, contact the state tax agency for the state in which the partnership return is filed.

Other Forms That May Be Required

● **Forms W-2** and **W-3,** Wage and Tax Statement; and Transmittal of Wage and Tax Statements.

● **Form 720,** Quarterly Federal Excise Tax Return. Use Form 720 to report environmental excise taxes, communications and air transportation taxes, fuel taxes, luxury tax on passenger vehicles, manufacturers' taxes, ship passenger tax, and certain other excise taxes.

Caution: *See* **Trust Fund Recovery Penalty** *on page 3.*

● **Form 940** or **Form 940-EZ,** Employer's Annual Federal Unemployment (FUTA) Tax Return. The partnership may be liable for FUTA tax and may have to file Form 940 or 940-EZ if it paid wages of $1,500 or more in any calendar quarter during the calendar year (or the preceding calendar year) or one or more employees worked for the partnership for some part of a day in any 20 different weeks during the calendar year (or the preceding calendar year).

● **Form 941,** Employer's Quarterly Federal Tax Return. Employers must file this form quarterly to report income tax withheld on wages and employer and employee social security and Medicare taxes. Agricultural employers must file **Form 943,** Employer's Annual Tax Return for Agricultural Employees, instead of Form 941, to report income tax

withheld and employer and employee social security and Medicare taxes on farmworkers.

Caution: *See* **Trust Fund Recovery Penalty** *on page 3.*

● **Form 945,** Annual Return of Withheld Federal Income Tax. Use this form to report income tax withheld from nonpayroll payments, including pensions, annuities, IRAs, gambling winnings, and backup withholding.

Caution: *See* **Trust Fund Recovery Penalty** *on page 3.*

● **Forms 1042** and **1042-S,** Annual Withholding Tax Return for U.S. Source Income of Foreign Persons; and Foreign Person's U.S. Source Income Subject to Withholding. Use these forms to report and send withheld tax on payments or distributions made to nonresident alien individuals, foreign partnerships, or foreign corporations to the extent such payments or distributions constitute gross income from sources within the United States that is not effectively connected with a U.S. trade or business. A domestic partnership must also withhold tax on a foreign partner's distributive share of such income, including amounts that are not actually distributed. Withholding on amounts not previously distributed to a foreign partner must be made and paid over by the earlier of **(a)** the date on which Schedule K-1 is sent to that partner or **(b)** the 15th day of the 3rd month after the end of the partnership's tax year. For more information, see sections 1441 and 1442 and get **Pub. 515,** Withholding of Tax on Nonresident Aliens and Foreign Corporations.

● **Form 1096,** Annual Summary and Transmittal of U.S. Information Returns.

● **Form 1098,** Mortgage Interest Statement. Use this form to report the receipt from any individual of $600 or more of mortgage interest and points in the course of the partnership's trade or business for any calendar year.

● **Forms 1099-A, B, INT, MISC, OID, R,** and **S.** You may have to file these information returns to report abandonments, acquisitions through foreclosure, proceeds from broker and barter exchange transactions, interest payments, medical and dental health care payments, direct sales of consumer goods for resale, miscellaneous income payments, nonemployee compensation, original issue discount, distributions from pensions, annuities, retirement or profit-sharing plans, IRAs, insurance contracts, etc., and proceeds from real estate transactions. Also, use these returns to report amounts that were received as a nominee on behalf of another person.

For more information, see the Instructions for Forms 1099, 1098, 5498, and W-2G.

Note: *Every partnership must file Forms 1099-MISC if, in the course of its trade or business, it makes payments of rents, commissions, or other fixed or determinable income (see section 6041) totaling $600 or more to any one person during the calendar year.*

● **Form 5471,** Information Return of U.S. Persons With Respect to Certain Foreign Corporations. A partnership may have to file Form 5471 if it **(a)** controls a foreign corporation; or **(b)** acquires, disposes of, or owns 5% or more in value of the outstanding stock of a foreign corporation; or **(c)** owns stock in a corporation that is a controlled foreign corporation for an uninterrupted period of 30 days or more during any tax year of the foreign corporation, and it owned that stock on the last day of that year.

• **Form 5713,** International Boycott Report, is used by persons having operations in, or related to, a "boycotting" country, company, or national of a country, to report those operations and figure the loss of certain tax benefits. The partnership must give each partner a copy of the Form 5713 filed by the partnership if there has been participation in, or cooperation with, an international boycott.

• **Form 8264,** Application for Registration of a Tax Shelter. Tax shelter organizers must file Form 8264 to get a tax shelter registration number from the IRS.

• **Form 8271,** Investor Reporting of Tax Shelter Registration Number. Partnerships that have acquired an interest in a tax shelter that is required to be registered use Form 8271 to report the tax shelter's registration number. Attach Form 8271 to any return on which a deduction, credit, loss, or other tax benefit attributable to a tax shelter is taken or any income attributable to a tax shelter is reported.

• **Form 8275,** Disclosure Statement. File Form 8275 to disclose items or positions, except those contrary to a regulation, that are not otherwise adequately disclosed on a tax return. The disclosure is made to avoid the parts of the accuracy-related penalty imposed for disregard of rules or substantial understatement of tax. Form 8275 is also used for disclosures relating to preparer penalties for understatements due to unrealistic positions or disregard of rules.

• **Form 8275-R,** Regulation Disclosure Statement, is used to disclose any item on a tax return for which a position has been taken that is contrary to Treasury regulations.

• **Forms 8288** and **8288-A,** U.S. Withholding Tax Return for Dispositions by Foreign Persons of U.S. Real Property Interests; and Statement of Withholding on Dispositions by Foreign Persons of U.S. Real Property Interests. Use these forms to report and send withheld tax on the sale of U.S. real property by a foreign person. See section 1445 and the related regulations for additional information.

• **Form 8300,** Report of Cash Payments Over $10,000 Received in a Trade or Business. File this form to report the receipt of more than $10,000 in cash or foreign currency in one transaction or a series of related transactions.

• **Form 8594,** Asset Acquisition Statement. Both the purchaser and seller of a group of assets constituting a trade or business must file this form if section 197 intangibles attach, or could attach, to such assets and if the purchaser's basis in the assets is determined only by the amount paid for the assets.

• **Form 8697,** Interest Computation Under the Look-Back Method for Completed Long-Term Contracts. Partnerships that are not closely held use this form to figure the interest due or to be refunded under the look-back method of section 460(b)(2) on certain long-term contracts that are accounted for under either the percentage of completion-capitalized cost method or the percentage of completion method. Closely held partnerships should see the instructions

on page 22 for line 25, item 10, of Schedule K-1 for details on the Form 8697 information they must provide to their partners.

• **Forms 8804, 8805,** and **8813,** Annual Return for Partnership Withholding Tax (Section 1446); Foreign Partner's Information Statement of Section 1446 Withholding Tax; and Partnership Withholding Tax Payment (Section 1446). File Forms 8804 and 8805 if the partnership had effectively connected gross income and foreign partners for the tax year. Use Form 8813 to send installment payments of withheld tax based on effectively connected taxable income allocable to foreign partners. However, publicly traded partnerships that do not elect to pay tax based on effectively connected taxable income do not file these forms. They must instead withhold tax on distributions to foreign partners and report and send payments using Forms 1042 and 1042-S. See section 1446 for more information.

Attachments

Attach schedules in alphabetical order and other forms in numerical order after Form 1065.

To assist us in processing the return, complete every applicable entry space on Form 1065 and Schedule K-1. **If you attach statements, do not write "See attached" instead of completing the entry spaces on the forms. Penalties may be assessed if the partnership files an incomplete return.**

If you need more space on the forms or schedules, attach separate sheets. Use the same size and format as on the printed forms. **But show your totals on the printed forms.** Be sure to put the partnership's name and employer identification number (EIN) on each sheet.

Separately Stated Items

Partners are required to take into account separately (under section 702(a)) their distributive shares of the following items (whether or not they are actually distributed):

1. Ordinary income or loss from trade or business activities.

2. Net income or loss from rental real estate activities.

3. Net income or loss from other rental activities.

4. Gains and losses from sales or exchanges of capital assets.

5. Gains and losses from sales or exchanges of property described in section 1231.

6. Charitable contributions.

7. Dividends (passed through to corporate partners) that qualify for the dividends-received deduction.

8. Taxes described in section 901 paid or accrued to foreign countries and to possessions of the United States.

9. Other items of income, gain, loss, deduction, or credit, to the extent provided by regulations. Examples of such items include nonbusiness expenses, intangible drilling and development costs, and soil and water conservation expenditures.

Elections Made by the Partnership

Generally, the partnership decides how to figure taxable income from its operations. For example, it chooses the accounting method and depreciation methods it will use. The partnership also makes elections under the following sections:

1. Section 179 (election to expense certain tangible property).

2. Section 614 (definition of property—mines, wells, and other natural deposits). This election must be made before the partners figure their individual depletion allowances under section 613A(c)(7)(D).

3. Section 754 (manner of electing optional adjustment to basis of partnership property).

Under section 754, a partnership may elect to adjust the basis of partnership property when property is distributed or when a partnership interest is transferred. If the election is made with respect to a transfer of a partnership interest (section 743(b)) and the assets of the partnership constitute a trade or business for purposes of section 1060(c), then the value of any goodwill transferred must be determined in the manner provided in Temporary Regulations section 1.1060-1T. Once an election is made under section 754, it applies both to all distributions and to all transfers made during the tax year and in all subsequent tax years unless the election is revoked (see Regulations section 1.754-1(c)).

This election must be made in a statement that is filed with the partnership's timely filed return (including any extension) for the tax year during which the distribution or transfer occurs. The statement must include **(a)** the name and address of the partnership; **(b)** a declaration that the partnership elects under section 754 to apply the provisions of section 734(b) and section 743(b); and **(c)** the signature of the general partner authorized to sign the partnership return.

The partnership can get an automatic 12-month extension to make the section 754 election provided corrective action is taken within 12 months of the original deadline for making the election. For details, see Temporary Regulations section 301.9100-2T.

See section 754 and the related regulations for more information.

Note: *If there is a distribution of property consisting of an interest in another partnership, see section 734(b).*

4. Section 1033 (involuntary conversions).

Elections Made by Each Partner

Elections under the following sections are made by each partner separately on the partner's tax return:

1. Section 59(e) (election to deduct ratably certain qualified expenditures such as intangible drilling costs, mining exploration expenses, or research and experimental expenditures).

2. Section 108 (income from discharge of indebtedness).

3. Section 617 (deduction and recapture of certain mining exploration expenditures paid or incurred).

4. Section 901 (foreign tax credit).

Page 5

Partner's Dealings With Partnership

If a partner engages in a transaction with his or her partnership, other than in his or her capacity as a partner, the partner is treated as not being a member of the partnership for that transaction. Special rules apply to sales or exchanges of property between partnerships and certain persons, as explained in Pub. 541.

Contributions to the Partnership

Generally, no gain (loss) is recognized to the partnership or any of the partners when property is contributed to the partnership in exchange for an interest in the partnership. This rule does not apply to any gain realized on a transfer of property to a partnership that would be treated as an investment company (within the meaning of section 351) if the partnership were incorporated. If, as a result of a transfer of property to a partnership, there is a direct or indirect transfer of money or other property to the transferring partner, the partner may have to recognize gain on the exchange.

The basis to the partnership of property contributed by a partner is the adjusted basis in the hands of the partner at the time it was contributed, plus any gain recognized (under section 721(b)) by the partner at that time. See section 723 for more information.

Dispositions of Contributed Property

If the partnership disposes of property contributed to the partnership by a partner, income, gain, loss, and deductions from that property must be allocated among the partners to take into account the difference between the property's basis and its fair market value at the time of the contribution.

For property contributed to the partnership, the contributing partner must recognize gain or loss on a distribution of the property to another partner within 5 years of being contributed. The gain or loss is equal to the amount that the contributing partner should have recognized if the property had been sold for its fair market value when distributed, because of the difference between the property's basis and its fair market value at the time of contribution.

See section 704(c) for details and other rules on dispositions of contributed property. See section 724 for the character of any gain or loss recognized on the disposition of unrealized receivables, inventory items, or capital loss property contributed to the partnership by a partner.

Recognition of Precontribution Gain on Certain Partnership Distributions

A partner who contributes appreciated property to the partnership must include in income any precontribution gain to the extent the fair market value of other property (other than money) distributed to the partner by the partnership exceeds the adjusted basis of his or her partnership interest just before the distribution. Precontribution gain is the net gain, if any, that would have been recognized under section 704(c)(1)(B) if the partnership

had distributed to another partner all the property that had been contributed to the partnership by the distributee partner within 5 years of the distribution and that was held by the partnership just before the distribution.

Appropriate basis adjustments are to be made to the adjusted basis of the distributee partner's interest in the partnership and the partnership's basis in the contributed property to reflect the gain recognized by the partner.

For more details and exceptions, see section 737.

Unrealized Receivables and Inventory Items

Generally, if a partner sells or exchanges a partnership interest where unrealized receivables or substantially appreciated inventory items are involved, the transferor partner must notify the partnership, in writing, within 30 days of the exchange. The partnership must then file **Form 8308,** Report of a Sale or Exchange of Certain Partnership Interests.

If a partnership distributes unrealized receivables or substantially appreciated inventory items in exchange for all or part of a partner's interest in other partnership property (including money), treat the transaction as a sale or exchange between the partner and the partnership. Treat the partnership gain (loss) as ordinary income (loss). The income (loss) is specially allocated only to partners other than the distributee partner.

If a partnership gives other property (including money) for all or part of that partner's interest in the partnership's unrealized receivables or substantially appreciated inventory items, treat the transaction as a sale or exchange of the property.

See Rev. Rul. 84-102, 1984-2 C.B. 119, for information on the tax consequences that result when a new partner joins a partnership that has liabilities and unrealized receivables. Also, see Pub. 541 for more information on unrealized receivables and substantially appreciated inventory items.

Passive Activity Limitations

In general, section 469 limits the amount of losses, deductions, and credits that partners may claim from "passive activities." The passive activity limitations do not apply to the partnership. Instead, they apply to each partner's share of any income or loss and credit attributable to a passive activity. Because the treatment of each partner's share of partnership income or loss and credit depends on the nature of the activity that generated it, the partnership must report income or loss and credits separately for each activity.

The instructions below (pages 6–9) and the instructions for Schedules K and K-1 (pages 15–23) explain the applicable passive activity limitation rules and specify the type of information the partnership must provide to its partners for each activity. If the partnership has more than one activity, it must report information for each activity on an attachment to Schedules K and K-1.

Generally, passive activities include **(a)** activities that involve the conduct of a

trade or business if the partner does not materially participate in the activity; and **(b)** all rental activities (defined on page 7), regardless of the partner's participation. For exceptions, see **Activities That Are Not Passive Activities** below. The level of each partner's participation in an activity must be determined by the partner.

The passive activity rules provide that losses and credits from passive activities can generally be applied only against income and tax from passive activities. Thus, passive losses and credits cannot be applied against income from salaries, wages, professional fees, or a business in which the taxpayer materially participates; against "portfolio income" (defined on page 8); or against the tax related to any of these types of income.

Special provisions apply to certain activities. First, the passive activity limitations must be applied separately with respect to a net loss from passive activities held through a publicly traded partnership. Second, special rules require that net income from certain activities that would otherwise be treated as passive income must be recharacterized as nonpassive income for purposes of the passive activity limitations.

To allow each partner to correctly apply the passive activity limitations, the partnership must report income or loss and credits separately for each of the following types of activities and income: trade or business activities, rental real estate activities, rental activities other than rental real estate, and portfolio income.

Activities That Are Not Passive Activities

Passive activities **do not** include:

1. Trade or business activities in which the partner materially participated for the tax year.

2. Any rental real estate activity in which the partner materially participated and met both of the following conditions for the tax year:

a. More than half of the personal services the partner performed in trades or businesses were performed in real property trades or businesses in which he or she materially participated, and

b. The partner performed more than 750 hours of services in real property trades or businesses in which he or she materially participated.

Note: *For a partner that is a closely held C corporation (defined in section 465(a)(1)(B)), the above conditions are treated as met if more than 50% of the corporation's gross receipts are from real property trades or businesses in which the corporation materially participated.*

For purposes of this rule, each interest in rental real estate is a separate activity, unless the partner elects to treat all interests in rental real estate as one activity.

If the partner is married filing jointly, either the partner or his or her spouse must separately meet both of the above conditions, without taking into account services performed by the other spouse.

A real property trade or business is any real property development, redevelopment, construction, reconstruction, acquisition, conversion, rental, operation, management, leasing, or brokerage trade or business. Services the partner performed as an employee are not treated as performed in a real property trade or business unless he or she owned more than 5% of the stock (or more than 5% of the capital or profits interest) in the employer.

3. An interest in an oil or gas well drilled or operated under a working interest if at any time during the tax year the partner held the working interest directly or through an entity that did not limit the partner's liability (e.g., an interest as a general partner). This exception applies regardless of whether the partner materially participated for the tax year.

4. The rental of a dwelling unit used by a partner for personal purposes during the year for more than the greater of 14 days or 10% of the number of days that the residence was rented at fair rental value.

5. An activity of trading personal property for the account of owners of interests in the activity. See Temporary Regulations section 1.469-1T(e)(6).

Trade or Business Activities

A trade or business activity is an activity (other than a rental activity or an activity treated as incidental to an activity of holding property for investment) that:

1. Involves the conduct of a trade or business (within the meaning of section 162),

2. Is conducted in anticipation of starting a trade or business, or

3. Involves research or experimental expenditures deductible under section 174 (or that would be if you chose to deduct rather than capitalize them).

If the partner does not materially participate in the activity, a trade or business activity held through a partnership is generally a passive activity of the partner. However, the passive activity limitations do not apply to any partner holding a working interest in an oil or gas well if the partner holds the interest through an entity that does not limit the partner's liability. See Temporary Regulations section 1.469-1T(e)(4) and Regulations section 1.469-1(e)(4) for more information.

Each partner must determine if he or she materially participated in an activity. As a result, while the partnership's overall trade or business income (loss) is reported on page 1 of Form 1065, the specific income and deductions from each separate trade or business activity must be reported on attachments to Form 1065. Similarly, while each partner's allocable share of the partnership's overall trade or business income (loss) is reported on line 1 of Schedule K-1, each partner's allocable share of the income and deductions from each trade or business activity must be reported on attachments to each Schedule K-1. See **Passive Activity Reporting Requirements** on page 9 for more information.

Rental Activities

Generally, except as noted below, if the gross income from an activity consists of amounts paid principally for the use of real or personal tangible property held by the partnership, the activity is a rental activity.

There are several exceptions to this general rule. Under these exceptions, an activity involving the use of real or personal tangible property is not a rental activity if **(a)** the average period of customer use (defined below) for such property is 7 days or less; **(b)** the average period of customer use for such property is 30 days or less and significant personal services (defined below) are provided by or on behalf of the partnership; **(c)** extraordinary personal services (defined below) are provided by or on behalf of the partnership; **(d)** the rental of such property is treated as incidental to a nonrental activity of the partnership under Temporary Regulations section 1.469-1T(e)(3)(vi) and Regulations section 1.469-1(e)(3)(vi); or **(e)** the partnership customarily makes the property available during defined business hours for nonexclusive use by various customers.

In addition, if the partnership provides property for use in a nonrental activity of a partnership or joint venture in its capacity as an owner of an interest in such partnership or joint venture, the provision of the property is not a rental activity. Consequently, the partnership's distributive share of income from the activity is not income from a rental activity. A guaranteed payment described in section 707(c) is not income from a rental activity under any circumstances. Whether the partnership provides property used in an activity of another partnership or of a joint venture in the partnership's capacity as an owner of an interest in the partnership or joint venture is determined on the basis of all the facts and circumstances.

Average period of customer use.—Figure the average period of customer use for a class of property by dividing the total number of days in all rental periods by the number of rentals during the tax year. If the activity involves renting more than one class of property, multiply the average period of customer use of each class by the ratio of the gross rental income from that class to the activity's total gross rental income. The activity's average period of customer use equals the sum of these class-by-class average periods weighted by gross income. See Regulations section 1.469-1(e)(3)(iii).

Significant personal services.—Personal services include only services performed by individuals. In determining whether personal services are significant personal services, consider all the relevant facts and circumstances. Relevant facts and circumstances include how often the services are provided, the type and amount of labor required to perform the services, and the value of the services in relation to the amount charged for use of the property.

The following services are not considered in determining whether personal services are significant: **(a)** services necessary to permit the lawful use of the rental property; **(b)** services performed in connection with improvements or repairs to the rental property that extend the useful life of the property substantially beyond the average rental period; and **(c)** services provided in connection with the use of any improved real property that are similar to those commonly provided in connection with long-term rentals of high-grade commercial or residential property (e.g., cleaning and maintenance of common areas, routine repairs, trash collection, elevator service, and security at entrances).

Extraordinary personal services.—Services provided in connection with making rental property available for customer use are extraordinary personal services only if the services are performed by individuals and the customers' use of the rental property is incidental to their receipt of the services. For example, a patient's use of a hospital room generally is incidental to the care received from the hospital's medical staff. Similarly, a student's use of a dormitory room in a boarding school is incidental to the personal services provided by the school's teaching staff.

Rental activity incidental to a nonrental activity.—An activity is not a rental activity if the rental of the property is incidental to a nonrental activity, such as the activity of holding property for investment, trade or business activity, or the activity of dealing in property.

Rental of property is incidental to an activity of holding property for investment if **(a)** the main purpose for holding the property is to realize a gain from the appreciation of the property, and **(b)** the gross rental income from such property for the tax year is less than 2% of the smaller of the property's unadjusted basis or its fair market value.

Rental of property is incidental to a trade or business activity if **(a)** the partnership owns an interest in the trade or business at all times during the year; **(b)** the rental property was mainly used in the trade or business activity during the tax year or during at least 2 of the 5 preceding tax years; and **(c)** the gross rental income from the property for the tax year is less than 2% of the smaller of the property's unadjusted basis or its fair market value.

The sale or exchange of property that is both rented and sold or exchanged during the tax year (where the gain or loss is recognized) is treated as incidental to the activity of dealing in property if, at the time of the sale or exchange, the property was held primarily for sale to customers in the ordinary course of the partnership's trade or business.

See Temporary Regulations section 1.469-1T(e)(3) and Regulations section 1.469-1(e)(3) for more information on the definition of rental activities for purposes of the passive activity limitations.

Reporting of rental activities.—In reporting the partnership's income or losses and credits from rental activities, the partnership must separately report **(a)** rental real estate activities, and **(b)** rental activities other than rental real estate activities.

Partners who actively participate in a rental real estate activity may be able to deduct part or all of their rental real estate losses (and the deduction equivalent of rental real estate credits) against income (or tax) from nonpassive activities. The combined amount of rental real estate losses and the deduction equivalent of rental real estate credits from all sources (including rental real estate activities not held through the partnership) that may be claimed is limited to $25,000. This $25,000 amount is generally reduced for high-income partners.

Report rental real estate activity income (loss) on **Form 8825,** Rental Real Estate Income and Expenses of a Partnership or an S Corporation, and line 2 of Schedules K and K-1 rather than on page 1 of Form 1065.

Page 7

Report credits related to rental real estate activities on lines 13b and 13c and low-income housing credits on line 13a of Schedules K and K-1.

Report income (loss) from rental activities other than rental real estate on line 3 and credits related to rental activities other than rental real estate on line 13d of Schedules K and K-1.

Portfolio Income

Generally, portfolio income includes all gross income, other than income derived in the ordinary course of a trade or business, that is attributable to interest; dividends; royalties; income from a real estate investment trust, a regulated investment company, a real estate mortgage investment conduit, a common trust fund, a controlled foreign corporation, a qualified electing fund, or a cooperative; income from the disposition of property that produces income of a type defined as portfolio income; and income from the disposition of property held for investment.

Solely for purposes of the preceding paragraph, gross income derived in the ordinary course of a trade or business includes (and portfolio income, therefore, does not include) only the following types of income:

• Interest income on loans and investments made in the ordinary course of a trade or business of lending money.

• Interest on accounts receivable arising from the performance of services or the sale of property in the ordinary course of a trade or business of performing such services or selling such property, but only if credit is customarily offered to customers of the business.

• Income from investments made in the ordinary course of a trade or business of furnishing insurance or annuity contracts or reinsuring risks underwritten by insurance companies.

• Income or gain derived in the ordinary course of an activity of trading or dealing in any property if such activity constitutes a trade or business (unless the dealer held the property for investment at any time before such income or gain is recognized).

• Royalties derived by the taxpayer in the ordinary course of a trade or business of licensing intangible property.

• Amounts included in the gross income of a patron of a cooperative by reason of any payment or allocation to the patron based on patronage occurring with respect to a trade or business of the patron.

• Other income identified by the IRS as income derived by the taxpayer in the ordinary course of a trade or business.

See Temporary Regulations section 1.469-2T(c)(3) for more information on portfolio income.

Report portfolio income on line 4 of Schedules K and K-1, rather than on page 1 of Form 1065. Report deductions related to portfolio income on line 10 of Schedules K and K-1.

Grouping Activities

Generally, one or more trade or business activities or rental activities may be treated as a single activity if the activities make up an appropriate economic unit for the

measurement of gain or loss under the passive activity rules. Whether activities make up an appropriate economic unit depends on all the relevant facts and circumstances. The factors given the greatest weight in determining whether activities make up an appropriate economic unit are:

1. Similarities and differences in types of trades or businesses,

2. The extent of common control,

3. The extent of common ownership,

4. Geographical location, and

5. Reliance between or among the activities.

Example. The partnership has a significant ownership interest in a bakery and a movie theater in Baltimore and a bakery and a movie theater in Philadelphia. Depending on the relevant facts and circumstances, there may be more than one reasonable method for grouping the partnership's activities. For instance, the following groupings may or may not be permissible: a single activity, a movie theater activity and a bakery activity, a Baltimore activity and a Philadelphia activity, or four separate activities.

Once the partnership chooses a grouping under these rules, it must continue using that grouping in later tax years unless a material change in the facts and circumstances makes it clearly inappropriate.

The IRS may regroup the partnership's activities if the partnership's grouping fails to reflect one or more appropriate economic units and one of the primary purposes of the grouping is to avoid the passive activity limitations.

Limitation on grouping certain activities.— The following activities may not be grouped together:

1. A rental activity with a trade or business activity unless the activities being grouped together make up an appropriate economic unit, and

a. The rental activity is insubstantial relative to the trade or business activity or vice versa, or

b. Each owner of the trade or business activity has the same proportionate ownership interest in the rental activity. If so, the portion of the rental activity involving the rental of property to be used in the trade or business activity may be grouped with the trade or business activity.

2. An activity involving the rental of real property with an activity involving the rental of personal property (except for personal property provided in connection with the real property or vice versa).

3. Any activity with another activity in a different type of business and in which the partnership holds an interest as a limited partner or as a limited entrepreneur (as defined in section 464(e)(2)) if that other activity engages in holding, producing, or distributing motion picture films or videotapes; farming; leasing section 1245 property; or exploring for (or exploiting) oil and gas resources or geothermal deposits.

Activities conducted through other partnerships.—Once a partnership determines its activities under these rules, the partnership as a partner may use these rules to group those activities with each other, with

activities conducted directly by the partnership, and with activities conducted through other partnerships. A partner may not treat as separate activities those activities grouped together by a partnership.

Recharacterization of Passive Income

Under Temporary Regulations section 1.469-2T(f) and Regulations section 1.469-2(f), net passive income from certain passive activities must be treated as nonpassive income. Net passive income is the excess of an activity's passive activity gross income over its passive activity deductions (current year deductions and prior year unallowed losses).

Income from the following six sources is subject to recharacterization. Note that any net passive income recharacterized as nonpassive income is treated as investment income for purposes of figuring investment interest expense limitations if it is from (a) an activity of renting substantially nondepreciable property from an equity-financed lending activity or (b) an activity related to an interest in a pass-through entity that licenses intangible property.

1. Significant participation passive activities.—A significant participation passive activity is any trade or business activity in which the partner both participates for more than 100 hours during the tax year and does not materially participate. Because each partner must determine the partner's level of participation, the partnership will not be able to identify significant participation passive activities.

2. Certain nondepreciable rental property activities.—Net passive income from a rental activity is nonpassive income if less than 30% of the unadjusted basis of the property used or held for use by customers in the activity is subject to depreciation under section 167.

3. Passive equity-financed lending activities.—If the partnership has net income from a passive equity-financed lending activity, the smaller of the net passive income or the equity-financed interest income from the activity is nonpassive income.

Note: The amount of income from the activities in paragraphs **1** through **3** above, that any partner will be required to recharacterize as nonpassive income may be limited under Temporary Regulations section 1.469-2T(f)(8). Because the partnership will not have information regarding all of a partner's activities, it must identify all partnership activities meeting the definitions in paragraphs **2** and **3** as activities that may be subject to recharacterization.

4. Rental of property incidental to a development activity.—Net rental activity income is nonpassive income for a partner if all of the following apply: (a) the partnership recognizes gain from the sale, exchange, or other disposition of the rental property during the tax year; (b) the use of the item of property in the rental activity started less than 12 months before the date of disposition (the use of an item of rental property begins on the first day that (i) the partnership owns an interest in the property; (ii) substantially all of the property is either rented or held out for rent and ready to be rented; and (iii) no significant value-enhancing services remain to be performed); and (c) the partner materially participated or significantly participated for any tax year in an activity that involved the performance of services for the purpose of enhancing the value of the property (or any other item of property, if the basis of the property disposed of is determined in whole or in part by reference to the basis of that item of property). "Net rental activity income" means the excess of passive activity gross income from renting or disposing of property over passive activity deductions (current year deductions and prior year unallowed losses) that are reasonably allocable to the rented property.

Because the partnership cannot determine a partner's level of participation, the partnership must identify net income from property described in items (a) and (b) of paragraph 4 as income that may be subject to recharacterization.

5. Rental of property to a nonpassive activity.—If a taxpayer rents property to a trade or business activity in which the taxpayer materially participates, the taxpayer's net rental activity income (defined above) from the property is nonpassive income.

6. Acquisition of an interest in a pass-through entity that licenses intangible property.—Generally, net royalty income from intangible property is nonpassive income if the taxpayer acquired an interest in the pass-through entity after the pass-through entity created the intangible property or performed substantial services, or incurred substantial costs in developing or marketing the intangible property. "Net royalty income" means the excess of passive activity gross income from licensing or transferring any right in intangible property over passive activity deductions (current year deductions and prior year unallowed losses) that are reasonably allocable to the intangible property.

See Temporary Regulations section 1.469-2T(f)(7)(iii) for exceptions to this rule.

Passive Activity Reporting Requirements

To allow partners to correctly apply the passive activity loss and credit rules, any partnership that carries on more than one activity must:

1. Provide an attachment for each activity conducted through the partnership that identifies the type of activity conducted (trade or business, rental real estate, rental activity other than rental real estate, or investment).

2. On the attachment for each activity, provide a schedule, using the same line numbers as shown on Schedule K-1, detailing the net income (loss), credits, and all items required to be separately stated under section 702(a) from each trade or business activity, from each rental real estate activity, from each rental activity other than a rental real estate activity, and from investments.

3. Identify the net income (loss) and credits from each oil or gas well drilled or operated under a working interest that any partner (other than a partner whose only interest in the partnership during the year is as a limited partner) holds through the partnership. Further, if any partner had an interest as a general partner in the partnership during less than the entire year, the partnership must identify both the disqualified deductions from each well that the partner must treat as

passive activity deductions, and the ratable portion of the gross income from each well that the partner must treat as passive activity gross income.

4. Identify the net income (loss) and the partner's share of partnership interest expense from each activity of renting a dwelling unit that any partner uses for personal purposes during the year for more than the greater of 14 days or 10% of the number of days that the residence is rented at fair rental value.

5. Identify the net income (loss) and the partner's share of partnership interest expense from each activity of trading personal property conducted through the partnership.

6. For any gain (loss) from the disposition of an interest in an activity or of an interest in property used in an activity (including dispositions before 1987 from which gain is being recognized after 1986):

a. Identify the activity in which the property was used at the time of disposition;

b. If the property was used in more than one activity during the 12 months preceding the disposition, identify the activities in which the property was used and the adjusted basis allocated to each activity; and

c. For gains only, if the property was substantially appreciated at the time of the disposition and the applicable holding period specified in Regulations section 1.469-2(c)(2)(iii)(A) was not satisfied, identify the amount of the nonpassive gain and indicate whether the gain is investment income under the provisions of Regulations section 1.469-2(c)(2)(iii)(F).

7. Specify the amount of gross portfolio income, the interest expense properly allocable to portfolio income, and expenses other than interest expense that are clearly and directly allocable to portfolio income.

8. Identify separately any of the following types of payments to partners:

a. Payments to a partner for services other than in the partner's capacity as a partner (under section 707(a));

b. Guaranteed payments to a partner for services (under section 707(c));

c. Guaranteed payments for use of capital;

d. If section 736(a)(2) payments are made for unrealized receivables or for goodwill, the amount of the payments and the activities to which the payments are attributable;

e. If section 736(b) payments are made, the amount of the payments and the activities to which the payments are attributable.

9. Identify the ratable portion of any section 481 adjustment (whether a net positive or a net negative adjustment) allocable to each partnership activity.

10. Identify the amount of gross income from each oil or gas property of the partnership.

11. Identify any gross income from sources that are specifically excluded from passive activity gross income, including:

a. Income from intangible property if the partner is an individual and the partner's personal efforts significantly contributed to the creation of the property;

b. Income from state, local, or foreign income tax refunds; and

c. Income from a covenant not to compete (in the case of a partner who is an individual and who contributed the covenant to the partnership).

12. Identify any deductions that are not passive activity deductions.

13. If the partnership makes a full or partial disposition of its interest in another entity, identify the gain (loss) allocable to each activity conducted through the entity, and the gain allocable to a passive activity that would have been recharacterized as nonpassive gain had the partnership disposed of its interest in property used in the activity (because the property was substantially appreciated at the time of the disposition, and the gain represented more than 10% of the partner's total gain from the disposition).

14. Identify the following items from activities that may be subject to the recharacterization rules under Temporary Regulations section 1.469-2T(f) and Regulations section 1.469-2(f):

a. Net income from an activity of renting substantially nondepreciable property;

b. The smaller of equity-financed interest income or net passive income from an equity-financed lending activity;

c. Net rental activity income from property that was developed (by the partner or the partnership), rented, and sold within 12 months after the rental of the property commenced;

d. Net rental activity income from the rental of property by the partnership to a trade or business activity in which the partner had an interest (either directly or indirectly); and

e. Net royalty income from intangible property if the partner acquired the partner's interest in the partnership after the partnership created the intangible property or performed substantial services, or incurred substantial costs in developing or marketing the intangible property.

15. Identify separately the credits from each activity conducted by or through the partnership.

Specific Instructions

These instructions follow the line numbers on the first page of Form 1065 and on the schedules that accompany it. Specific instructions for most of the lines are provided on the following pages. Lines that are not discussed in the instructions are self-explanatory.

Fill in all applicable lines and schedules.

Enter any items specially allocated to the partners on the appropriate line of the applicable partner's Schedule K-1. Enter the total amount on the appropriate line of Schedule K. Do not enter separately stated amounts on the numbered lines on Form 1065, page 1, or on Schedule A or D.

Be sure to file all four pages of Form 1065. However, if the answer to Question 5 of Schedule B is "Yes," the completion of page 4 is optional. Also attach a Schedule K-1 to Form 1065 for each partner.

File only one Form 1065 for each partnership. Mark "duplicate copy" on any copy you give to a partner.

Page 9

If a syndicate, pool, joint venture, or similar group files Form 1065, it must attach a copy of the agreement and all amendments to the return, unless a copy has previously been filed.

General Information

Name, Address, and Employer Identification Number

Use the label that was mailed to the partnership. Cross out any errors and print the correct information on the label.

Name.—If the partnership did not receive a label, print or type the legal name of the partnership as it appears in the partnership agreement.

Address.—Include the suite, room, or other unit number after the street address. If a preaddressed label is used, include this information on the label.

If the Post Office does not deliver mail to the street address and the partnership has a P.O. box, show the box number instead of the street address.

If the partnership has had a change of address, check box G(3).

If the partnership's address is outside the United States or its possessions or territories, enter the information on the line for "City or town, state, and ZIP code" in the following order: city, province or state, foreign postal code, and the name of the foreign country. **Do not** abbreviate the country name.

If the partnership changes its mailing address after filing its return, it can notify the IRS by filing **Form 8822,** Change of Address.

Employer identification number (EIN).—Show the correct EIN in item D on page 1 of Form 1065. If the partnership does not have an EIN, it must apply for one on **Form SS-4,** Application for Employer Identification Number. Form SS-4 can be obtained at most IRS or Social Security Administration offices. If the partnership has not received its EIN by the time the return is due, write "Applied for" in the space for the EIN. Get **Pub. 583,** Starting a Business and Keeping Records, for more information.

Items A and C

Enter the applicable activity name and code number from the list on page 24.

For example, if, as its principal business activity, the partnership **(a)** purchases raw materials, **(b)** subcontracts out for labor to make a finished product from the raw materials, and **(c)** retains title to the goods, the partnership is considered to be a manufacturer and must enter "Manufacturer" in item A and enter in item C one of the codes (2000 through 3970) listed under "Manufacturing" on page 24.

You are not required to complete item C if the business code on the label is correct.

Item F—Total Assets

You are not required to complete item F if the answer to Question 5 of Schedule B is "Yes."

If you are required to complete this item, enter the partnership's total assets at the end of the tax year, as determined by the accounting method regularly used in keeping the partnership's books and records. If there were no assets at the end of the tax year,

enter the total assets as of the beginning of the tax year.

Income

Caution: *Report only trade or business activity income on lines 1a through 8.* **Do not report rental activity income or portfolio income on these lines.** *(See the instructions on* **Passive Activity Limitations** *beginning on page 6 for definitions of rental income and portfolio income.) Rental activity income and portfolio income are reported on Schedules K and K-1 (rental real estate activities are also reported on Form 8825).*

Do not include any tax-exempt income on lines 1a through 8. A partnership that receives any tax-exempt income other than interest, or holds any property or engages in any activity that produces tax-exempt income reports the amount of this income on line 20 of Schedules K and K-1.

Report tax-exempt interest income, including exempt-interest dividends received as a shareholder in a mutual fund or other regulated investment company, on line 19 of Schedules K and K-1.

See **Deductions** on page 11 for information on how to report expenses related to tax-exempt income.

If the partnership has had debt discharged resulting from a title 11 bankruptcy proceeding or while insolvent, get **Form 982,** Reduction of Tax Attributes Due to Discharge of Indebtedness, and **Pub. 908,** Bankruptcy Tax Guide.

Line 1a—Gross Receipts or Sales

Enter the gross receipts or sales from all trade or business operations except those that must be reported on lines 4 through 7. For example, do not include gross receipts from farming on this line. Instead, show the net profit (loss) from farming on line 5. Also, do not include on line 1a rental activity income or portfolio income. See section 460 for special rules that apply to long-term contracts.

Installment sales.—Generally, the installment method cannot be used for dealer dispositions of property. A "dealer disposition" is any disposition of personal property by a person who regularly sells or otherwise disposes of personal property of the same type on the installment plan or any disposition of real property held for sale to customers in the ordinary course of the taxpayer's trade or business. The disposition of property used or produced in a farming business is not included as a dealer disposition. See section 453(l) for details and exceptions.

Enter on line 1a the gross profit on collections from installment sales for any of the following:

● Dealer dispositions of property before March 1, 1986.

● Dispositions of property used or produced in the trade or business of farming.

● Certain dispositions of timeshares and residential lots reported under the installment method.

Attach a schedule showing the following information for the current year and the 3 preceding years: **(a)** gross sales, **(b)** cost of goods sold, **(c)** gross profits, **(d)** percentage of gross profits to gross sales, **(e)** amount

collected, and **(f)** gross profit on amount collected.

Line 2—Cost of Goods Sold

See the instructions for Schedule A on page 13.

Line 4—Ordinary Income (Loss) From Other Partnerships, Estates, and Trusts

Enter the amount shown on Schedule K-1 (Form 1065) or Schedule K-1 (Form 1041). Be sure to show the partnership's, estate's, or trust's name, address, and EIN on a separate statement attached to this return. If the amount entered is from more than one source, identify the amount from each source.

Do not include portfolio income or rental activity income (loss) from other partnerships, estates, or trusts on this line. Instead, report these amounts on the applicable lines of Schedules K and K-1, or on line 20a of Form 8825 if the amount is from a rental real estate activity.

Ordinary income or loss from another partnership that is a publicly traded partnership is not reported on this line. Instead, report the amount separately on line 7 of Schedules K and K-1.

Treat shares of other items separately reported on Schedule K-1 issued by the other entity as if the items were realized or incurred by this partnership.

If there is a loss from another partnership, the amount of the loss that may be claimed is subject to the at-risk and basis limitations as appropriate.

If the tax year of your partnership does not coincide with the tax year of the other partnership, estate, or trust, include the ordinary income (loss) from the other entity in the tax year in which the other entity's tax year ends.

Line 5—Net Farm Profit (Loss)

Enter the partnership's net farm profit (loss) from **Schedule F (Form 1040),** Profit or Loss From Farming. Attach Schedule F (Form 1040) to Form 1065. **Do not** include on this line any farm profit (loss) from other partnerships. Report those amounts on line 4. In figuring the partnership's net farm profit (loss), do not include any section 179 expense deduction; this amount must be separately stated.

Also report the partnership's fishing income on this line.

For a special rule concerning the method of accounting for a farming partnership with a corporate partner and for other tax information on farms, get **Pub. 225,** Farmer's Tax Guide.

Note: *Because the election to deduct the expenses of raising any plant with a preproductive period of more than 2 years is made by the partner and not the partnership, farm partnerships that are not required to use an accrual method should not capitalize such expenses. Instead, state them separately on an attachment to Schedule K, line 24, and on Schedule K-1, line 25, Supplemental Information. See Temporary Regulations section 1.263A-4T(c) for more information.*

Line 6—Net Gain (Loss) From Form 4797

Caution: *Include only ordinary gains or losses from the sale, exchange, or involuntary conversion of assets used in a trade or business activity. Ordinary gains or losses from the sale, exchange, or involuntary conversion of rental activity assets are reported separately on line 19 of Form 8825 or line 3 of Schedules K and K-1, generally as a part of the net income (loss) from the rental activity.*

A partnership that is a partner in another partnership must include on **Form 4797, Sales of Business Property,** its share of ordinary gains (losses) from sales, exchanges, or involuntary conversions (other than casualties or thefts) of the other partnership's trade or business assets.

Do not include any recapture of section 179 expense deduction. See the instructions for Schedule K-1, line 25, Supplemental Information, item 4, and the Instructions for Form 4797 for more information.

Line 7—Other Income (Loss)

Enter on line 7 trade or business income (loss) that is not included on lines 1a through 6. Examples of such income include:

1. Interest income derived in the ordinary course of the partnership's trade or business, such as interest charged on receivable balances.

2. Recoveries of bad debts deducted in earlier years under the specific charge-off method.

3. Taxable income from insurance proceeds.

4. The amount of credit figured on **Form 6478,** Credit for Alcohol Used as Fuel.

5. All section 481 income adjustments resulting from changes in accounting methods. Show the computation of the section 481 adjustments on an attached schedule.

6. The amount of any deduction previously taken under section 179A that is subject to recapture. See Pub. 535 for details, including how to figure the recapture.

7. The recapture amount for section 280F if the business use of listed property drops to 50% or less. To figure the recapture amount, the partnership must complete Part IV of Form 4797.

Do not include items requiring separate computations that must be reported on Schedules K and K-1. See the instructions for Schedules K and K-1 later in these instructions.

Do not report portfolio or rental activity income (loss) on this line.

Deductions

Caution: *Report only trade or business activity deductions on lines 9 through 21.*

Do not report rental activity expenses or deductions allocable to portfolio income on these lines. Rental activity expenses are separately reported on Form 8825 or line 3b of Schedule K. Deductions allocable to portfolio income are separately reported on line 10 of Schedules K and K-1. See **Passive Activity Limitations** beginning on page 6 for more information on rental activities and portfolio income.

Do not report any nondeductible amounts (such as expenses connected with the production of tax-exempt income) on lines 9 through 21. Instead, report nondeductible expenses on line 21 of Schedules K and K-1. If an expense is connected with both taxable income and nontaxable income, allocate a reasonable part of the expense to each kind of income.

Do not take a deduction for any qualified expenditures to which an election under section 59(e) may apply. See the instructions on page 21 for Schedules K and K-1, lines 18a and 18b, for information on how to report these amounts.

Do not deduct in this section items which section 702 and the regulations require that the partnership state separately and which require separate computations by the partners. For example, expenses incurred for the production of income instead of in a trade or business must be separately stated. Other items that must be separately stated include charitable contributions, foreign taxes paid, intangible drilling and development costs, soil and water conservation expenditures, and exploration expenditures. The distributive shares of these expenses are reported as separate items to each partner on Schedule K-1.

Limitations on Deductions

Section 263A uniform capitalization rules.— The uniform capitalization rules of section 263A require partnerships to capitalize or include in inventory certain costs incurred in connection with the production of real and personal tangible property held in inventory or held for sale in the ordinary course of business. Tangible personal property produced by a partnership includes a film, sound recording, videotape, book, or similar property. The rules also apply to personal property (tangible and intangible) acquired for resale. Partnerships subject to the rules are required to capitalize not only direct costs but an allocable portion of most indirect costs (including taxes) that benefit the assets produced or acquired for resale. Interest expense paid or incurred during the production period of certain property must be capitalized and is governed by special rules. For more information, see Regulations sections 1.263A-8 through 1.263A-15. The uniform capitalization rules also apply to the production of property constructed or improved by a partnership for use in its trade or business or in an activity engaged in for profit.

Section 263A does not apply to personal property acquired for resale if the taxpayer's average annual gross receipts for the 3 prior tax years are $10 million or less. It does not apply to timber or to most property produced under a long-term contract. Special rules apply to certain partnerships engaged in farming (see the note at the end of line 5 instructions). The rules do not apply to property that is produced for use by the taxpayer if substantial construction occurred before March 1, 1986.

In the case of inventory, some of the indirect expenses that must be capitalized are: administration expenses; taxes; depreciation; insurance; compensation paid to officers attributable to services; rework labor; and

contributions to pension, stock bonus, and certain profit-sharing, annuity, or deferred compensation plans.

The costs required to be capitalized under section 263A are not deductible until the property to which the costs relate is sold, used, or otherwise disposed of by the partnership.

Research and experimental costs under section 174; intangible drilling costs for oil, gas, and geothermal property; and mining exploration and development costs are reported separately to partners for purposes of determinations under section 59(e).

Regulations section 1.263A-1(e)(3) specifies other indirect costs that may be currently deducted and those that must be capitalized with respect to production or resale activities.

For more information, see Regulations sections 1.263A-1 through 1.263A-3.

Transactions between related taxpayers.— Generally, an accrual basis partnership may deduct business expenses and interest owed to a related party (including any partner) only in the tax year of the partnership that includes the day on which the payment is includible in the income of the related party. See section 267 for details.

Business start-up expenses.—Business start-up expenses must be capitalized. An election may be made to amortize them over a period of not less than 60 months. See Pub. 535.

Organization costs.—Amounts paid or incurred to organize a partnership are capital expenditures. They are not deductible as a current expense.

The partnership may elect to amortize organization expenses over a period of 60 or more months, beginning with the month in which the partnership begins business. Include the amortization expense on line 20. On the balance sheet (Schedule L) show the unamortized balance of organization costs. See the instructions on page 12 for line 10 for the treatment of organization expenses paid to a partner. See Pub. 535 for more information.

Syndication costs.—Costs for issuing and marketing interests in the partnership, such as commissions, professional fees, and printing costs, must be capitalized. They cannot be depreciated or amortized. See the instructions on page 12 for line 10 for the treatment of syndication fees paid to a partner.

Reducing certain expenses for which credits are allowable.—For each of the credits listed below, the partnership must reduce the otherwise allowable deductions for expenses used to figure the credit by the amount of the current year credit:

1. The work opportunity credit,

2. The credit for increasing research activities,

3. The enhanced oil recovery credit,

4. The disabled access credit,

5. The empowerment zone employment credit,

6. The Indian employment credit,

7. The credit for employer social security and Medicare taxes paid on certain employee tips, and

Page 11

8. The orphan drug credit.

If the partnership has any of these credits, be sure to figure each current year credit before figuring the deductions for expenses on which the credit is based.

Line 9—Salaries and Wages

Enter on line 9 the salaries and wages paid or incurred for the tax year, reduced by any applicable employment credits from **Form 5884,** Work Opportunity Credit, **Form 8844,** Empowerment Zone Employment Credit, and **Form 8845,** Indian Employment Credit. See the instructions for these forms for more information.

Do not include salaries and wages reported elsewhere on the return, such as amounts included in cost of goods sold, elective contributions to a section 401(k) cash or deferred arrangement, or amounts contributed under a salary reduction SEP agreement.

Line 10—Guaranteed Payments to Partners

Deduct payments or credits to a partner for services or for the use of capital if the payments or credits are determined without regard to partnership income and are allocable to a trade or business activity. Also include on line 10 amounts paid during the tax year for insurance that constitutes medical care for a partner, a partner's spouse, or a partner's dependents.

Do not include any payments and credits that should be capitalized. For example, although payments or credits to a partner for services rendered in organizing or syndicating a partnership may be guaranteed payments, they are not deductible on line 10. They are capital expenditures. However, they should be separately reported on Schedules K and K-1, line 5.

Do not include distributive shares of partnership profits.

Report the guaranteed payments to the appropriate partners on Schedule K-1, line 5.

Line 11—Repairs and Maintenance

Enter the costs of incidental repairs and maintenance that do not add to the value of the property or appreciably prolong its life, but only to the extent that such costs relate to a trade or business activity and are not claimed elsewhere on the return.

New buildings, machinery, or permanent improvements that increase the value of the property are not deductible. They are chargeable to capital accounts and may be depreciated or amortized.

Line 12—Bad Debts

Enter the total debts that became worthless in whole or in part during the year, but only to the extent such debts relate to a trade or business activity. Report deductible nonbusiness bad debts as a short-term capital loss on Schedule D (Form 1065).

Caution: Cash method partnerships cannot take a bad debt deduction unless the amount was previously included in income.

Line 13—Rent

Enter rent paid on business property used in a trade or business activity. Do not deduct rent for a dwelling unit occupied by any partner for personal use.

If the partnership rented or leased a vehicle, enter the total annual rent or lease expense paid or incurred in the trade or business activities of the partnership. Also complete Part V of **Form 4562,** Depreciation and Amortization. If the partnership leased a vehicle for a term of 30 days or more, the deduction for vehicle lease expense may have to be reduced by an amount called the **inclusion amount.** You may have an inclusion amount if—

The lease term began:	And the vehicle's fair market value on the first day of the lease exceeded:
After 12/31/94	$15,500
After 12/31/93 but before 1/1/95	$14,600
After 12/31/92 but before 1/1/94	$14,300
After 12/31/91 but before 1/1/93	$13,700

If the lease term began before January 1, 1992, get **Pub. 463,** Travel, Entertainment, Gift, and Car Expenses, to find out if the partnership has an inclusion amount.

See Pub. 463 for instructions on figuring the inclusion amount.

Line 14—Taxes and Licenses

Enter taxes and licenses paid or incurred in the trade or business activities of the partnership if not reflected in cost of goods sold. Federal import duties and Federal excise and stamp taxes are deductible only if paid or incurred in carrying on the trade or business of the partnership.

Do not deduct taxes, including state and local sales taxes, paid or accrued in connection with the acquisition or disposition of business property. These taxes must be added to the cost of the property, or, in the case of a disposition, subtracted from the amount realized.

Do not deduct taxes assessed against local benefits to the extent that they increase the value of the property assessed (such as for paving, etc.), Federal income taxes, or taxes reported elsewhere on the return.

Do not deduct section 901 foreign taxes. Report these taxes separately on Schedules K and K-1, line 17e.

Do not report on line 14 taxes allocable to portfolio income or to a rental activity. Taxes allocable to a rental real estate activity are reported on Form 8825. Taxes allocable to a rental activity other than a rental real estate activity are reported on line 3b of Schedule K. Taxes allocable to portfolio income are reported on line 10 of Schedules K and K-1.

Do not deduct on line 14 taxes paid or incurred for the production or collection of income, or for the management, conservation, or maintenance of property held to produce income. Report these taxes separately on line 11 of Schedules K and K-1.

See section 263A(a) for rules on capitalization of allocable costs (including taxes) for any property.

Line 15—Interest

Include only interest incurred in the trade or business activities of the partnership that is not claimed elsewhere on the return.

Do not include interest expense on debt required to be allocated to the production of qualified property. Interest that is allocable to certain property produced by a partnership for its own use or for sale must be capitalized. In addition, a partnership must also capitalize any interest on debt that is allocable to an asset used to produce the above property. A partner may have to capitalize interest that the partner incurs during the tax year with respect to the production expenditures of the partnership. Similarly, interest incurred by a partnership may have to be capitalized by a partner with respect to the partner's own production expenditures. The information required by the partner to properly capitalize interest for this purpose must be provided by the partnership in an attachment to Schedule K-1. See section 263A(f) and Regulations sections 1.263A-8 through 1.263A-15.

Do not include interest expense on debt used to purchase rental property or debt used in a rental activity. Interest allocable to a rental real estate activity is reported on Form 8825 and is used in arriving at net income (loss) from rental real estate activities on line 2 of Schedules K and K-1. Interest allocable to a rental activity other than a rental real estate activity is included on line 3b of Schedule K and is used in arriving at net income (loss) from a rental activity (other than a rental real estate activity). This net amount is reported on line 3c of Schedule K and line 3 of Schedule K-1.

Do not include interest expense on debt used to buy property held for investment. Do not include interest expense that is clearly and directly allocable to interest, dividend, royalty, or annuity income not derived in the ordinary course of a trade or business. Interest paid or incurred on debt used to purchase or carry investment property is reported on line 12a of Schedules K and K-1. See the instructions for line 12a of Schedules K and K-1 and **Form 4952,** Investment Interest Expense Deduction, for more information on investment property.

Do not include interest on debt proceeds allocated to distributions made to partners during the tax year. Instead, report such interest on line 11 of Schedules K and K-1. To determine the amount to allocate to distributions to partners, see Notice 89-35, 1989-1 C.B. 675.

Temporary Regulations section 1.163-8T gives rules for allocating interest expense among activities so that the limitations on passive activity losses, investment interest, and personal interest can be properly figured. Generally, interest expense is allocated in the same manner that debt is allocated. Debt is allocated by tracing disbursements of the debt proceeds to specific expenditures, as provided in the regulations.

Note: Interest paid by a partnership to a partner for the use of capital should be entered on line 10 as guaranteed payments. Prepaid interest can only be deducted over the period to which the prepayment applies. Interest incurred during construction or improvement of real property, personal property that has a class life of 20 years or more, or other tangible property requiring more than 2 years (1 year in the case of property costing more than $1 million) to produce or construct generally must be capitalized. See Regulations sections 1.263A-8 through 1.263A-15 for more information. The limitations on deductions for

Page 12

unpaid interest are in Regulations section 1.267(b)-1(b).

Line 16—Depreciation

On line 16a, enter **only** the depreciation claimed on assets used in a trade or business activity. Enter on line 16b the depreciation reported elsewhere on the return (e.g., on Schedule A) that is attributable to assets used in trade or business activities. See the Instructions for Form 4562 or **Pub. 946,** How To Depreciate Property, to figure the amount of depreciation to enter on this line.

For depreciation, you must complete and attach Form 4562 only if the partnership placed property in service during 1996 or claims depreciation on any car or other listed property.

Do not include any section 179 expense deduction on this line. This amount is not deducted by the partnership. Instead, it is passed through to the partners on line 9 of Schedule K-1.

Line 17—Depletion

If the partnership claims a deduction for timber depletion, complete and attach **Form T,** Forest Activities Schedules.

Caution: *Do not deduct depletion for oil and gas properties. Each partner figures depletion on oil and gas properties. See the instructions for Schedule K-1, line 25, item 3, for the information on oil and gas depletion that must be supplied to the partners by the partnership.*

Line 18—Retirement Plans, etc.

Do not deduct payments for partners to retirement or deferred compensation plans including IRAs, Keoghs, and simplified employee pension (SEP) plans on this line. These amounts are reported on Schedule K-1, line 11, and are deducted by the partners on their own returns.

Enter the deductible contributions not claimed elsewhere on the return made by the partnership for its common-law employees under a qualified pension, profit-sharing, annuity, or SEP plan, and under any other deferred compensation plan.

If the partnership contributes to an individual retirement arrangement (IRA) for employees, include the contribution in salaries and wages on page 1, line 9, or Schedule A, line 3, and not on line 18.

Employers who maintain a pension, profit-sharing, or other funded deferred compensation plan (other than a SEP), whether or not the plan is qualified under the Internal Revenue Code and whether or not a deduction is claimed for the current year, generally must file one of the following forms:

- **Form 5500,** Annual Return/Report of Employee Benefit Plan, for each plan with 100 or more participants.

- **Form 5500-C/R,** Return/Report of Employee Benefit Plan, for each plan with fewer than 100 participants.

- **Form 5500-EZ,** Annual Return of One-Participant (Owners and Their Spouses) Retirement Plan, for each plan that covers only partners or partners and their spouses.

There are penalties for not filing these forms on time.

Line 19—Employee Benefit Programs

Enter the partnership's contributions to employee benefit programs not claimed elsewhere on the return (e.g., insurance, health, and welfare programs) that are not part of a pension, profit-sharing, etc., plan included on line 18.

Do not include amounts paid during the tax year for insurance that constitutes medical care for a partner, a partner's spouse, or a partner's dependents. Instead, include these amounts on line 10 as guaranteed payments and on Schedule K, line 5, and Schedule K-1, line 5, of each partner on whose behalf the amounts were paid. Also report these amounts on Schedule K, line 11, and Schedule K-1, line 11, of each partner on whose behalf the amounts were paid.

Line 20—Other Deductions

Attach your own schedule, listing by type and amount, all allowable deductions related to a trade or business activity for which there is no separate line on page 1 of Form 1065. Enter the total on this line. Do not include items that must be reported separately on Schedules K and K-1.

A partnership is not allowed the deduction for net operating losses.

Do not include qualified expenditures to which an election under section 59(e) may apply.

Include on line 20 the deduction taken for amortization. You must complete and attach Form 4562 if the partnership is claiming amortization of costs that begins during its 1996 tax year. The instructions for Form 4562 provide code section references for specific amortizable property. See Pub. 535 for more information on amortization.

Do not deduct amounts paid or incurred to participate or intervene in any political campaign on behalf of a candidate for public office, or to influence the general public regarding legislative matters, elections, or referendums. In addition, partnerships generally cannot deduct expenses paid or incurred to influence Federal or state legislation, or to influence the actions or positions of certain Federal executive branch officials. However, certain in-house lobbying expenditures that do not exceed $2,000 are deductible. See section 162(e) for more details.

Do not deduct fines or penalties paid to a government for violating any law.

A deduction is allowed for part of the cost of qualified clean-fuel vehicle property and qualified clean-fuel vehicle refueling property. For more details, see section 179A.

Meals, travel, and entertainment.— Generally, the partnership can deduct only 50% of the amount otherwise allowable for meals and entertainment expenses paid or incurred in its trade or business. In addition, meals must not be lavish or extravagant; a bona fide business discussion must occur during, immediately before, or immediately after the meal; and a partner or employee of the partnership must be present at the meal. See Pub. 463 for exceptions.

Additional limitations apply to deductions for gifts, skybox rentals, luxury water travel, convention expenses, and entertainment tickets.

Partnerships are not allowed to deduct amounts paid or incurred for membership dues in any club organized for business, pleasure, recreation, or other social purpose. This includes country clubs, golf and athletic clubs, airline and hotel clubs, and clubs operated to provide meals under conditions favorable to business discussion. But it does not include civic or public service organizations, professional organizations (such as bar and medical associations), business leagues, trade associations, chambers of commerce, boards of trade, and real estate boards, unless a principal purpose of the organization is to entertain, or provide entertainment facilities for, members or their guests.

In addition, no deduction is allowed for travel expenses paid or incurred for a partner's or employee's spouse or dependent or other individual accompanying a partner or employee of the partnership, unless that spouse, dependent, or other individual is an employee of the partnership, and that person's travel is for a bona fide business purpose and would otherwise be deductible by that person.

Generally, a partnership can deduct all other ordinary and necessary travel and entertainment expenses paid or incurred in its trade or business. However, it cannot deduct an expense paid or incurred for a facility (such as a yacht or hunting lodge) that is used for an activity that is usually considered entertainment, amusement, or recreation.

Note: *The partnership may be able to deduct otherwise nondeductible meals, travel, and entertainment expenses if the amounts are treated as compensation and reported on Form W-2 for an employee or on Form 1099-MISC for an independent contractor.*

See Pub. 463 for more details.

Schedule A—Cost of Goods Sold

Inventories are required at the beginning and end of each tax year if the production, purchase, or sale of merchandise is an income-producing factor. See Regulations section 1.471-1.

Section 263A Uniform Capitalization Rules

The uniform capitalization rules of section 263A are discussed under **Limitations on Deductions** on page 11. See those instructions before completing Schedule A.

Line 1—Inventory at Beginning of Year

This figure should match the ending inventory reported on the partnership's 1995 Form 1065, Schedule A, line 7. If it is different, attach an explanation.

Line 2—Purchases

Reduce purchases by items withdrawn for personal use. The cost of these items should be shown on line 23 of Schedules K and K-1 as distributions to partners.

Line 4—Additional Section 263A Costs

An entry is required on this line only for partnerships that have elected a simplified method.

For partnerships that have elected the simplified production method, additional section 263A costs are generally those costs,

Page 13

other than interest, that were not capitalized under the partnership's method of accounting immediately prior to the effective date of section 263A that are now required to be capitalized under section 263A. Interest is to be accounted for separately. For new partnerships, additional section 263A costs are the costs, other than interest, that must be capitalized under section 263A, but which the partnership would not have been required to capitalize if it had existed before the effective date of section 263A. For more details, see Regulations section 1.263A-2(b).

For partnerships that have elected the simplified resale method, additional section 263A costs are generally those costs incurred with respect to the following categories: **(a)** off-site storage or warehousing; **(b)** purchasing; **(c)** handling, processing, assembly, and repackaging; and **(d)** general and administrative costs (mixed service costs). For more details, see Regulations section 1.263A-3(d).

Enter on line 4 the balance of section 263A costs paid or incurred during the tax year not included on lines 2, 3, and 5. Attach a schedule listing these costs.

Line 5—Other Costs

Enter on line 5 any other inventoriable costs paid or incurred during the tax year not entered on lines 2 through 4. Attach a schedule.

Line 7—Inventory at End of Year

See Regulations sections 1.263A-1 through 1.263A-3 for details on figuring the costs to be included in ending inventory.

Lines 9a through 9c—Inventory Valuation Methods

Inventories can be valued at:

● Cost,

● Cost or market value (whichever is lower), or

● Any other method approved by the IRS that conforms to the requirements of the applicable regulations.

The average cost (rolling average) method of valuing inventories generally does not conform to the requirements of the regulations. See Rev. Rul. 71-234, 1971-1 C.B. 148.

Partnerships that use erroneous valuation methods must change to a method permitted for Federal tax purposes. To make this change, use Form 3115.

On line 9a, check the methods used for valuing inventories. Under lower of cost or market, the term "market" (for normal goods) means the current bid price prevailing on the inventory valuation date for the particular merchandise in the volume usually purchased by the taxpayer. For a manufacturer, market applies to the basic elements of cost—raw materials, labor, and burden. If section 263A applies to the taxpayer, the basic elements of cost must reflect the current bid price of all direct costs and all indirect costs properly allocable to goods on hand at the inventory date.

Inventory may be valued below cost when the merchandise is unsalable at normal prices or unusable in the normal way because the goods are subnormal due to damage, imperfections, shop wear, etc., within the

meaning of Regulations section 1.471-2(c). These goods may be valued at the current bona fide selling price minus the direct cost of disposition (but not less than scrap value) if such a price can be established.

If this is the first year the last-in first-out (LIFO) inventory method was either adopted or extended to inventory goods not previously valued under the LIFO method, attach **Form 970,** Application To Use LIFO Inventory Method, or a statement with the information required by Form 970. Also check the box on line 9c.

If the partnership has changed or extended its inventory method to LIFO and has had to write up its opening inventory to cost in the year of election, report the effect of this write-up as income (line 7, page 1, Form 1065) proportionately over a 3-year period that begins in the tax year of the LIFO election.

For more information on inventory valuation methods, see Pub. 538.

Schedule B—Other Information
Question 1

Check box **(d)** for any other type of entity and state the type (e.g., limited liability partnership).

Question 4—Consolidated Audit Procedures

Generally, the tax treatment of partnership items is determined at the partnership level in a consolidated audit proceeding, rather than in separate proceedings with individual partners.

Answer "Yes" to Question 4 if **ANY** of the following apply:

● The partnership had more than 10 partners at any one time during the tax year (for purposes of this question, a husband and wife—and their estates—count as one person); or

● Any partner was a nonresident alien or was other than a natural person or estate; or

● Any partner's share of any partnership item was different from his or her share of any other partnership item; or

● The partnership is a "small partnership" that has elected to be subject to the rules for consolidated audit proceedings. "Small partnerships" as defined in section 6231(a)(1)(B) are not subject to the rules for consolidated audit proceedings, but may make an irrevocable election under Temporary Regulations section 301.6231(a)(1)-1T(b)(2) to be covered by them.

Note: *The partnership does not make this election when it answers "Yes" to Question 4. The election must be made separately.*

If a partnership return is filed by an entity for a tax year, but it is determined that the entity is not a partnership for that tax year, the consolidated partnership audit procedures will generally apply to that entity and to persons holding an interest in that entity. See Temporary Regulations section 301.6233-1T for details and exceptions.

Question 6—Foreign Partners

Answer "Yes" to Question 6 if the partnership had any foreign partners (for purposes of

section 1446) at any time during the tax year. Otherwise, answer "No."

If the partnership had gross income effectively connected with a trade or business in the United States **and** foreign partners, it may be required to withhold tax under section 1446 on income allocable to foreign partners (without regard to distributions) and file Forms 8804, 8805, and 8813.

Question 7

Answer "Yes" to Question 7 if interests in the partnership are traded on an established securities market or are readily tradable on a secondary market (or its substantial equivalent).

Question 8

Organizers of certain tax shelters are required to register the tax shelters by filing Form 8264 no later than the day on which an interest in the shelter is first offered for sale. Organizers filing a properly completed Form 8264 will receive a tax shelter registration number that they must furnish to their investors. See the Instructions for Form 8264 for the definition of a tax shelter and the investments exempted from tax shelter registration.

Question 9—Foreign Accounts

Answer "Yes" to Question 9 if either **1** OR **2** below applies to the partnership. Otherwise, check the "No" box.

1. At any time during calendar year 1996, the partnership had an interest in or signature or other authority over a bank account, securities account, or other financial account in a foreign country; **AND**

● The combined value of the accounts was more than $10,000 at any time during the calendar year; **AND**

● The accounts were NOT with a U.S. military banking facility operated by a U.S. financial institution.

2. The partnership owns more than 50% of the stock in any corporation that would answer the question "Yes," based on item **1** above.

Get **Form TD F 90-22.1,** Report of Foreign Bank and Financial Accounts, to see if the partnership is considered to have an interest in or signature or other authority over a bank account, securities account, or other financial account in a foreign country.

If you answered "Yes" to Question 9, file Form TD F 90-22.1 by June 30, 1997, with the Department of the Treasury at the address shown on the form. Because Form TD F 90-22.1 is not a tax return, **do not** file it with Form 1065. You may order Form TD F 90-22.1 by calling 1-800-829-3676.

Question 10

If the partnership received a distribution from a foreign trust after August 20, 1996, it must provide additional information. For this purpose, a loan of cash or marketable securities generally is considered to be a distribution. See **Pub. 553,** Highlights of 1996 Tax Changes, for details.

If the partnership was the grantor of, or the transferor to, a foreign trust that existed during the tax year, it may have to file **Form 3520,** Creation of or Transfers to Certain Foreign Trusts; **Form 3520-A,** Annual Return of Foreign Trust With U.S. Beneficiaries; or

Page 14

Form 926, Return by a U.S. Transferor of Property to a Foreign Corporation, Foreign Estate or Trust, or Foreign Partnership.

Designation of Tax Matters Partner (TMP)

If the partnership is subject to the rules for consolidated audit proceedings in sections 6221 through 6233, the partnership may designate a partner as the TMP for the tax year for which the return is filed by completing the **Designation of Tax Matters Partner** section on page 2 of Form 1065. See the instructions for Question 4, consolidated audit procedures, to determine if the partnership is subject to these rules. The designated TMP must be a general partner and, in most cases, must also be a U.S. person. For details, see Temporary Regulations section 301.6231(a)(7)-1T.

General Instructions for Schedules K and K-1— Partners' Shares of Income, Credits, Deductions, etc.

Purpose of Schedules

Although the partnership is not subject to income tax, the partners are liable for tax on their shares of the partnership income, whether or not distributed, and must include their shares on their tax returns.

Schedule K (page 3 of Form 1065) is a summary schedule of all the partners' shares of the partnership's income, credits, deductions, etc.

Schedule K-1 (Form 1065) shows each partner's separate share. Attach a copy of each Schedule K-1 to the Form 1065 filed with the IRS; keep a copy with a copy of the partnership return as a part of the partnership's records; and furnish a copy to each partner. If a partnership interest is held by a nominee on behalf of another person, the partnership may be required to furnish Schedule K-1 to the nominee. See Temporary Regulations sections 1.6031(b)-1T and 1.6031(c)-1T for more information.

Be sure to give each partner a copy of either the Partner's Instructions for Schedule K-1 (Form 1065) or specific instructions for each item reported on the partner's Schedule K-1 (Form 1065).

Substitute Forms

The partnership does not need IRS approval to use a substitute Schedule K-1 if it is an exact copy of the IRS schedule, or if it contains only those lines the taxpayer is required to use. The lines must use the same numbers and titles and must be in the same order and format as on the comparable IRS Schedule K-1. The substitute schedule must include the OMB number. The partnership must provide each partner with the Partner's Instructions for Schedule K-1 (Form 1065) or other prepared specific instructions.

The partnership must request IRS approval to use other substitute Schedules K-1. To request approval, write to Internal Revenue Service, Attention: Substitute Forms Program Coordinator, T:FP:S, 1111 Constitution Avenue, N.W., Washington, DC 20224.

Each partner's information must be on a separate sheet of paper. Therefore, separate all continuously printed substitutes before you file them with the IRS.

The partnership may be subject to a penalty if it files Schedules K-1 that do not conform to the specifications of Rev. Proc. 96-48, 1996-39 I.R.B. 10.

How Income Is Shared Among Partners

Income (loss) is allocated to a partner only for the part of the year in which that person is a member of the partnership. The partnership will either allocate on a daily basis or divide the partnership year into segments and allocate income, loss, or special items in each segment among the persons who were partners during that segment. Partnerships that report their income on the cash basis must allocate interest expense, taxes, and any payment for services or for the use of property on a daily basis if there is any change in any partner's interest during the year. See Pub. 541 for more information and for information on the tax consequences of the termination of a partner's interest.

Allocate shares of income, gain, loss, deduction, or credit among the partners according to the partnership agreement for sharing income or loss generally. Partners may agree to allocate specific items in a ratio different from the ratio for sharing income or loss. For instance, if the net income exclusive of specially allocated items is divided evenly among three partners but some special items are allocated 50% to one, 30% to another, and 20% to the third partner, report the specially allocated items on the appropriate line of the applicable partner's Schedule K-1 and the total on the appropriate line of Schedule K, instead of on the numbered lines on page 1 of Form 1065 or Schedules A or D.

Special rules on the allocation of income, gain, loss, and deductions generally apply if a partner contributes property to the partnership and the fair market value of that property at the time of contribution differs from the contributing partner's adjusted tax basis. Under these rules, the partnership must use a reasonable method of making allocations of income, gain, loss, and deductions from the property so that the contributing partner receives the tax burdens and benefits of any built-in gain or loss (i.e., precontribution appreciation or diminution of value of the contributed property). See Regulations section 1.704-3 for details on how to make these allocations, including a description of specific allocation methods that are generally reasonable.

See **Dispositions of Contributed Property** on page 6 for special rules on the allocation of income, gain, loss, and deductions on the disposition of property contributed to the partnership by a partner.

If the partnership agreement does not provide for the partner's share of income, gain, loss, deduction, or credit, or if the allocation under the agreement does not have substantial economic effect, the partner's share is determined according to the partner's interest in the partnership. See Regulations section 1.704-1 for more information.

Note: *If a partner's interest changed during the year, see section 706(d) before*

determining each partner's distributive share of any item of income, gain, loss, deduction, etc.

Specific Instructions (Schedule K Only)

All partnerships must complete Schedule K. Rental activity income (loss) and portfolio income are not reported on page 1 of Form 1065. These amounts are not combined with trade or business activity income (loss). Schedule K is used to report the totals of these and other amounts.

Specific Instructions (Schedule K-1 Only)
General Information

Prepare and give a Schedule K-1 to each person who was a partner in the partnership at any time during the year. **Schedule K-1 must be provided to each partner on or before the day on which the partnership return is required to be filed.**

Note: *Generally, any person who holds an interest in a partnership as a nominee for another person must furnish to the partnership the name, address, etc., of the other person.*

On each Schedule K-1, enter the names, addresses, and identifying numbers of the partner and partnership and the partner's distributive share of each item.

For an individual partner, enter the partner's social security number. For all other partners, enter the partner's EIN. However, if a partner is an individual retirement arrangement (IRA), enter the identifying number of the custodian of the IRA. Do not enter the social security number of the person for whom the IRA is maintained.

If a husband and wife each had an interest in the partnership, prepare a separate Schedule K-1 for each of them. If a husband and wife held an interest together, prepare one Schedule K-1 if the two of them are considered to be one partner.

Note: *There is space on line 25 of Schedule K-1 for you to provide information to the partners. This space may be used instead of of attachments.*

Specific Items and Questions
Question A

Answer Question A on all Schedules K-1. If a partner holds interests as both a general and limited partner, check the first two boxes and attach a schedule for each activity that shows the amounts allocable to the partner's interest as a limited partner.

Question B—What Type of Entity Is This Partner?

State on this line whether the partner is an individual, a corporation, an estate, a trust, a partnership, an exempt organization, or a nominee (custodian). If the partner is a nominee, use one of the following codes to indicate the type of entity the nominee represents: I—Individual; C—Corporation; F—Estate or Trust; P—Partnership; E—Exempt Organization; or IRA—Individual Retirement Arrangement.

Page 15

Question C—Domestic/Foreign Partner

Check the foreign partner box if the partner is a nonresident alien individual, foreign partnership, foreign corporation, or a foreign estate or trust. Otherwise, check the domestic partner box.

Item D—Partner's Profit, Loss, and Capital Sharing Percentages

Enter in Item D, column (ii), the appropriate percentages as of the end of the year. However, if a partner's interest terminated during the year, enter in column (i) the percentages that existed immediately before the termination. When the profit or loss sharing percentage has changed during the year, show the percentage before the change in column (i) and the end-of-year percentage in column (ii). If there are multiple changes in the profit and loss sharing percentage during the year, attach a statement giving the date and percentage before each change.

"Ownership of capital" means the portion of the capital that the partner would receive if the partnership was liquidated at the end of the year by the distribution of undivided interests in partnership assets and liabilities.

Item F—Partner's Share of Liabilities

Enter each partner's share of nonrecourse liabilities, partnership-level qualified nonrecourse financing, and other liabilities.

"Nonrecourse liabilities" are those liabilities of the partnership for which no partner bears the economic risk of loss. The extent to which a partner bears the economic risk of loss is determined under the rules of Regulations section 1.752-2. Do not include partnership-level qualified nonrecourse financing (defined below) on the line for nonrecourse liabilities.

If the partner terminated his or her interest in the partnership during the year, enter the share that existed immediately before the total disposition. In all other cases, enter it as of the end of the year.

If the partnership is engaged in two or more different types of at-risk activities, or a combination of at-risk activities and any other activity, attach a statement showing the partner's share of nonrecourse liabilities, partnership-level qualified nonrecourse financing, and other liabilities for **each** activity. See Pub. 925 to determine if the partnership is engaged in more than one at-risk activity.

The at-risk rules of section 465 generally apply to any activity carried on by the partnership as a trade or business or for the production of income. These rules generally limit the amount of loss and other deductions a partner can claim from any partnership activity to the amount for which that partner is considered at risk. However, for partners who acquired their partnership interests before 1987, the at-risk rules do not apply to losses from an activity of holding real property the partnership placed in service before 1987. The activity of holding mineral property does not qualify for this exception. Identify on an attachment to Schedule K-1 the amount of any losses that are not subject to the at-risk rules.

If a partnership is engaged in an activity subject to the limitations of section 465(c)(1)

(i.e., films or videotapes, leasing section 1245 property, farming, or oil and gas property), give each partner his or her share of the total pre-1976 losses from that activity for which there existed a corresponding amount of nonrecourse liability at the end of each year in which the losses occurred. Get **Form 6198,** At-Risk Limitations, and related instructions for more information.

Qualified nonrecourse financing secured by real property used in an activity of holding real property that is subject to the at-risk rules is treated as an amount at risk. "Qualified nonrecourse financing" generally includes financing for which no one is personally liable for repayment that is borrowed for use in an activity of holding real property and that is loaned or guaranteed by a Federal, state, or local government or that is borrowed from a "qualified" person. Qualified persons include any person actively and regularly engaged in the business of lending money, such as a bank or savings and loan association. Qualified persons generally do not include related parties (unless the nonrecourse financing is commercially reasonable and on substantially the same terms as loans involving unrelated persons), the seller of the property, or a person who receives a fee for the partnership's investment in the real property. See section 465 for more information on qualified nonrecourse financing.

The partner as well as the partnership must meet the qualified nonrecourse rules. Therefore, the partnership must enter on an attached statement any other information the partner needs to determine if the qualified nonrecourse rules are also met at the partner level.

Item G—Tax Shelter Registration Number

If the partnership is a registration-required tax shelter, it must enter its tax shelter registration number in Item G. If the partnership invested in a registration-required shelter, the partnership must also furnish a copy of its Form 8271 to its partners. See Form 8271 for more information.

Item J—Analysis of Partner's Capital Account

You are not required to complete Item J if the answer to Question 5 of Schedule B is "Yes." If you are required to complete this item, see the instructions for Schedule M-2 on page 23.

Specific Instructions (Schedules K and K-1, Except as Noted)

Schedules K and K-1 have the same line numbers for lines 1 through 23.

Special Allocations

An item is specially allocated if it is allocated to a partner in a ratio different from the ratio for sharing income or loss generally.

Report specially allocated ordinary gain (loss) on Schedules K and K-1, line 7. Report other specially allocated items on the applicable lines of the partner's Schedule K-1, with the total amount on the applicable line of Schedule K. For example, specially allocated long-term capital gain is entered on line 4e of the partner's Schedule K-1, and the

total is entered on line 4e of Schedule K, along with any net long-term capital gain (or loss) from line 11 of Schedule D (Form 1065).

Income (Loss)

Line 1—Ordinary Income (Loss) From Trade or Business Activities

Enter the amount from page 1, line 22. Enter the income or loss without reference to **(a)** the basis of the partners' interests in the partnership, **(b)** the partners' at-risk limitations, or **(c)** the passive activity limitations. These limitations, if applicable, are determined at the partner level.

If the partnership has more than one trade or business activity, identify on an attachment to Schedule K-1 the amount from each separate activity. See **Passive Activity Reporting Requirements** on page 9.

Line 1 should not include rental activity income (loss) or portfolio income (loss).

Line 2—Net Income (Loss) From Rental Real Estate Activities

Enter the net income or loss from rental real estate activities of the partnership from Form 8825. Attach this form to Form 1065. If the partnership has more than one rental real estate activity, identify on an attachment to Schedule K-1 the amount attributable to each activity.

Line 3—Net Income (Loss) From Other Rental Activities

On Schedule K, line 3a, enter gross income from rental activities other than rental real estate activities. See page 7 of these instructions and Pub. 925 for the definition of rental activities. Include on line 3a, the gain (loss) from line 20 of Form 4797 that is attributable to the sale, exchange, or involuntary conversion of an asset used in a rental activity other than a rental real estate activity.

On line 3b of Schedule K, enter the deductible expenses of the activity. Attach a schedule of these expenses to Form 1065.

Enter the net income (loss) on line 3c of Schedule K. Enter each partner's share on line 3 of Schedule K-1.

If the partnership has more than one rental activity reported on line 3, identify on an attachment to Schedule K-1 the amount from each activity.

Lines 4a Through 4f—Portfolio Income (Loss)

Enter portfolio income (loss) on lines 4a through 4f.

See page 8 of these instructions for a definition of portfolio income. Do not reduce portfolio income by deductions allocable to it. Report such deductions (other than interest expense) on line 10 of Schedules K and K-1. Interest expense allocable to portfolio income is generally investment interest expense and is reported on line 12a of Schedules K and K-1.

Lines 4a and 4b.—Enter only taxable interest and dividends on these lines. Taxable interest is interest from all sources except interest exempt from tax and interest on tax-free covenant bonds.

Lines 4d and 4e.—Enter on line 4d of Schedule K the amount on line 5 of Schedule

D (Form 1065) plus any short-term capital gain (loss) that is specially allocated to partners. Report each partner's share on line 4d of Schedule K-1.

The amount reported for line 4e of Schedule K is the amount on line 11 of Schedule D (Form 1065) plus any long-term capital gain (loss) that is specially allocated to partners. Report each partner's share on line 4e of Schedule K-1.

Caution: *If any short-term or long-term capital gain or loss is from the disposition of nondepreciable personal property used in a trade or business, it may not be treated as portfolio income. Report such gain or loss on line 7 of Schedules K and K-1.*

Line 4f.—Report and identify other portfolio income or loss on an attachment for line 4f.

For example, income reported to the partnership from a real estate mortgage investment conduit (REMIC), in which the partnership is a residual interest holder, would be reported on an attachment for line 4f. If the partnership holds a residual interest in a REMIC, report on the attachment for line 4f the partner's share of:

1. Taxable income (net loss) from the REMIC (line 1b of Schedules Q (Form 1066)),

2. "Excess inclusion" (line 2c of Schedules Q (Form 1066)), and

3. Section 212 expenses (line 3b of Schedules Q (Form 1066)). Do not report these section 212 expenses on line 10 of Schedules K and K-1.

Because Schedule Q (Form 1066) is a quarterly statement, the partnership must follow the Schedule Q instructions to figure the amounts to report to the partner for the partnership's tax year.

Line 5—Guaranteed Payments to Partners

Guaranteed payments to partners include:

1. Payments for salaries, health insurance, and interest deducted by the partnership and reported on Form 1065, page 1, line 10; Form 8825; or on Schedule K, line 3b; and

2. Payments the partnership must capitalize. See the Instructions for Form 1065, line 10.

Generally, amounts reported on line 5 are not considered to be related to a passive activity. For example, guaranteed payments for personal services paid to a partner would not be passive activity income. Likewise, interest paid to any partner is not passive activity income.

Line 6—Net Gain (Loss) Under Section 1231 (Other Than Due to Casualty or Theft)

Enter on line 6 the amount shown on line 8 of Form 4797. Do not include specially allocated ordinary gains and losses or net gains or losses from involuntary conversions due to casualties or thefts on this line. Instead, report them on line 7. If the partnership has more than one activity, attach a statement to Schedule K-1 that identifies the activity to which the section 1231 gain (loss) relates.

Line 7—Other Income (Loss)

Use line 7 to report other items of income, gain, or loss not included on lines 1 through 6. If the partnership has more than one activity, identify on an attachment the amount and the activity to which each amount relates.

Items to be reported on line 7 include:

● Gains from the disposition of farm recapture property (see Form 4797) and other items to which section 1252 applies.

● Gains from the disposition of an interest in oil, gas, geothermal, or other mineral properties (section 1254).

● Any net gain or loss from section 1256 contracts from **Form 6781**, Gains and Losses From Section 1256 Contracts and Straddles.

● Recoveries of tax benefit items (section 111).

● Gambling gains and losses (subject to the limitations in section 165(d)).

● Any income, gain, or loss to the partnership under section 751(b).

● Specially allocated ordinary gain (loss).

● Net gain (loss) from involuntary conversions due to casualty or theft. The amount for this line is shown on **Form 4684,** Casualties and Thefts, line 38a, 38b, or 39.

Each partner's share must be entered on Schedule K-1. Give each partner a schedule that shows the amounts to be reported on the partner's Form 4684, line 34, columns (b)(i), (b)(ii), and (c).

If there was a gain (loss) from a casualty or theft to property not used in a trade or business or for income-producing purposes, notify the partner. The partnership should not complete Form 4684 for this type of casualty or theft. Instead, each partner will complete his or her own Form 4684.

Deductions

Line 8—Charitable Contributions

Enter the total amount of charitable contributions made by the partnership during its tax year on Schedule K. Enter each partner's distributive share on Schedule K-1. On an attachment to Schedules K and K-1, show separately the dollar amount of contributions subject to each of the 50%, 30%, and 20% of adjusted gross income limits. For additional information, get **Pub. 526,** Charitable Contributions.

Generally, no deduction is allowed for any contribution of $250 or more unless the partnership obtains a written acknowledgment from the charitable organization that shows the amount of cash contributed, describes any property contributed, and gives an estimate of the value of any goods or services provided in return for the contribution. The acknowledgment must be obtained by the due date (including extensions) of the partnership return, or, if earlier, the date the partnership files its return. Do not attach the acknowledgment to the tax return, but keep it with the partnership's records. These rules apply in addition to the filing requirements for Form 8283 described below.

Certain contributions made to an organization conducting lobbying activities are not deductible. See section 170(f)(9) for more details.

Form 8283, Noncash Charitable Contributions, must be completed and attached to Form 1065 if the deduction claimed for noncash contributions exceeds

$500. The partnership must give a copy of its Form 8283 to every partner if the deduction for an item or group of similar items of contributed property exceeds $5,000. Each partner must be furnished a copy even if the amount allocated to any partner is $5,000 or less.

If the deduction for an item or group of similar items of contributed property is $5,000 or less, the partnership should pass through each partner's share of the amount of noncash contributions so the partners will be able to complete their own Forms 8283. See the Instructions for Form 8283 for additional information.

If the partnership made a qualified conservation contribution, include the fair market value of the underlying property before and after the donation and describe the conservation purpose furthered by the donation. Give a copy of this information to each partner.

Line 9—Section 179 Expense Deduction

A partnership may elect to expense part of the cost of certain tangible property the partnership purchased this year for use in its trade or business or certain rental activities. See Pub. 946 for a definition of what kind of property qualifies for the section 179 deduction.

Complete Part I of Form 4562 to figure the partnership's section 179 expense deduction. The partnership does not claim the deduction itself but instead passes it through to the partners. Attach Form 4562 to Form 1065 and show the total section 179 expense deduction on Schedule K, line 9. Report each partner's allocable share on Schedule K-1, line 9. Do not complete line 9 of Schedule K-1 for any partner that is an estate or trust.

If the partnership is an enterprise zone business, also report on an attachment to Schedules K and K-1 the cost of section 179 property placed in service during the year that is qualified zone property.

See the instructions for line 25 of Schedule K-1, item 4, for any recapture of a section 179 amount.

Note: *See the Instructions for Form 4562 for limitations on the section 179 deduction that the partnership is allowed to claim.*

Line 10—Deductions Related to Portfolio Income

Enter on line 10 and attach an itemized list of the deductions clearly and directly allocable to portfolio income (other than interest expense and section 212 expenses from a REMIC). Interest expense related to portfolio income is investment interest expense and is reported on line 12a of Schedules K and K-1. Section 212 expenses from the partnership's interest in a REMIC are reported on an attachment for line 4f of Schedules K and K-1.

No deduction is allowable under section 212 for expenses allocable to a convention, seminar, or similar meeting.

Line 11—Other Deductions

Use line 11 to report deductions not included on lines 8, 9, 10, 17e, and 18b. On an attachment, identify the deduction and amount, and if the partnership has more than

Page 17

one activity, the activity to which the deduction relates.

Examples of items to be reported on an attachment to line 11 include:

• Amounts paid by the partnership that would be allowed as itemized deductions on any of the partners' income tax returns if they were paid directly by a partner for the same purpose. However, do not enter expenses related to portfolio income or investment interest expense on this line.

If there was a loss from an involuntary conversion due to casualty or theft of income-producing property, include in the total amount for this line the relevant amount from Form 4684, line 32.

• Any penalty on early withdrawal of savings.

• Soil and water conservation expenditures (section 175).

• Expenditures for the removal of architectural and transportation barriers to the elderly and handicapped and which the partnership has elected to treat as a current expense (section 190).

• Any amounts paid during the tax year for health insurance coverage for a partner (including that partner's spouse and dependents). For 1996, a partner may be allowed to deduct up to 30% of such amounts on Form 1040, line 26.

• Payments for a partner to an IRA, Keogh, or SEP plan. If there is a defined benefit plan (Keogh), attach to the Schedule K-1 for each partner a statement showing the amount of benefit accrued for the tax year.

• Interest expense allocated to debt-financed distributions. See Notice 89-35 for more information.

• Interest paid or accrued on debt properly allocable to each general partner's share of a working interest in any oil or gas property (if the partner's liability is not limited). General partners that did not materially participate in the oil or gas activity treat this interest as investment interest; for other general partners, it is trade or business interest.

Investment Interest

Lines 12a through 12b(2) must be completed for all partners.

Line 12a—Interest Expense on Investment Debts

Include on this line interest paid or accrued on debt properly allocable to property held for investment. Property held for investment includes property that produces income (unless derived in the ordinary course of a trade or business) from interest, dividends, annuities, or royalties; and gains from the disposition of property that produces those types of income or is held for investment.

Property held for investment also includes each general partner's share of a working interest in any oil or gas property for which the partner's liability is not limited and in which the partner did not materially participate. However, the level of each partner's participation in an activity is determined by the partner and not by the partnership. As a result, interest allocable to a general partner's share of a working interest in any oil or gas property (if the partner's liability is not limited) should not be reported

on line 12a. Instead, report this interest on line 11.

Investment interest does not include interest expense allocable to a passive activity.

The amount on line 12a will be deducted (after applying the investment interest expense limitations of section 163(d)) by individual partners on Schedule A (Form 1040), line 13.

For more information, get **Form 4952,** Investment Interest Expense Deduction.

Lines 12b(1) and 12b(2)—Investment Income and Expenses

Enter on line 12b(1) only the investment income included on lines 4a, 4b, 4c, and 4f of Schedules K and K-1. Do not include other portfolio gains or losses on this line.

Enter on line 12b(2) only the investment expense included on line 10 of Schedules K and K-1.

If there are other items of investment income or expense included in the amounts that are required to be passed through separately to the partner on Schedule K-1, such as net short-term capital gain or loss, net long-term capital gain or loss, and other portfolio gains or losses, give each partner a schedule identifying these amounts.

Investment income includes gross income from property held for investment, the excess of net gain from the disposition of property held for investment over net capital gain from the disposition of property held for investment, and any net capital gain from the disposition of property held for investment that each partner elects to include in investment income under section 163(d)(4)(B)(iii). Generally, investment income and investment expenses do not include any income or expenses from a passive activity.

Property subject to a net lease is not treated as investment property because it is subject to the passive loss rules. Do not reduce investment income by losses from passive activities.

Investment expenses are deductible expenses (other than interest) directly connected with the production of investment income. See the Form 4952 instructions for more information on investment income and expenses.

Credits

Line 13a—Low-Income Housing Credit

Section 42 provides a credit that may be claimed by owners of low-income residential rental buildings. If the partners are eligible to take the low-income housing credit, complete and attach **Form 8586,** Low-Income Housing Credit; **Form 8609,** Low-Income Housing Credit Allocation Certification; and **Schedule A (Form 8609),** Annual Statement, to Form 1065.

Report on line 13a(1) the total low-income housing credit for property placed in service before 1990 with respect to which a partnership is to be treated under section 42(j)(5) as the taxpayer to which the low-income housing credit was allowed. Report any other low-income housing credit for property placed in service before 1990 on line 13a(2). On lines 13a(3) and (4), report the

low-income housing credit for property placed in service after 1989.

Line 13b—Qualified Rehabilitation Expenditures Related to Rental Real Estate Activities

Enter total qualified rehabilitation expenditures related to rental real estate activities of the partnership. Also complete the applicable lines of **Form 3468,** Investment Credit, that apply to qualified rehabilitation expenditures for property related to rental real estate activities of the partnership for which income or loss is reported on line 2 of Schedule K. See Form 3468 for details on qualified rehabilitation expenditures. Attach Form 3468 to Form 1065.

For line 13b of Schedule K-1, enter each partner's distributive share of the expenditures. On the dotted line to the left of the entry space for line 13b, enter the line number of Form 3468 on which the partner should report the expenditures. If there is more than one type of expenditure, or the expenditures are from more than one rental real estate activity, report this information separately for each expenditure or activity on an attachment to Schedules K and K-1.

Note: *Qualified rehabilitation expenditures for property not related to rental real estate activities must be listed separately on line 25 of Schedule K-1.*

Line 13c—Credits (Other Than Credits Shown on Lines 13a and 13b) Related to Rental Real Estate Activities

Report any information that the partners need to figure credits related to a rental real estate activity, other than the low-income housing credit and qualified rehabilitation expenditures. On the dotted line to the left of the entry space for line 13c (or in the margin), identify the type of credit. If there is more than one type of credit or the credit is from more than one activity, report this information separately for each credit or activity on an attachment to Schedules K and K-1.

Line 13d—Credits Related to Other Rental Activities

Use this line to report information that the partners need to figure credits related to a rental activity other than a rental real estate activity. On the dotted line to the left of the entry space for line 13d, identify the type of credit. If there is more than one type of credit or the credit is from more than one activity, report this information separately for each credit or activity on an attachment to Schedules K and K-1.

Line 14—Other Credits

Enter on line 14 any other credit, except credits or expenditures shown or listed for lines 13a through 13d of Schedules K and K-1. On the dotted line to the left of the entry space for line 14, identify the type of credit. If there is more than one type of credit or the credit is from more than one activity, report this information separately for each credit or activity on an attachment to Schedules K and K-1. The credits to be reported on line 14 and other required attachments are as follows:

• Credit for backup withholding on dividends, interest, or patronage dividends.

• Nonconventional source fuel credit. The credit is figured at the partnership level and

Page 18

then is apportioned to the partners based on their distributive shares of partnership income attributable to sales of qualified fuels. Attach a separate schedule to the return to show the computation of the credit. See section 29 for more information.

- Qualified electric vehicle credit (Form 8834).
- Unused credits from cooperatives. The unused credits are apportioned to persons who were partners in the partnership on the last day of the partnership's tax year.
- Work opportunity credit (Form 5884). This credit is apportioned among the partners according to their interest in the partnership at the time the wages on which the credit is figured were paid or accrued.
- Credit for alcohol used as fuel (Form 6478). This credit is apportioned to persons who were partners on the last day of the partnership's tax year. The credit must be included in income on page 1, line 7, of Form 1065. See section 40(f) for an election the partnership can make to not have the credit apply.

If this credit includes the small ethanol producer credit, identify on a statement attached to each Schedule K-1 **(a)** the amount of the small producer credit included in the total credit allocated to the partner, **(b)** the number of gallons of qualified ethanol fuel production allocated to the partner, and **(c)** the partner's share in gallons of the partnership's productive capacity for alcohol.

- Credit for increasing research activities (Form 6765).
- Enhanced oil recovery credit (Form 8830).
- Disabled access credit (Form 8826).
- Renewable electricity production credit (Form 8835).
- Empowerment zone employment credit (Form 8844).
- Indian employment credit (Form 8845).
- Credit for employer social security and Medicare taxes paid on certain employee tips (Form 8846).

- Orphan drug credit (Form 8820).
- Credit for contributions to selected community development corporations (Form 8847).

Note: *See the instructions for line 25, item 13 of Schedule K-1 to report expenditures qualifying for the **(a)** rehabilitation credit not related to rental real estate activities, **(b)** energy credit, or **(c)** reforestation credit.*

Self-Employment

Note: *If the partnership is an options dealer or a commodities dealer, see section 1402(i) before completing lines 15a, b, and c, to determine the amount of any adjustment that may have to be made to the amounts shown on the **Worksheet for Figuring Net Earnings (Loss) From Self-Employment** below. If the partnership is engaged solely in the operation of a group investment program, earnings from the operation are not self-employment earnings for either general or limited partners.*

General partners.—General partners' net earnings (loss) from self-employment do not include:

- Dividends on any shares of stock and interest on any bonds, debentures, notes, etc., unless the dividends or interest are received in the course of a trade or business, such as a dealer in stocks or securities or interest on notes or accounts receivable.
- Rentals from real estate, except rentals of real estate held for sale to customers in the course of a trade or business as a real estate dealer or payments for rooms or space when significant services are provided.
- Royalty income, except royalty income received in the course of a trade or business.

See the instructions for **Schedule SE (Form 1040),** Self-Employment Tax, for more information.

Limited partners.—Generally, a limited partner's share of partnership income (loss) is not included in net earnings (loss) from self-employment. Limited partners treat as self-employment earnings only guaranteed

payments for services they actually rendered to, or on behalf of, the partnership to the extent that those payments are payment for those services.

Worksheet Instructions

Line 1b.—Include on line 1b any part of the net income (loss) from rental real estate activities from Schedule K, line 2, that is from:

1. Rentals of real estate held for sale to customers in the course of a trade or business as a real estate dealer, or

2. Rentals for which services were rendered to the occupants (other than services usually or customarily rendered for the rental of space for occupancy only). The supplying of maid service is such a service; but the furnishing of heat and light, the cleaning of public entrances, exits, stairways and lobbies, trash collection, etc., are not considered services rendered to the occupants.

Lines 3b and 4b.—Allocate the amounts on these lines in the same way Form 1065, page 1, line 22, is allocated to these particular partners.

Line 4a.—Include in the amount on line 4a any guaranteed payments to partners reported on Schedules K and K-1, line 5, and derived from a trade or business as defined in section 1402(c). Also include other ordinary income and expense items (other than expense items subject to separate limitations at the partner level, such as the section 179 expense deduction) reported on Schedules K and K-1 that are used to figure self-employment earnings under section 1402.

Line 15a—Net Earnings (Loss) From Self-Employment

Schedule K.—Enter on line 15a the amount from line 5 of the worksheet.

Schedule K-1.—Do not complete this line for any partner that is an estate, trust, corporation, exempt organization, or individual retirement arrangement (IRA).

Worksheet for Figuring Net Earnings (Loss) From Self-Employment

1a Ordinary income (loss) (Schedule K, line 1)	**1a**	
b Net income (loss) from **CERTAIN** rental real estate activities (see instructions) . . .	**1b**	
c Net income (loss) from other rental activities (Schedule K, line 3c)	**1c**	
d Net loss from Form 4797, Part II, line 20, included on line 1a above. Enter as a positive amount	**1d**	
e Combine lines 1a through 1d	**1e**	
2 Net gain from Form 4797, Part II, line 20, included on line 1a above	**2**	
3a Subtract line 2 from line 1e. If line 1e is a loss, increase the loss on line 1e by the amount on line 2	**3a**	
b Part of line 3a allocated to limited partners, estates, trusts, corporations, exempt organizations, and IRAs	**3b**	
c Subtract line 3b from line 3a. If line 3a is a loss, reduce the loss on line 3a by the amount on line 3b. Include each individual general partner's share on line 15a of Schedule K-1 .		**3c**
4a Guaranteed payments to partners (Schedule K, line 5) derived from a trade or business as defined in section 1402(c) (see instructions)	**4a**	
b Part of line 4a allocated to individual limited partners for **other than** services and to estates, trusts, corporations, exempt organizations, and IRAs	**4b**	
c Subtract line 4b from line 4a. Include each individual general partner's share and each individual limited partner's share on line 15a of Schedule K-1		**4c**
5 Net earnings (loss) from self-employment. Combine lines 3c and 4c. Enter here and on Schedule K, line 15a		**5**

Page 19

Enter on line 15a of Schedule K-1 each individual general partner's share of the amount shown on line 5 of the worksheet and each individual limited partner's share of the amount shown on line 4c of the worksheet.

Line 15b—Gross Farming or Fishing Income

Enter the partnership's gross farming or fishing income from self-employment. Individual partners need this amount to figure net earnings from self-employment under the farm optional method in Section B, Part II of Schedule SE (Form 1040).

Line 15c—Gross Nonfarm Income

Enter the partnership's gross nonfarm income from self-employment. Individual partners need this amount to figure net earnings from self-employment under the nonfarm optional method in Section B, Part II of Schedule SE (Form 1040).

Adjustments and Tax Preference Items

Lines 16a through 16e must be completed for all partners.

Enter items of income and deductions that are adjustments or tax preference items. Get **Form 6251**, Alternative Minimum Tax—Individuals; **Form 4626**, Alternative Minimum Tax—Corporations; or Schedule I of **Form 1041**, U.S. Income Tax Return for Estates and Trusts, to determine the amounts to enter and for other information.

Do not include as a tax preference item any qualified expenditures to which an election under section 59(e) may apply. Instead, report these expenditures on lines 18a and 18b. Because these expenditures are subject to an election by each partner, the partnership cannot figure the amount of any tax preference related to them.

Line 16a—Depreciation Adjustment on Property Placed in Service After 1986

Figure the adjustment for line 16a based only on tangible property placed in service after 1986 (and tangible property placed in service after July 31, 1986, and before 1987 for which the partnership elected to use the General Depreciation System). **Do not** make an adjustment for motion picture films, videotapes, sound recordings, certain public utility property (as defined in section 168(f)(2)), or property depreciated under the unit-of-production method (or any other method not expressed in a term of years).

Using the same convention you used for regular tax purposes, refigure depreciation as follows:

• For property that is neither real property nor property depreciated using the straight line method, use the 150% declining balance method over the property's class life (instead of the recovery period), switching to straight line for the first tax year that method gives a better result. See Pub. 946 for a table of class lives. For property having no class life, use 12 years.

• For property depreciated using the straight line method (other than real property), use the straight line method over the property's class life (instead of the recovery period). For property having no class life, use 12 years.

• For residential rental and nonresidential real property, use the straight line method over 40 years.

Determine the depreciation adjustment by subtracting the refigured depreciation from the depreciation claimed on Form 4562. If the refigured depreciation exceeds the depreciation claimed on Form 4562, enter the difference as a negative amount. See Form 6251 for more information.

Line 16b—Adjusted Gain or Loss

If the partnership disposed of any tangible property placed in service after 1986 (or after July 31, 1986, if an election was made to use the General Depreciation System), or if it disposed of a certified pollution control facility placed in service after 1986, refigure the gain or loss from the disposition using the adjusted basis for the alternative minimum tax (AMT). The property's adjusted basis for the AMT is its cost or other basis minus all depreciation or amortization deductions allowed or allowable for the AMT during the current tax year and previous tax years. Enter on this line the difference between the regular tax gain (or loss) and the AMT gain (or loss). If the AMT gain is less than the regular tax gain, OR the AMT loss is more than the regular tax loss, OR there is an AMT loss and a regular tax gain, enter the difference as a negative amount.

If any part of the adjustment is allocable to net short-term capital gain (loss), net long-term capital gain (loss), or net gain (loss) under section 1231, attach a schedule that identifies the amount of the adjustment allocable to each type of gain or loss. No schedule is required if the adjustment is allocable solely to ordinary gain (loss).

Line 16c—Depletion (Other Than Oil and Gas)

Do not include any depletion on oil and gas wells. The partners must figure their depletion deductions and preference items separately.

Refigure the depletion deduction under section 611 for mines, wells (other than oil and gas wells), and other natural deposits for the AMT. Percentage depletion is limited to 50% of the taxable income from the property as figured under section 613(a), using only income and deductions allowed for the AMT. Also, the deduction is limited to the property's adjusted basis at the end of the year, as refigured for the AMT. Figure this limit separately for each property. When refiguring the property's adjusted basis, take into account any AMT adjustments made this year or in previous years that affect basis (other than the current year's depletion).

Enter the difference between the regular tax and AMT deduction. If the AMT deduction is greater, enter the difference as a negative amount.

Lines 16d(1) and 16d(2)

Enter only the income and deductions for oil, gas, and geothermal properties that are used to figure the partnership's ordinary income or loss (line 22 of Form 1065). If there are items of income or deduction for oil, gas, and geothermal properties included in the amounts required to be passed through separately to the partners on Schedule K-1 (items not reported on line 1 of Schedule K-1), give each partner a schedule identifying these amounts.

Figure the amount for lines 16d(1) and (2) separately for oil and gas properties that are not geothermal deposits and for all properties that are geothermal deposits.

Give each partner a schedule that shows the separate amounts that are included in the computation of the amounts on lines 16d(1) and (2).

Line 16d(1). Gross income from oil, gas, and geothermal properties.—Enter the aggregate amount of gross income (within the meaning of section 613(a)) from all oil, gas, and geothermal properties that was received or accrued during the tax year and included on page 1, Form 1065.

Line 16d(2). Deductions allocable to oil, gas, and geothermal properties.—Enter the amount of any deductions allowed for the AMT that are allocable to oil, gas, and geothermal properties.

Line 16e—Other Adjustments and Tax Preference Items

Attach a schedule that shows each partner's share of other items not shown on lines 16a through 16d(2) that are adjustments or tax preference items or that the partner needs to complete Form 6251, Form 4626, or Schedule I of Form 1041. See these forms and their instructions to determine the amount to enter.

Other adjustments or tax preference items include the following:

• Accelerated depreciation of real property under pre-1987 rules.

• Accelerated depreciation of leased personal property under pre-1987 rules.

• Long-term contracts entered into after February 28, 1986. Except for certain home construction contracts, the taxable income from these contracts must be figured using the percentage of completion method of accounting for the AMT.

• Installment sales after March 1, 1986, of property held primarily for sale to customers in the ordinary course of the partnership's trade or business. Generally, the installment method may not be used for these sales in figuring alternative minimum taxable income.

• Losses from tax shelter farm activities. No loss from any tax shelter farm activity is allowed for the AMT.

Foreign Taxes

Lines 17a through 17g must be completed whether or not a partner is eligible for the foreign tax credit if the partnership has foreign income, deductions, or losses or has paid or accrued foreign taxes.

In addition to the instructions below, see the following for more information:

• **Form 1116**, Foreign Tax Credit (Individual, Estate, Trust, or Nonresident Alien Individual), and the related instructions.

• **Form 1118**, Foreign Tax Credit—Corporations, and the related instructions.

• **Pub. 514**, Foreign Tax Credit for Individuals.

Line 17a—Type of Income

Enter the type of income from outside the United States as follows:

• Passive income.

• High withholding tax interest.

- Financial services income.
- Shipping income.
- Dividends from a DISC or former DISC.
- Distributions from a foreign sales corporation (FSC) or former FSC.
- Dividends from each noncontrolled section 902 corporation.
- Taxable income attributable to foreign trade income (within the meaning of section 923(b)).
- General limitation income—all other income from sources outside the United States (including income from sources within U.S. possessions).

If, for the country or U.S. possession shown on line 17b, the partnership had **more than one** type of income, enter **"See attached"** and attach a schedule for each type of income for lines 17c through 17g.

Line 17b—Foreign Country or U.S. Possession

Enter the name of the foreign country or U.S. possession. If, for the type of income shown on line 17a, the partnership had income from, or paid taxes to, **more than one** foreign country or U.S. possession, enter **"See attached"** and attach a schedule for each country for lines 17a and 17c through 17g.

Line 17c—Total Gross Income From Sources Outside the United States

Enter in U.S. dollars the total gross income from sources outside the United States. Attach a schedule that shows each type of income listed in the instructions for line 17a.

See section 904(d) for types of income that must be reported to partners for figuring their foreign tax credit.

Line 17d—Total Applicable Deductions and Losses

Enter in U.S. dollars the total applicable deductions and losses attributable to income on line 17c. Attach a schedule that shows each type of deduction or loss as follows:

- Expenses directly allocable to each type of income listed above.
- Pro rata share of all other deductions not directly allocable to specific items of income.
- Pro rata share of losses from other separate limitation categories.

Line 17e—Total Foreign Taxes

Enter in U.S. dollars the total foreign taxes (described in section 901) that were paid or accrued by the partnership to foreign countries or U.S. possessions. Attach a schedule that shows the dates the taxes were paid or accrued, and the amount in both foreign currency and in U.S. dollars, as follows:

- Taxes withheld at source on dividends.
- Taxes withheld at source on rents and royalties.
- Other foreign taxes paid or accrued.

Line 17f—Reduction in Taxes Available for Credit

Enter in U.S. dollars the total reduction in taxes available for credit. Attach a schedule that shows separately the:

- Reduction for foreign mineral income (section 901(e)).

- Reduction for failure to furnish returns required under section 6038.
- Reduction for taxes attributable to boycott operations (section 908).
- Reduction for foreign oil and gas extraction income (section 907(a)).
- Reduction for any other items (specify).

Line 17g—Other Foreign Tax Information

Enter in U.S. dollars any items not covered on lines 17c through 17f. For noncorporate partners, enter gross income from all sources. Noncorporate partners need this information to complete Form 1116. For corporate partners, enter gross income and definitely allocable deductions from sources outside the United States and for foreign branches. Corporations need this information to complete Form 1118, Schedule F.

Other

Lines 18a and 18b

Generally, section 59(e) allows each partner to make an election to deduct the partner's distributive share of the partnership's otherwise deductible qualified expenditures ratably over 10 years (3 years for circulation expenditures), beginning with the tax year in which the expenditures were made (or for intangible drilling and development costs, over the 60-month period beginning with the month in which such costs were paid or incurred). The term "qualified expenditures" includes only the following types of expenditures paid or incurred during the tax year: circulation expenditures, research and experimental expenditures, intangible drilling and development costs, and mining exploration and development costs. If a partner makes this election, these items are not treated as tax preference items.

Because the partners are generally allowed to make this election, the partnership cannot deduct these amounts or include them as adjustments or tax preference items on Schedule K-1. Instead, on lines 18a and 18b of Schedule K-1, the partnership passes through the information the partners need to figure their separate deductions.

On line 18a, enter the type of expenditures claimed on line 18b. Enter on line 18b the qualified expenditures paid or incurred during the tax year to which an election under section 59(e) may apply. Enter this amount for all partners whether or not any partner makes an election under section 59(e). If the expenditures are for intangible drilling and development costs, enter the month in which the expenditures were paid or incurred (after the type of expenditure on line 18a). If there is more than one type of expenditure included in the total shown on line 18b (or intangible drilling and development costs were paid or incurred for more than 1 month), report this information separately for each type of expenditure (or month) on an attachment to Schedules K and K-1.

Line 19—Tax-Exempt Interest Income

Enter on line 19 tax-exempt interest income, including any exempt-interest dividends received from a mutual fund or other regulated investment company. This information must be reported by individuals on line 8b of Form 1040. The adjusted basis of the partner's interest is increased by the

amount shown on this line under section 705(a)(1)(B).

Line 20—Other Tax-Exempt Income

Enter on line 20 all income of the partnership exempt from tax other than tax-exempt interest (e.g., life insurance proceeds). The adjusted basis of the partner's interest is increased by the amount shown on this line under section 705(a)(1)(B).

Line 21—Nondeductible Expenses

Enter on line 21 nondeductible expenses paid or incurred by the partnership. Do not include separately stated deductions shown elsewhere on Schedules K and K-1, capital expenditures, or items the deduction for which is deferred to a later tax year. The adjusted basis of the partner's interest is decreased by the amount shown on this line under section 705(a)(2)(B).

Line 22—Distributions of Money (Cash and Marketable Securities)

Enter on line 22 the total distributions to each partner of cash and marketable securities that are treated as money under section 731(c)(1). Generally, marketable securities are valued at fair market value on the date of distribution. However, the value of marketable securities does not include the distributee partner's share of the gain on the securities distributed to that partner. See section 731(c)(3)(B) for details.

If the amount on line 22 includes marketable securities treated as money, state separately on an attachment to Schedules K and K-1 **(a)** the partnership's adjusted basis of those securities immediately before the distribution and **(b)** the fair market value of those securities on the date of distribution (excluding the distributee partner's share of the gain on the securities distributed to that partner).

Line 23—Distributions of Property Other Than Money

Enter on line 23 the total distributions to each partner of property not included on line 22. The property is valued at its adjusted basis to the partnership immediately before the distribution.

Line 24 (Schedule K Only)

Attach a statement to report the partnership's total income, expenditures, or other information for the items listed under **Supplemental Information (Schedule K-1 Only)** on page 22.

Lines 24a and 24b (Schedule K-1 Only)—Recapture of Low-Income Housing Credit

If recapture of part or all of the low-income housing credit is required because: **(a)** prior year qualified basis of a building decreased, or **(b)** the partnership disposed of a building or part of its interest in a building, get **Form 8611**, Recapture of Low-Income Housing Credit. The instructions for Form 8611 indicate when the form is completed by the partnership and what information is provided to partners when recapture is required.

Note: *If a partner's ownership interest in a building decreased because of a transaction at the partner level, the partnership must provide the necessary information to the*

Page 21

partner to enable the partner to figure the recapture.

Report on line 24a the total low-income housing credit recapture with respect to a partnership treated under section 42(j)(5) as the taxpayer to which the low-income housing credit was allowed. Report any other low-income housing credit recapture on line 24b.

If the partnership filed **Form 8693,** Low-Income Housing Credit Disposition Bond, to avoid recapture of the low-income housing credit, no entry should be made on line 24 of Schedule K-1.

See Form 8586, Form 8611, and section 42 for more information.

Analysis (Schedule K Only)

Lines 25a and 25b

For each type of partner shown, enter the portion of the amount shown on line 25a of Schedule K that was allocated to that type of partner. Report all amounts for limited liability company members on the line for limited partners. The sum of the amounts shown on line 25b must equal the amount shown on line 25a. In addition, the amount on line 25a must equal the amount on line 9, Schedule M-1 (if the partnership is required to complete Schedule M-1).

In classifying partners who are individuals as "active" or "passive," the partnership should apply the rules below. In applying these rules, a partnership should classify each partner to the best of its knowledge and belief. It is assumed that in most cases the level of a particular partner's participation in an activity will be apparent:

1. If the partnership's principal activity is a trade or business, classify a general partner as "active" if the partner materially participated in all partnership trade or business activities; otherwise, classify a general partner as "passive."

2. If the partnership's principal activity consists of a working interest in an oil or gas well, classify a general partner as "active."

3. If the partnership's principal activity is a rental real estate activity, classify a general partner as "active" if the partner actively participated in all of the partnership's rental real estate activities; otherwise, classify a general partner as "passive."

4. Classify as "passive" all partners in a partnership whose principal activity is a rental activity other than a rental real estate activity.

5. If the partnership's principal activity is a portfolio activity, classify all partners as "active."

6. Classify as "passive" all limited partners and limited liability company members in a partnership whose principal activity is a trade or business or rental activity.

7. If the partnership cannot make a reasonable determination whether a partner's participation in a trade or business activity is material or whether a partner's participation in a rental real estate activity is active, classify the partner as "passive."

Supplemental Information (Schedule K-1 Only)

Line 25

Enter in the line 25 Supplemental Information space of Schedule K-1, or on an attached schedule if more space is needed, each partner's share of any information asked for on lines 1 through 24b that must be reported in detail, and items **1** through **17** below. Identify the applicable line number next to the information entered in the Supplemental Information space. Show income or gains as a positive number. Show losses in parentheses.

1. Taxes paid on undistributed capital gains by a regulated investment company. As a shareholder of a regulated investment company, the partnership will receive notice on **Form 2439,** Notice to Shareholder of Undistributed Long-Term Capital Gains, that the company paid tax on undistributed capital gains.

2. The number of gallons of each fuel used during the tax year in a use qualifying for the credit for taxes paid on fuels and the applicable credit per gallon. Also, each partner's share of the credit for qualified diesel-powered highway vehicles purchased before August 21, 1996. Get **Form 4136,** Credit for Federal Tax Paid on Fuels, for details.

3. The partner's share of gross income from each property, share of production for the tax year, etc., needed to figure the partner's depletion deduction for oil and gas wells. The partnership should also allocate to each partner a proportionate share of the adjusted basis of each partnership oil or gas property. The allocation of the basis of each property is made as specified in section 613A(c)(7)(D).

The partnership cannot deduct depletion on oil and gas wells. The partner must determine the allowable amount to report on his or her return. See Pub. 535 for more information.

4. Recapture of section 179 expense deduction. For property placed in service after 1986, the section 179 expense deduction is recaptured at any time the business use of the property drops to 50% or less. Enter the amount that was originally passed through to the partners and the partnership's tax year in which the amount was passed through. Tell the partner if the recapture amount was caused by the disposition of the section 179 property. Do not include this amount in the partnership's income.

5. Recapture of certain mining exploration expenditures (section 617).

6. Any information or statements a partner needs to comply with section 6111 (registration of tax shelters) or section 6662(d)(2)(B)(ii) (regarding adequate disclosure of items that may cause an understatement of income tax).

7. The partner's share of preproductive period farm expenses, if the partnership is not required to use the accrual method of accounting. See Temporary Regulations section 1.263A-4T(c).

8. Any information needed by a partner to figure the interest due under section 453(l)(3). If the partnership elected to report the disposition of certain timeshares and

residential lots on the installment method, each partner's tax liability must be increased by the partner's allocable share of the interest on tax attributable to the installment payments received during the tax year.

9. Any information needed by a partner to figure interest due under section 453A(c). If an obligation arising from the disposition of property to which section 453A applies is outstanding at the close of the year, report each partner's allocable share of the outstanding installment obligation to which section 453A(b) applies.

10. For closely held partnerships (as defined in section 460(b)(4)), provide the information needed by a partner to figure the partner's allocable share of any interest due or to be refunded under the look-back method of section 460(b)(2) on certain long-term contracts that are accounted for under either the percentage of completion-capitalized cost method or the percentage of completion method. Also attach to Form 1065 the information specified in the instructions for Form 8697, Part II, lines 1 and 3, for each tax year in which such a long-term contract is completed.

11. Any information needed by a partner relating to interest expense that the partner is required to capitalize. Under section 263A, a partner may be required to capitalize interest expense incurred by the partner during the tax year with respect to the production expenditures of the partnership. Similarly, interest incurred by a partnership may have to be capitalized by a partner with respect to the partner's own production expenditures. The information required by the partner to properly capitalize interest for this purpose must be provided on an attachment to Schedule K-1. See Regulations sections 1.263A-8 through 1.263A-15 for more information.

12. Any information a partner that is a tax-exempt organization may need to figure that partner's share of unrelated business taxable income under section 512(a)(1) (but excluding any modifications required by paragraphs (8) through (15) of section 512(b)).

Note: *Partners are required to notify the partnership of their tax-exempt status.*

13. Expenditures qualifying for the **(a)** rehabilitation credit not related to rental real estate activities, **(b)** energy credit, or **(c)** reforestation credit. Complete and attach Form 3468 to Form 1065. See Form 3468 and the related instructions for information on eligible property and the lines on Form 3468 to complete. Do not include that part of the cost of the property the partnership has elected to expense under section 179. Attach to each Schedule K-1 a separate schedule in a format similar to that shown on Form 3468 detailing each partner's share of qualified expenditures. Also indicate the lines of Form 3468 on which the partners should report these amounts.

14. Recapture of investment credit. Complete and attach **Form 4255,** Recapture of Investment Credit, when investment credit property is disposed of, or it no longer qualifies for the credit, before the end of the recapture period or the useful life applicable to the property. State the type of property at the top of Form 4255 and complete lines 2, 3, 4, and 8, whether or not any partner is subject to recapture of the credit. Attach to each Schedule K-1 a separate schedule providing the information the partnership is required to show on Form 4255, but list only the partner's distributive share of the cost of the property subject to recapture. Also indicate the lines of Form 4255 on which the partners should report these amounts.

15. Any information a partner may need to figure the recapture of the qualified electric vehicle credit. See Pub. 535 for more information.

16. Any information a partner may need to figure recapture of the Indian employment credit. Generally, if a partnership terminates a qualified employee less than 1 year after the date of initial employment, any Indian employment credit allowed for a prior tax year by reason of wages paid or incurred to that employee must be recaptured. For details, see section 45A(d).

17. Any other information a partner may need to file his or her return that is not shown anywhere else on Schedule K-1. For example, if one of the partners is a pension plan, that partner may need special information to properly file its tax return.

Specific Instructions

Note: *Schedules L, M-1, and M-2 are not required to be completed if the partnership answered "Yes" to Question 5 of Schedule B.*

Schedule L—Balance Sheets per Books

The balance sheets should agree with the partnership's books and records. Attach a statement explaining any differences.

Partnerships reporting to the Interstate Commerce Commission or to any national, state, municipal, or other public officer may send copies of their balance sheets prescribed by the Commission or state or municipal authorities, as of the beginning and end of the tax year, instead of completing Schedule L. However, statements filed under this procedure must contain sufficient information to enable the IRS to reconstruct a balance sheet similar to that contained on Form 1065 without contacting the partnership during processing.

Line 5—Tax-Exempt Securities

Include on this line:

1. State and local government obligations, the interest on which is excludable from gross income under section 103(a), and

2. Stock in a mutual fund or other regulated investment company that distributed exempt-interest dividends during the tax year of the partnership.

Line 18—All Nonrecourse Loans

Nonrecourse loans are those liabilities of the partnership for which no partner bears the economic risk of loss.

Schedule M-1—Reconciliation of Income (Loss) per Books With Income (Loss) per Return

Line 3—Guaranteed Payments

Include on this line guaranteed payments shown on Schedule K, line 5 (other than amounts paid for insurance that constitutes medical care for a partner, a partner's spouse, and a partner's dependents).

Line 4b—Travel and Entertainment

Include on this line:

- 50% of meals and entertainment not allowed under section 274(n).
- Expenses for the use of an entertainment facility.
- The part of business gifts over $25.
- Expenses of an individual allocable to conventions on cruise ships over $2,000.
- Employee achievement awards over $400.
- The part of the cost of entertainment tickets that exceeds face value (also subject to 50% disallowance).
- The part of the cost of skyboxes that exceeds the face value of nonluxury box seat tickets.

- The part of the cost of luxury water travel not allowed under section 274(m).
- Expenses for travel as a form of education.
- Nondeductible club dues.
- Other travel and entertainment expenses not allowed as a deduction.

Schedule M-2—Analysis of Partners' Capital Accounts

Show what caused the changes during the tax year in the partners' capital accounts as reflected on the partnership's books and records. The amounts on Schedule M-2 should equal the total of the amounts reported in Item J of all the partners' Schedules K-1.

The partnership may, but is not required to, use the rules in Regulations section 1.704-1(b)(2)(iv) to determine the partners' capital accounts in Schedule M-2 and Item J of the partners' Schedules K-1. If the beginning and ending capital accounts reported under these rules differ from the amounts reported on Schedule L, attach a statement reconciling any differences.

Line 2—Capital Contributed During Year

Include on line 2 the amount of money and property contributed by each partner to the partnership as reflected on the partnership's books and records.

Line 3—Net Income per Books

Enter on line 3 the net income shown on the partnership books from Schedule M-1, line 1.

Line 6—Distributions

1. On line 6a, enter the amount of money distributed to each partner by the partnership.

2. On line 6b, enter the amount of property distributed to each partner by the partnership as reflected on the partnership's books and records. Include withdrawals from inventory for the personal use of a partner.

Codes for Principal Business Activity and Principal Product or Service

These codes for the Principal Business Activity are designed to classify an enterprise by the type of activity in which it is engaged to facilitate the administration of the Internal Revenue Code. Though similar in format and structure to the

Standard Industrial Classification Codes (SIC), they should not be used as SIC codes.

Using the list below, enter on page 1, Item C, the code for the specific industry group for which the largest percentage of "total assets (Schedule L, line 14, column (d))" is used.

In Item A, state the principal business activity. In Item B, state the principal product or service that accounts for the largest percentage of total assets. For example, if the principal business activity is "Retail food store," the principal product or service may be "dairy products."

Agriculture, Forestry, and Fishing

Code

Farms:
0120 Field crop.
0160 Vegetable and melon farms.
0170 Fruit and nut tree farms.
0180 Horticultural specialty.
0211 Beef cattle feedlots.
0212 Beef cattle, except feedlots.
0215 Hogs, sheep, and goats.
0240 Dairy farms.
0250 Poultry and eggs.
0260 General livestock (except animal specialty).
0270 Animal specialty.

Agricultural services and forestry:
0740 Veterinary services.
0753 Livestock breeding.
0754 Animal services, except livestock breeding and veterinary.
0780 Landscape and horticultural services.
0790 Other agricultural services.
0800 Forestry, except logging.
2400 Logging.

Fishing, hunting, and trapping:
0930 Commercial fishing, hatcheries, and preserves.
0970 Hunting, trapping, and game propagation.

Mining
1000 Metal mining.
1200 Coal mining.
1300 Oil and gas extraction.
1400 Nonmetallic minerals except fuel.

Construction

General building contractors and operative builders.
1510 General building contractors.
1531 Operative builders.

Heavy construction contractors:
1611 Highway and street construction.
1620 Heavy construction, except highway.

Special trade contractors:
1711 Plumbing, heating, and air conditioning.
1721 Painting, paperhanging, and decorating.
1731 Electrical work.
1740 Masonry, drywall, stone, tile.
1750 Carpentering and flooring.
1761 Roofing, siding, and sheet metal.
1771 Concrete work.
1781 Water well drilling.
1790 Other building trade contractors (excavation, glazing, etc.)

Manufacturing
2000 Food and kindred products.
2200 Textile mill products.
2300 Apparel and other textile products.
2400 Lumber and wood products, except furniture.
2500 Furniture and fixtures.
2700 Printing, publishing, and allied industries.
2800 Chemicals and allied products.
3000 Rubber and plastic products.
3100 Leather and leather products.
3200 Stone, clay, and glass products.
3300 Primary metal industries.
3400 Fabricated metal products.
3500 Machinery, except electrical.
3600 Electrical and electronic equipment.
3700 Transportation equipment.
3970 Other manufacturing industries.

Code

Transportation, Communication, Electric, Gas, and Sanitary Services

Local and interurban passenger transit:
4121 Taxicabs.
4189 Other passenger transportation.

Trucking and warehousing:
4210 Trucking (local and long distance), except trash collection.
4216 Trash collection without own dump.
4220 Public warehousing.

Other transportation including transportation services:
4400 Water transportation.
4540 Transportation by air.
4722 Passenger transportation arrangement.
4799 Other transportation services.
4800 Communication.
4900 Utilities, including dumps, snowplowing, etc.

Wholesale Trade—Selling Goods to Other Businesses, Government, or Institutions, etc.

Durable goods, including machinery, equipment, wood, metals, etc.:
5001 Selling for your own account.
5002 Agent or broker for other firms—more than 50% of gross sales on commission.

Nondurable goods, including food, fiber, chemicals, etc.:
5101 Selling for your own account.
5102 Agent or broker for other firms—more than 50% of gross sales on commission.

Retail Trade

Building materials, hardware, garden supply, and mobile home dealers:
5211 Lumber and other building materials dealers.
5231 Paint, glass, and wallpaper stores.
5251 Hardware stores.
5261 Retail nurseries and garden stores.
5271 Mobile home dealers.

General merchandise:
5331 Variety stores.
5398 Other general merchandise stores.

Food stores:
5411 Grocery stores.
5420 Meat and fish markets freezer provisioners.
5431 Fruit stores and vegetable markets.
5441 Candy, nut, and confectionery stores.
5451 Dairy products stores.
5460 Retail bakeries.
5490 Other food stores.

Automotive dealers and service stations:
5511 New car dealers (franchised).
5521 Used car dealers.
5531 Auto and home supply stores.
5541 Gasoline service stations.
5551 Boat dealers.
5561 Recreational vehicle dealers.
5571 Motorcycle dealers.
5599 Aircraft and other automotive dealers.

Apparel and accessory stores:
5611 Men's and boys' clothing and furnishings.
5621 Women's ready-to-wear stores.
5631 Women's accessory and specialty stores.
5641 Children's and infants' wear stores.
5651 Family clothing stores.
5661 Shoe stores.
5681 Furriers and fur shops.
5699 Other apparel and accessory stores.

Code

Furniture, home furnishings, and equipment stores:
5712 Furniture stores.
5713 Floor covering stores.
5714 Drapery, curtain, and upholstery stores.
5719 Home furnishings, except appliances.
5722 Household appliance stores.
5732 Radio and television stores.
5733 Music stores.
5734 Computer and software stores.

Eating and drinking places:
5812 Eating places.
5813 Drinking places.

Miscellaneous retail stores:
5912 Drug stores and proprietary stores.
5921 Liquor stores.
5932 Used merchandise and antique stores (except motor vehicle parts).
5941 Sporting goods stores and bicycle shops.
5942 Book stores.
5943 Stationery stores.
5944 Jewelry stores.
5945 Hobby, toy, and game shops.
5946 Camera and photographic supply stores.
5947 Gift, novelty, and souvenir shops.
5948 Luggage and leather goods stores.
5949 Sewing, needlework, and piece goods stores.
5961 Mail order houses.
5962 Merchandising machine operators.
5963 Direct selling organizations.
5983 Fuel oil dealers.
5984 Liquefied petroleum gas (bottled gas) dealers.
5989 Other fuel dealers (except gasoline)
5992 Florists.
5996 Other miscellaneous retail stores.

Finance, Insurance, and Real Estate
6000 Banking.
6100 Credit agencies other than banks.
Security and commodity brokers, dealers, exchanges, and services:
6212 Security underwriting syndicates.
6218 Security brokers and dealers, except underwriting syndicates.
6299 Commodity contracts brokers and dealers; security and commodity exchanges; and allied services.
6411 Insurance agents, brokers, and services.

Real estate:
6511 Real estate operators (except developers) and lessors of buildings.
6520 Lessors of real property other than buildings.
6531 Real estate agents, brokers, and managers.
6541 Title abstract offices.
6552 Subdividers and developers, except cemeteries.
6553 Cemetery subdividers and developers.

Holding and other investment companies:
6746 Investment clubs.
6747 Common trust funds.
6748 Other holding and investment companies.

Services

Hotels and other lodging places:
7012 Hotels.
7013 Motels, motor hotels, and tourist courts.
7021 Rooming and boarding houses.
7032 Sporting and recreational camps.
7033 Trailer parks and camp sites.

Code

Personal services:
7215 Coin-operated laundries and dry cleaning.
7219 Other laundry, cleaning, and garment services.
7221 Photographic studios and portrait studios.
7231 Beauty shops.
7241 Barber shops.
7251 Shoe repair and hat cleaning shops.
7261 Funeral services and crematories.
7291 Income tax preparation.
7299 Miscellaneous personal services.

Business services:
7310 Advertising.
7340 Janitorial and window cleaning.
7350 Equipment rental and leasing.
7370 Computer and data processing services.
7398 Other business services.

Automotive repair and services:
7510 Automotive rentals and leasing, without drivers.
7520 Automobile parking.
7538 General automobile repair shops.
7539 Other automotive repair shops.
7540 Automotive services, except repair.

Miscellaneous repair services:
7622 Radio and TV repair shops.
7628 Electrical repair shops, except radio and TV.
7641 Reupholstery and furniture repair.
7680 Other miscellaneous repair shops.

Motion picture:
7812 Other motion picture and TV film and tape activities.
7830 Motion picture theaters.
7840 Video tape rental stores.

Amusement and recreation services:
7920 Producers, orchestras, and entertainers.
7933 Bowling alleys.
7941 Professional sports clubs and promoters.
7948 Racing, including track operation.
7980 Other amusement and recreation services.
7991 Physical fitness facilities.

Medical and health services:
8011 Offices and clinics of medical doctors (MDs).
8021 Offices and clinics of dentists.
8031 Offices of osteopathic physicians.
8041 Offices of chiropractors.
8042 Offices of optometrists.
8047 Other licensed health practitioners.
8048 Registered and practical nurses.
8050 Nursing and personal care facilities.
8060 Hospitals.
8072 Dental laboratories.
8098 Other medical and health services.

Other services:
8111 Legal services.
8200 Educational services.
8351 Child day care.
8722 Certified public accountants.
8723 Other accounting, auditing, and bookkeeping services.
8740 Management, consulting, and public relations services.
8911 Engineering and architectural services.
8999 Other services not classified elsewhere.

Printed on recycled paper

SCHEDULE D
(Form 1065)

Department of the Treasury
Internal Revenue Service

Capital Gains and Losses

▶ **Attach to Form 1065.**

OMB No. 1545-0099

1996

Name of partnership

Employer identification number

Part I — Short-Term Capital Gains and Losses—Assets Held 1 Year or Less

(a) Description of property (e.g., 100 shares 7% preferred of "Z" Co.)	(b) Date acquired (month, day, year)	(c) Date sold (month, day, year)	(d) Sales price (see instructions)	(e) Cost or other basis (see instructions)	(f) Gain (loss) ((d) minus (e))
1					

2 Short-term capital gain from installment sales from Form 6252, line 26 or 37 . . . . | **2** |

3 Short-term capital gain (loss) from like-kind exchanges from Form 8824 . . . . | **3** |

4 Partnership's share of net short-term capital gain (loss), including specially allocated short-term capital gains (losses), from other partnerships, estates, and trusts . . . . , ... | **4** |

5 Net short-term capital gain (loss). Combine lines 1 through 4. Enter here and on Form 1065, Schedule K, line 4d or 7 . . . . | **5** |

Part II — Long-Term Capital Gains and Losses—Assets Held More Than 1 Year

6					

7 Long-term capital gain from installment sales from Form 6252, line 26 or 37 . . . . | **7** |

8 Long-term capital gain (loss) from like-kind exchanges from Form 8824 . . . . | **8** |

9 Partnership's share of net long-term capital gain (loss), including specially allocated long-term capital gains (losses), from other partnerships, estates, and trusts . . . . | **9** |

10 Capital gain distributions . . . . | **10** |

11 Net long-term capital gain (loss). Combine lines 6 through 10. Enter here and on Form 1065, Schedule K, line 4e or 7 . . . . | **11** |

General Instructions

Section references are to the Internal Revenue Code.

Purpose of Schedule

Use Schedule D (Form 1065) to report sales or exchanges of capital assets, capital gain distributions, and nonbusiness bad debts. Do not report on Schedule D capital gains (losses) specially allocated to any partners.

Enter capital gains (losses) specially allocated to the partnership as a partner in other partnerships and from estates and trusts on Schedule D, line 4 or 9, whichever applies. Enter capital gains (losses) of the partnership that are specially allocated to partners directly on line 4d, 4e, or 7 of Schedules K and K-1, whichever applies. See **How Income Is Shared Among Partners** in the Instructions for Form 1065 for more information.

To report sales or exchanges of property other than capital assets, including the sale or exchange of property used in a trade or business and involuntary conversions (other than casualties and thefts), get **Form 4797**, Sales of Business Property, and related instructions. If property is involuntarily converted because of a casualty or theft, use **Form 4684**, Casualties and Thefts.

For amounts received from an installment sale, the holding period rule in effect in the year of sale will determine the treatment of the amounts received as long-term or short-term capital gain.

Report every sale or exchange of property in detail, even if there is no gain or loss.

For more information, get **Pub. 544**, Sales and Other Dispositions of Assets.

What Are Capital Assets?

Each item of property the partnership held (whether or not connected with its trade or business) is a capital asset **except:**

1. Assets that can be inventoried or property held mainly for sale to customers.

2. Depreciable or real property used in the trade or business.

3. Certain copyrights; literary, musical, or artistic compositions; letters or memoranda; or similar property.

4. Accounts or notes receivable acquired in the ordinary course of trade or business for services rendered or from the sale of property described in **1** above.

5. U.S. Government publications, including the Congressional Record, that the partnership received from the government, other than by purchase at the normal sales price, or that the partnership got from another taxpayer who had received it in a similar way, if the partnership's basis is determined by reference to the previous owner.

Items for Special Treatment and Special Cases

The following items may require special treatment:

● Transactions by a securities dealer. See section 1236.

● Bonds and other debt instruments. Get **Pub. 550,** Investment Income and Expenses.

● Certain real estate subdivided for sale that may be considered a capital asset. See section 1237.

● Gain on the sale of depreciable property to a more than 50%-owned entity, or to a trust in which the partnership is a beneficiary, is treated as ordinary gain.

● Liquidating distributions from a corporation. See Pub. 550 for details.

● Gain on disposition of stock in an Interest Charge Domestic International Sales Corporation. See section 995(c).

For Paperwork Reduction Act Notice, see page 1 of the Instructions for Form 1065.   Cat. No. 11393G   Schedule D (Form 1065) 1996

- Gain on the sale or exchange of stock in certain foreign corporations. See section 1248.

- Gain or loss on options to buy or sell, including closing transactions. See Pub. 550 for details.

- Transfer of property to a foreign corporation as paid-in surplus or as a contribution to capital, or to a foreign estate, trust, or partnership. Get **Form 926,** Return by a U.S. Transferor of Property to a Foreign Corporation, Foreign Estate or Trust, or Foreign Partnership.

- Transfer of property to a partnership that would be treated as an investment company if the partnership were incorporated. Get **Pub. 541,** Partnerships, for details.

- Transfer of property to a political organization if the fair market value of the property exceeds the partnership's adjusted basis in such property. See section 84.

- Any loss on the disposition of converted wetland or highly erodible cropland that is first used for farming after March 1, 1986, is reported as a long-term capital loss on Schedule D, but any gain on such a disposition is reported as ordinary income on Form 4797. See section 1257 for details.

- Conversion of a general partnership interest into a limited partnership interest in the same partnership. See Rev. Rul. 84-52, 1984-1 C.B. 157.

- Transfer of partnership assets and liabilities to a newly formed corporation in exchange for all of its stock. See Rev. Rul. 84-111, 1984-2 C.B. 88.

- Contribution of limited partnership interests in exchange for limited partnership interests in another partnership. See Rev. Rul. 84-115, 1984-2 C.B. 118.

- Disposition of foreign investment in a U.S. real property interest. See section 897.

- Any loss from a sale or exchange of property between the partnership and certain related persons is not allowed, except for distributions in complete liquidation of a corporation. See sections 267 and 707(b) for details.

- Any loss from securities that are capital assets that become worthless during the year is treated as a loss from the sale or exchange of a capital asset on the last day of the tax year.

- Gain from the sale or exchange of stock in a collapsible corporation is not a capital gain. See section 341.

- A nonbusiness bad debt must be treated as a short-term capital loss and can be deducted only in the year the debt becomes totally worthless. For each bad debt, enter the name of the debtor and "schedule attached" in column (a) of line 1 and the amount of the bad debt as a loss in column (f). Also attach a statement of facts to support each bad debt deduction.

- Any loss from a wash sale of stock or securities (including contracts or options to acquire or sell stock or securities) cannot be deducted unless the partnership is a dealer in stock or securities and the loss was sustained in a transaction made in the ordinary course of the partnership's trade or business. A wash sale occurs if the partnership acquires (by purchase or exchange), or has a contract or option to acquire, substantially identical stock or securities within 30 days before or after the date of the sale or exchange. See section 1091 for more information.

- Gains and losses from section 1256 contracts and straddles are reported on **Form 6781,** Gains and Losses From Section 1256 Contracts and Straddles.

If there are limited partners, see section 1256(e)(4) for the limitation on losses from hedging transactions.

- Gains from the sale of property (other than publicly traded stock or securities) for which any payment is to be received in a tax year after the year of sale must be reported using the installment method on **Form 6252,** Installment Sale Income, unless the partnership elects to report the entire gain in the year of sale. The partnership should also use Form 6252 if it received a payment this year from a sale made in an earlier year on the installment method.

If the partnership wants to elect out of the installment method for installment gain that **is not** specially allocated among the partners, it must report the full amount of the gain on a timely filed return (including extensions).

If the partnership wants to elect out of the installment method for installment gain that **is** specially allocated among the partners, it must do the following on a timely filed return (including extensions):

1. For a **short-term capital gain,** report the full amount of the gain on Schedule K, line 4d or 7.

For a **long-term capital gain,** report the full amount of the gain on Schedule K, line 4e or 7.

2. Enter each partner's share of the full amount of the gain on Schedule K-1, line 4d, 4e, or 7, whichever applies.

- An exchange of business or investment property for property of a like kind is reported on **Form 8824,** Like-Kind Exchanges.

Specific Instructions

Columns (b) and (c)—Date Acquired and Date Sold

Use the trade dates for date acquired and date sold for stocks and bonds traded on an exchange or over-the-counter market.

Column (d)—Sales Price

Enter in this column either the gross sales price or the net sales price from the sale. On sales of stocks and bonds, report the gross amount as reported to the partnership by the partnership's broker on

Form 1099-B, Proceeds From Broker and Barter Exchange Transactions, or similar statement. However, if the broker advised the partnership that gross proceeds (gross sales price) less commissions and option premiums were reported to the IRS, enter that net amount in column (d).

Column (e)—Cost or Other Basis

In general, the cost or other basis is the cost of the property plus purchase commissions and improvements and minus depreciation, amortization, and depletion. If the partnership got the property in a tax-free exchange, involuntary conversion, or wash sale of stock, it may not be able to use the actual cash cost as the basis. If the partnership does not use cash cost, attach an explanation of the basis.

When selling stock, adjust the basis by subtracting all the stock-related nontaxable distributions received before the sale. This includes nontaxable distributions from utility company stock and mutual funds. Also adjust the basis for any stock splits or stock dividends.

If a charitable contribution deduction is passed through to a partner because of a sale of property to a charitable organization, the adjusted basis for determining gain from the sale is an amount that has the same ratio to the adjusted basis as the amount realized has to the fair market value.

See section 852(f) for the treatment of certain load charges incurred in acquiring stock in a mutual fund with a reinvestment right.

If the gross sales price is reported in column (d), increase the cost or other basis by any expense of sale, such as broker's fees, commissions, or option premiums, before making an entry in column (e).

For more information, get **Pub. 551,** Basis of Assets.

Lines 4 and 9—Capital Gains and Losses From Other Partnerships, Estates, and Trusts

See the Schedule K-1 or other information supplied to you by the other partnership, estate, or trust.

Line 10—Capital Gain Distributions

On line 10, report as capital gain distributions **(a)** capital gain dividends and **(b)** the partnership's share of undistributed capital gains from a regulated investment company. Report the partnership's share of taxes paid on undistributed capital gains by a regulated investment company on Schedule K, line 24, and Schedule K-1, line 25.

SCHEDULE K-1 (Form 1065) Department of the Treasury Internal Revenue Service	Partner's Share of Income, Credits, Deductions, etc. ▶ See separate instructions.	OMB No. 1545-0099 1996
	For calendar year 1996 or tax year beginning _____ 1996, and ending _____ , 19 __	

Partner's identifying number ▶ *123-00-6789* | Partnership's identifying number ▶ *10:9876543*

Partner's name, address, and ZIP code	Partnership's name, address, and ZIP code
FRANK W. ABLE *10 GREEN STREET* *ORANGE, MD 20904*	*ABLEBAKER BOOK STORE* *334 WEST MAIN STREET* *ORANGE, MD 20904*

A This partner is a ☑ general partner ☐ limited partner
☐ limited liability company member

B What type of entity is this partner? ▶ *INDIVIDUAL*

C Is this partner a ☑ domestic or a ☐ foreign partner?

D Enter partner's percentage of:

	(i) Before change or termination	(ii) End of year
Profit sharing	*50* %	*50* %
Loss sharing	*50* %	*50* %
Ownership of capital	*50* %	*50* %

E IRS Center where partnership filed return: *PHILADELPHIA*

F Partner's share of liabilities (see instructions):
Nonrecourse . . . . $ ....
Qualified nonrecourse financing . $ ....
Other . . . . $ *10,900*

G Tax shelter registration number . ▶ *N/A*

H Check here if this partnership is a publicly traded partnership as defined in section 469(k)(2) . . . . ☐

I Check applicable boxes: **(1)** ☐ Final K-1 **(2)** ☐ Amended K-1

J Analysis of partner's capital account:

(a) Capital account at beginning of year	(b) Capital contributed during year	(c) Partner's share of lines 3, 4, and 7, Form 1065, Schedule M-2	(d) Withdrawals and distributions	(e) Capital account at end of year (combine columns (a) through (d))
14,050		*24,460*	(*26,440*)	*12,070*

		(a) Distributive share item		(b) Amount	(c) 1040 filers enter the amount in column (b) on:
Income (Loss)	1	Ordinary income (loss) from trade or business activities . . .	1	*24,685*	See pages 5 and 6 of Partner's Instructions for Schedule K-1 (Form 1065).
	2	Net income (loss) from rental real estate activities	2		
	3	Net income (loss) from other rental activities	3		
	4	Portfolio income (loss):			
	a	Interest	4a		Sch. B, Part I, line 1
	b	Dividends	4b	*75*	Sch. B, Part II, line 5
	c	Royalties	4c		Sch. E, Part I, line 4
	d	Net short-term capital gain (loss)	4d		Sch. D, line 5, col. (f) or (g)
	e	Net long-term capital gain (loss)	4e		Sch. D, line 13, col. (f) or (g)
	f	Other portfolio income (loss) (attach schedule)	4f		Enter on applicable line of your return.
	5	Guaranteed payments to partner	5	*20,000*	See page 6 of Partner's Instructions for Schedule K-1 (Form 1065).
	6	Net gain (loss) under section 1231 (other than due to casualty or theft)	6		
	7	Other income (loss) (attach schedule)	7		Enter on applicable line of your return
Deductions	8	Charitable contributions (see instructions) (attach schedule) . .	8	*325*	Sch. A, line 15 or 16
	9	Section 179 expense deduction	9		See page 7 of Partner's Instructions for Schedule K-1 (Form 1065).
	10	Deductions related to portfolio income (attach schedule) . . .	10		
	11	Other deductions (attach schedule)	11		
Investment Interest	12a	Interest expense on investment debts	12a		Form 4952, line 1
	b	**(1)** Investment income included on lines 4a, 4b, 4c, and 4f above	b(1)	*75*	See page 7 of Partner's Instructions for Schedule K-1 (Form 1065).
		(2) Investment expenses included on line 10 above	b(2)		
Credits	13a	Low-income housing credit:			
		(1) From section 42(j)(5) partnerships for property placed in service before 1990	a(1)		Form 8586, line 5
		(2) Other than on line 13a(1) for property placed in service before 1990	a(2)		
		(3) From section 42(j)(5) partnerships for property placed in service after 1989	a(3)		
		(4) Other than on line 13a(3) for property placed in service after 1989	a(4)		
	b	Qualified rehabilitation expenditures related to rental real estate activities	13b		
	c	Credits (other than credits shown on lines 13a and 13b) related to rental real estate activities	13c		See page 8 of Partner's Instructions for Schedule K-1 (Form 1065).
	d	Credits related to other rental activities	13d		
	14	Other credits	14		

For Paperwork Reduction Act Notice, see Instructions for Form 1065.　　Cat. No. 11394R　　Schedule K-1 (Form 1065) 1996

Schedule K-1 (Form 1065) 1996   Page **2**

(a) Distributive share item		(b) Amount	(c) 1040 filers enter the amount in column (b) on:
Self-employment	**15a** Net earnings (loss) from self-employment	**15a** *44,685*	Sch. SE, Section A or B
	b Gross farming or fishing income	**15b**	See page 8 of Partner's
	c Gross nonfarm income	**15c**	Instructions for Schedule K-1 (Form 1065).
Adjustments and Tax Preference Items	**16a** Depreciation adjustment on property placed in service after 1986	**16a**	See pages 8 and 9 of Partner's Instructions for Schedule K-1 (Form 1065) and Instructions for Form 6251.
	b Adjusted gain or loss	**16b**	
	c Depletion (other than oil and gas)	**16c**	
	d (1) Gross income from oil, gas, and geothermal properties . .	**d(1)**	
	(2) Deductions allocable to oil, gas, and geothermal properties	**d(2)**	
	e Other adjustments and tax preference items (attach schedule)	**16e**	
Foreign Taxes	**17a** Type of income ▶		Form 1116, check boxes
	b Name of foreign country or U.S. possession ▶		
	c Total gross income from sources outside the United States (attach schedule)	**17c**	Form 1116, Part I
	d Total applicable deductions and losses (attach schedule) . . .	**17d**	
	e Total foreign taxes (check one): ▶ ☐ Paid ☐ Accrued . . .	**17e**	Form 1116, Part II
	f Reduction in taxes available for credit (attach schedule) . . .	**17f**	Form 1116, Part III
	g Other foreign tax information (attach schedule)	**17g**	See Instructions for Form 1116.
Other	**18** Section 59(e)(2) expenditures: **a** Type ▶		See page 9 of Partner's Instructions for Schedule K-1 (Form 1065).
	b Amount	**18b**	
	19 Tax-exempt interest income	**19** *25*	Form 1040, line 8b
	20 Other tax-exempt income	**20**	See page 9 of Partner's Instructions for Schedule K-1 (Form 1065).
	21 Nondeductible expenses	**21**	
	22 Distributions of money (cash and marketable securities) . . .	**22** *26,440*	
	23 Distributions of property other than money	**23**	
	24 Recapture of low-income housing credit:		
	a From section 42(j)(5) partnerships	**24a**	Form 8611, line 8
	b Other than on line 24a	**24b**	

25 Supplemental information required to be reported separately to each partner (attach additional schedules if more space is needed):

Supplemental Information

....

....

....

....

....

....

....

....

....

....

....

....

....

....

....

*U.S. Government Printing Office: 1997 - 417-677/60116   ✪ Printed on recycled paper

Department of the Treasury
Internal Revenue Service

Partner's Instructions for Schedule K-1 (Form 1065)

Partner's Share of Income, Credits, Deductions, etc.

(For Partner's Use Only)

Section references are to the Internal Revenue Code unless otherwise noted.

General Instructions

Purpose of Schedule K-1

The partnership uses Schedule K-1 to report your share of the partnership's income, credits, deductions, etc. **Keep it for your records. Do not file it with your tax return.** The partnership has filed a copy with the IRS.

Although the partnership is not subject to income tax, you are liable for tax on your share of the partnership income, whether or not distributed. Include your share on your tax return if a return is required. Use these instructions to help you report the items shown on Schedule K-1 on your tax return.

The amount of loss and deduction that you may claim on your tax return may be less than the amount reported on Schedule K-1. **It is the partner's responsibility to consider and apply any applicable limitations. See Limitations on Losses, Deductions, and Credits** beginning on page 2 for more information.

Where "attach schedule" appears beside a line item on Schedule K-1, see either the schedule that the partnership has attached for that line or line 25 of Schedule K-1.

Inconsistent Treatment of Items

Generally, you must report partnership items shown on your Schedule K-1 (and any attached schedules) the same way that the partnership treated the items on its return. This rule does not apply if your partnership is within the "small partnership exception" and does not elect to have the tax treatment of partnership items determined at the partnership level.

If the treatment on your original or amended return is inconsistent with the partnership's treatment, or if the partnership was required to but has not filed a return, you must file **Form 8082**, Notice of Inconsistent Treatment or Amended Return (Administrative Adjustment Request (AAR)), with your original or amended return to identify and explain any inconsistency (or to note that a partnership return has not been filed).

If you are required to file Form 8082 but fail to do so, you may be subject to the accuracy-related penalty. This penalty is in addition to any tax that results from making your amount or treatment of the item consistent with that shown on the partnership's return. Any deficiency that results from making the amounts consistent may be assessed immediately.

Errors

If you believe the partnership has made an error on your Schedule K-1, notify the partnership and ask for a corrected Schedule K-1. Do not change any items on your copy of Schedule K-1. Be sure that the partnership sends a copy of the corrected Schedule K-1 to the IRS. If you are a partner in a partnership that does not meet the small partnership exception and you report any partnership item on your return in a manner different from the way the partnership reported it, you must file Form 8082.

Sale or Exchange of Partnership Interest

Generally, a partner who sells or exchanges a partnership interest in a section 751(a) exchange must notify the partnership, in writing, within 30 days of the exchange (or, if earlier, by January 15 of the calendar year following the calendar year in which the exchange occurred). A "section 751(a) exchange" is any sale or exchange of a partnership interest in which any money or other property received by the partner in exchange for that partner's interest is attributable to unrealized receivables (as defined in section 751(c)) or substantially appreciated inventory items (as defined in section 751(d)).

The written notice to the partnership must include the names and addresses of both parties to the exchange, the identifying numbers of the transferor and (if known) of the transferee, and the exchange date.

An exception to this rule is made for sales or exchanges of publicly traded partnership interests for which a broker is required to file **Form 1099-B**, Proceeds From Broker and Barter Exchange Transactions.

If a partner is required to notify the partnership of a section 751(a) exchange but fails to do so, a $50 penalty may be imposed for each such failure. However, no penalty will be imposed if the partner can show that the failure was due to reasonable cause and not willful neglect.

Nominee Reporting

Any person who holds, directly or indirectly, an interest in a partnership as a nominee for another person must furnish a written statement to the partnership by the last day of the month following the end of the partnership's tax year. This statement must include the name, address, and identifying number of the nominee and such other person, description of the partnership interest held as nominee for that person, and other information required by Temporary Regulations section 1.6031(c)-1T. A nominee that fails to furnish this statement must furnish to the person for whom the nominee holds the partnership interest a copy of Schedule K-1 and related information within 30 days of receiving it from the partnership.

Note: *A nominee who fails to furnish when due all the information required by Temporary Regulations section 1.6031(c)-1T, or who furnishes incorrect information, is subject to a $50 penalty for each statement for which a failure occurs. The maximum penalty is $100,000 for all such failures during a calendar year. If the nominee intentionally disregards the requirement to report correct information, each $50 penalty increases to $100 or, if greater, 10% of the aggregate amount of items required to be reported (and the $100,000 maximum does not apply).*

U.S. Persons With Interests in Foreign Partnerships

If you are a U.S. person in a foreign partnership that does not file a partnership return, you may be required to furnish information necessary to determine your correct income (loss) from the partnership.

International Boycotts

Every partnership that had operations in, or related to, a boycotting country, company,

Cat. No. 11396N

or a national of a country must file **Form 5713**, International Boycott Report.

If the partnership cooperated with an international boycott, it must give you a copy of its Form 5713. You must file your own Form 5713 to report the partnership's activities and any other boycott operations that you may have. You may lose certain tax benefits if the partnership participated in, or cooperated with, an international boycott. See Form 5713 and the instructions for more information.

Definitions

General Partner

A general partner is a partner who is personally liable for partnership debts.

Limited Partner

A limited partner is a partner in a partnership formed under a state limited partnership law, whose personal liability for partnership debts is limited to the amount of money or other property that the partner contributed or is required to contribute to the partnership. Some members of other entities, such as domestic or foreign business trusts or limited liability companies that are classified as partnerships, may be treated as limited partners for certain purposes. See, for example, Temporary Regulations section 1.469-5T(e)(3), which treats all members with limited liability as limited partners for purposes of section 469(h)(2).

Nonrecourse Loans

Nonrecourse loans are those liabilities of the partnership for which no partner bears the economic risk of loss.

Elections

Generally, the partnership decides how to figure taxable income from its operations. However, certain elections are made by you separately on your income tax return and not by the partnership. These elections are made under the following code sections:

• Section 59(e) (deduction of certain qualified expenditures ratably over the period of time specified in that section). For more information, see the instructions for lines 18a and 18b of Schedule K-1 on page 9.

• Section 108(b)(5) (income from the discharge of indebtedness).

• Section 617 (deduction and recapture of certain mining exploration expenditures).

• Section 901 (foreign tax credit).

Additional Information

For more information on the treatment of partnership income, credits, deductions, etc., get **Pub. 541**, Partnerships; and **Pub. 535**, Business Expenses.

You can get the above publications and other publications referenced throughout these instructions at most IRS offices. To order publications and forms, call 1-800-TAX-FORM (1-800-829-3676).

Limitations on Losses, Deductions, and Credits

There are three separate potential limitations on the amount of partnership losses that you may deduct on your return. These limitations and the order in which you must apply them are as follows: the basis rules, the at-risk limitations, and the passive activity limitations. Each of these limitations is discussed separately below.

Note: *Other limitations may apply to specific deductions (e.g., the section 179 expense deduction). These limitations on specific deductions generally apply before the basis, at-risk, and passive loss limitations.*

Basis Rules

Generally, you may **not** claim your share of a partnership loss (including a capital loss) to the extent that it is greater than the adjusted basis of your partnership interest at the end of the partnership's tax year.

The partnership is not responsible for keeping the information needed to figure the basis of your partnership interest. Although the partnership does provide an analysis of the changes to your capital account in Item J of Schedule K-1, that information is based on the partnership's books and records and cannot be used to figure your basis.

You can compute the adjusted basis of your partnership interest by adding items that increase your basis and then subtracting items that decrease your basis.

Items that **increase** your basis are:

• Money and your adjusted basis in property contributed to the partnership.

• Your share of the increase in the partnership's liabilities (or your individual liabilities caused by your assumption of partnership liabilities).

• Your share of the partnership's income (including tax-exempt income).

• Your share of the excess of the deductions for depletion over the basis of the property subject to depletion.

Items that **decrease** your basis (but not below zero) are:

• Money and the adjusted basis of property distributed to you.

• Your share of the decrease in the partnership's liabilities (or your individual liabilities assumed by the partnership).

• Your share of the partnership's losses (including capital losses).

• Your share of the partnership's section 179 expense deduction (even if you cannot deduct all of it).

• Your share of the partnership's nondeductible expenses.

• The amount of your deduction for depletion of any partnership oil and gas property (not to exceed your allocable share of the adjusted basis of that property).

For more details on the basis rules, see Pub. 541.

At-Risk Limitations

Generally, if you have **(a)** a loss or other deduction from any activity carried on as a trade or business or for the production of income by the partnership, and **(b)** amounts in the activity for which you are not at risk, you will have to complete **Form 6198,** At-Risk Limitations, to figure your allowable loss.

The at-risk rules generally limit the amount of loss and other deductions that you can claim to the amount you could actually lose in the activity. These losses and deductions include a loss on the disposition of assets and the section 179 expense deduction. However, if you acquired your partnership interest before 1987, the at-risk rules do not apply to losses from an activity of holding real property placed in service before 1987 by the partnership. The activity of holding mineral property does not qualify for this exception. The partnership should identify on an attachment to Schedule K-1 the amount of any losses that are not subject to the at-risk limitations.

Generally, you are not at risk for amounts such as the following:

• Nonrecourse loans used to finance the activity, to acquire property used in the activity, or to acquire your interest in the activity, that are not secured by your own property (other than the property used in the activity). See the instructions for item F on page 5 for the exception for qualified nonrecourse financing secured by real property.

• Cash, property, or borrowed amounts used in the activity (or contributed to the activity, or used to acquire your interest in the activity) that are protected against loss by a guarantee, stop-loss agreement, or other similar arrangement (excluding casualty insurance and insurance against tort liability).

• Amounts borrowed for use in the activity from a person who has an interest in the activity, other than as a creditor, or who is related, under section 465(b)(3), to a person (other than you) having such an interest.

To help you complete Form 6198, the partnership should specify on an attachment to Schedule K-1 your share of the total pre-1976 losses from a section 465(c)(1) activity for which there existed a corresponding amount of nonrecourse liability at the end of the year in which the losses occurred. Also, you should get a separate statement of income, expenses, etc., for each activity from the partnership.

Passive Activity Limitations

Section 469 provides rules that limit the deduction of certain losses and credits. These rules apply to partners who:

• Are individuals, estates, trusts, closely held corporations, or personal service corporations, and

• Have a passive activity loss or credit for the tax year.

Generally, passive activities include:

1. Trade or business activities in which you did not materially participate, and

2. Activities that meet the definition of rental activities under Temporary Regulations section 1.469-1T(e)(3) and Regulations section 1.469-1(e)(3).

Passive activities **do not** include:

1. Trade or business activities in which you materially participated.

2. Rental real estate activities in which you materially participated if you were a "real estate professional" for the tax year. You were a real estate professional only if you met both of the following conditions:

a. More than half of the personal services you performed in trades or businesses were performed in real property trades or businesses in which you materially participated, and

b. You performed more than 750 hours of services in real property trades or businesses in which you materially participated.

Note: *For a closely held C corporation (defined in section 465(a)(1)(B)), the above conditions are treated as met if more than 50% of the corporation's gross receipts were from real property trades or businesses in which the corporation materially participated.*

For purposes of this rule, each interest in rental real estate is a separate activity, unless you elect to treat all interests in rental real estate as one activity.

If you are married filing jointly, either you or your spouse must separately meet both of the above conditions, without taking into account services performed by the other spouse.

A real property trade or business is any real property development, redevelopment, construction, reconstruction, acquisition, conversion, rental, operation, management, leasing, or brokerage trade or business. Services you performed as an employee are not treated as performed in a real property trade or business unless you owned more than 5% of the stock (or more than 5% of the capital or profits interest) in the employer.

3. Working interests in oil or gas wells if you were a general partner.

4. The rental of a dwelling unit any partner used for personal purposes during the year for more than the greater of 14 days or 10% of the number of days that the residence was rented at fair rental value.

5. Activities of trading personal property for the account of owners of interests in the activities.

If you are an individual, an estate, or a trust, and you have a passive activity loss or credit, get **Form 8582**, Passive Activity Loss Limitations, to figure your allowable passive losses and **Form 8582-CR**, Passive Activity Credit Limitations, to figure your allowable passive credits. For a corporation, get **Form 8810**, Corporate Passive Activity Loss and Credit Limitations. See the instructions for these forms for more information.

If the partnership had more than one activity, it will attach a statement to your Schedule K-1 that identifies each activity (trade or business activity, rental real estate activity, rental activity other than rental real estate, etc.) and specifies the income (loss), deductions, and credits from each activity.

Material participation.—You must determine if you materially participated **(a)** in each trade or business activity held through the partnership and **(b)** if you were a real estate professional (defined above), in each rental real estate activity held through the partnership. **All determinations of material participation are made regarding your participation during the partnership's tax year.**

Material participation standards for partners who are individuals are listed below. Special rules apply to certain retired or disabled farmers and to the surviving spouses of farmers. See the Instructions for Form 8582 for details.

Corporations should refer to the Instructions for Form 8810 for the material participation standards that apply to them.

Individuals (other than limited partners).—If you are an individual (either a general partner or a limited partner who owned a general partnership interest at all times during the tax year), you materially participated in an activity only if one or more of the following apply:

1. You participated in the activity for more than 500 hours during the tax year.

2. Your participation in the activity for the tax year constituted substantially all the participation in the activity of all individuals (including individuals who are not owners of interests in the activity).

3. You participated in the activity for more than 100 hours during the tax year, and your participation in the activity for the tax year was not less than the participation in the activity of any other individual (including individuals who were not owners of interests in the activity) for the tax year.

4. The activity was a significant participation activity for the tax year, and you participated in all significant participation activities (including activities outside the partnership) during the year for more than 500 hours. A "significant participation activity" is any trade or business activity in which you participated for more than 100 hours during the year and in which you did not materially participate under any of the material participation tests (other than this test **4**).

5. You materially participated in the activity for any 5 tax years (whether or not consecutive) during the 10 tax years that immediately precede the tax year.

6. The activity was a personal service activity and you materially participated in the activity for any 3 tax years (whether or not consecutive) preceding the tax year. A "personal service activity" involves the performance of personal services in the fields of health, law, engineering, architecture, accounting, actuarial science, performing arts, consulting, or any other

trade or business in which capital is not a material income-producing factor.

7. Based on all the facts and circumstances, you participated in the activity on a regular, continuous, and substantial basis during the tax year.

Limited partners.—If you are a limited partner, you do not materially participate in an activity unless you meet one of the tests in paragraphs **1, 5,** or **6** above.

Work counted toward material participation.—Generally, any work that you or your spouse does in connection with an activity held through a partnership (where you own your partnership interest at the time the work is done) is counted toward material participation. However, work in connection with the activity is not counted toward material participation if either of the following applies.

1. The work is not the sort of work that owners of the activity would usually do and one of the principal purposes of the work that you or your spouse does is to avoid the passive loss or credit limitations.

2. You do the work in your capacity as an investor and you are not directly involved in the day-to-day operations of the activity. Examples of work done as an investor that would not count toward material participation include **(a)** studying and reviewing financial statements or reports on operations of the activity; **(b)** preparing or compiling summaries or analyses of the finances or operations of the activity for your own use; and **(c)** monitoring the finances or operations of the activity in a nonmanagerial capacity.

Effect of determination.—If you determine that you materially participated in **(a)** a trade or business activity of the partnership, or **(b)** if you were a real estate professional (defined above) in a rental real estate activity of the partnership, report the income (loss), deductions, and credits from that activity as indicated in either column **(c)** of Schedule K-1 or the instructions for each line.

If you determine that you did not materially participate in a trade or business activity of the partnership or if you have income (loss), deductions, or credits from a rental activity of the partnership (other than a rental real estate activity in which you materially participated as a real estate professional), the amounts from that activity are passive. Report passive income (losses), deductions, and credits as follows:

1. If you have an overall gain (the excess of income over deductions and losses, including any prior year unallowed loss) from a passive activity, report the income, deductions, and losses from the activity as indicated on Schedule K-1 or in these instructions.

2. If you have an overall loss (the excess of deductions and losses, including any prior year unallowed loss, over income) or credits from a passive activity, report the income, deductions, losses, and credits from **all** passive activities following the Instructions for Form 8582 or Form

Page 3

8582-CR (or Form 8810), to see if your deductions, losses, and credits are limited under the passive activity rules.

Publicly traded partnerships.—The passive activity limitations are applied separately for items (other than the low-income housing credit and the rehabilitation credit) from each publicly traded partnership (PTP). Thus, a net passive loss from a PTP may not be deducted from other passive income. Instead, a passive loss from a PTP is suspended and carried forward to be applied against passive income from the same PTP in later years. If the partner's entire interest in the PTP is completely disposed of, any unused losses are allowed in full in the year of disposition.

If you have an overall gain from a PTP, the net gain is nonpassive income. In addition, the nonpassive income is included in investment income to figure your investment interest expense deduction.

Do not report passive income, gains, or losses from a PTP on Form 8582. Instead, use the following rules to figure and report on the proper form or schedule your income, gains, and losses from passive activities that you held through each PTP you owned during the tax year:

1. Combine any current year income, gains and losses, and any prior year unallowed losses to see if you have an overall gain or loss from the PTP. Include only the same types of income and losses you would include in figuring your net income or loss from a non-PTP passive activity. Get **Pub. 925,** Passive Activity and At-Risk Rules, for more details.

2. If you have an overall gain, the net gain portion (total gain minus total losses) is nonpassive income. On the form or schedule you normally use, report the net gain portion as nonpassive income and the remaining income and the total losses as passive income and loss. To the left of the entry space, write **"From PTP."** It is important to identify the nonpassive income because the nonpassive portion is included in modified adjusted gross income for purposes of figuring on Form 8582 the "special allowance" for active participation in a non-PTP rental real estate activity. In addition, the nonpassive income is included in investment income when figuring your investment interest expense deduction on Form 4952.

Example. If you have Schedule E income of $8,000, and a Form 4797 prior year unallowed loss of $3,500 from the passive activities of a particular PTP, you have a $4,500 overall gain ($8,000–$3,500). On Schedule E, Part II, report the $4,500 net gain as nonpassive income in column (k). In column (h), report the remaining Schedule E gain of $3,500 ($8,000–$4,500). On the appropriate line of Form 4797, report the prior year unallowed loss of $3,500. Be sure to write **"From PTP"** to the left of each entry space.

3. If you have an overall loss (but did not dispose of your entire interest in the PTP to an unrelated person in a fully taxable transaction during the year), the losses are

allowed to the extent of the income, and the excess loss is carried forward to use in a future year when you have income to offset it. Report as a passive loss on the schedule or form you normally use the portion of the loss equal to the income. Report the income as passive income on the form or schedule you normally use.

Example. You have a Schedule E loss of $12,000 (current year losses plus prior year unallowed losses) and a Form 4797 gain of $7,200. Report the $7,200 gain on the appropriate line of Form 4797. On Schedule E, Part II, report $7,200 of the losses as a passive loss in column (g). Carry forward to 1997 the unallowed loss of $4,800 ($12,000–$7,200).

If you have unallowed losses from more than one activity of the PTP or from the same activity of the PTP that must be reported on different forms, you must allocate the unallowed losses on a pro rata basis to figure the amount allowed from each activity or on each form.

Tax tip. To allocate and keep a record of the unallowed losses, use Worksheets 4, 5, and 6 of Form 8582. List each activity of the PTP in Worksheet 4. Enter the overall loss from each activity in column (a). Complete column (b) of Worksheet 4 according to its instructions. Multiply the total unallowed loss from the PTP by each ratio in column (b) and enter the result in column (c) of Worksheet 4. Then complete Worksheet 5 if all the loss from the same activity is to be reported on one form or schedule. Use Worksheet 6 instead of Worksheet 5 if you have more than one loss to be reported on different forms or schedules for the same activity. Enter the net loss plus any prior year unallowed losses in column (a) of Worksheet 5 (or Worksheet 6 if applicable). The losses in column (c) of Worksheet 5 (column (e) of Worksheet 6) are the allowed losses to report on the forms or schedules. Report both these losses and any income from the PTP on the forms and schedules you normally use.

4. If you have an overall loss and you disposed of your entire interest in the PTP to an unrelated person in a fully taxable transaction during the year, your losses (including prior year unallowed losses) allocable to the activity for the year are not limited by the passive loss rules. A fully taxable transaction is one in which you recognize all your realized gain or loss. Report the income and losses on the forms and schedules you normally use.

Note: *For rules on the disposition of an entire interest reported using the installment method, see the Instructions for Form 8582.*

Active participation in a rental real estate activity.—If you actively participated in a rental real estate activity, you may be able to deduct up to $25,000 of the loss from the activity from nonpassive income. This "special allowance" is an exception to the general rule disallowing losses in excess of income from passive activities. The special allowance is not available if you were married, file a separate return for the year,

and did not live apart from your spouse at all times during the year.

Only individuals and qualifying estates can actively participate in a rental real estate activity. Estates (other than qualifying estates), trusts, and corporations cannot actively participate. Limited partners cannot actively participate unless future regulations provide an exception.

You are not considered to actively participate in a rental real estate activity if at any time during the tax year your interest (including your spouse's interest) in the activity was less than 10% (by value) of all interests in the activity.

Active participation is a less stringent requirement than material participation. You may be treated as actively participating if you participated, for example, in making management decisions or arranging for others to provide services (such as repairs) in a significant and bona fide sense. Management decisions that can count as active participation include approving new tenants, deciding rental terms, approving capital or repair expenditures, and other similar decisions.

An estate is a qualifying estate if the decedent would have satisfied the active participation requirement for the activity for the tax year the decedent died. A qualifying estate is treated as actively participating for tax years ending less than 2 years after the date of the decedent's death.

The maximum special allowance that single individuals and married individuals filing a joint return can qualify for is $25,000. The maximum is $12,500 for married individuals who file separate returns and who lived apart all times during the year. The maximum special allowance for which an estate can qualify is $25,000 reduced by the special allowance for which the surviving spouse qualifies.

If your modified adjusted gross income (defined below) is $100,000 or less ($50,000 or less if married filing separately), your loss is deductible up to the amount of the maximum special allowance referred to in the preceding paragraph. If your modified adjusted gross income is more than $100,000 (more than $50,000 if married filing separately), the special allowance is limited to 50% of the difference between $150,000 ($75,000 if married filing separately) and your modified adjusted gross income. When modified adjusted gross income is $150,000 or more ($75,000 or more if married filing separately), there is no special allowance.

Modified adjusted gross income is your adjusted gross income figured without taking into account any passive activity loss, any rental real estate loss allowed under section 469(c)(7) to real estate professionals (as defined on page 3), any taxable social security or equivalent railroad retirement benefits, any deductible contributions to an IRA or certain other qualified retirement plans under section 219, the deduction allowed under section 164(f) for one-half of self-employment taxes, the exclusion from income of interest from Series EE U.S. Savings

Page 4

Bonds used to pay higher education expenses, or the exclusion of amounts received under an employer's adoption assistance program.

Special rules for certain other activities.—If you have net income (loss), deductions, or credits from any activity to which special rules apply, the partnership will identify the activity and all amounts relating to it on Schedule K-1 or on an attachment.

If you have net income subject to recharacterization under Temporary Regulations section 1.469-2T(f) and Regulations section 1.469-2(f), report such amounts according to the Instructions for Form 8582 (or Form 8810).

If you have net income (loss), deductions, or credits from any of the following activities, treat such amounts as nonpassive and report them as instructed in column (c) of Schedule K-1 or in these instructions:

1. Working interests in oil and gas wells if you are a general partner.

2. The rental of a dwelling unit any partner used for personal purposes during the year for more than the greater of 14 days or 10% of the number of days that the residence was rented at fair rental value.

3. Trading personal property for the account of owners of interests in the activity.

Specific Instructions

General Information and Questions

Item F

Item F should show your share of the partnership's nonrecourse liabilities, partnership-level qualified nonrecourse financing, and other liabilities as of the end of the partnership's tax year. If you terminated your interest in the partnership during the tax year, Item F should show the share that existed immediately before the total disposition. A partner's "other liability" is any partnership liability for which a partner is personally liable.

Use the total of the three amounts for computing the adjusted basis of your partnership interest.

Generally, you may use only the amounts shown next to "Qualified nonrecourse financing" and "Other" to compute your amount at risk. Do not include any amounts that are not at risk if such amounts are included in either of these categories.

If your partnership is engaged in two or more different types of activities subject to the at-risk provisions, or a combination of at-risk activities and any other activity, the partnership should give you a statement showing your share of nonrecourse liabilities, partnership-level qualified nonrecourse financing, and other liabilities for each activity.

Qualified nonrecourse financing secured by real property used in an activity of holding real property that is subject to the at-risk rules is treated as an amount at risk. Qualified nonrecourse financing generally includes financing for which no one is personally liable for repayment that is borrowed for use in an activity of holding real property and that is loaned or guaranteed by a Federal, state, or local government or borrowed from a "qualified" person. Qualified persons include any persons actively and regularly engaged in the business of lending money, such as a bank or savings and loan association. Qualified persons generally do not include related parties (unless the nonrecourse financing is commercially reasonable and on substantially the same terms as loans involving unrelated persons), the seller of the property, or a person who receives a fee for the partnership's investment in the real property. See Pub. 925 for more information on qualified nonrecourse financing.

Both the partnership and you must meet the qualified nonrecourse rules on this debt before you can include the amount shown next to "Qualified nonrecourse financing" in your at-risk computation.

See **Limitations on Losses, Deductions, and Credits** beginning on page 2 for more information on the at-risk limitations.

Item G

If the partnership is a registration-required tax shelter or has invested in a registration-required tax shelter, it should have completed Item G. If you claim or report any income, loss, deduction, or credit from a tax shelter, you must attach Form 8271 to your tax return. If the partnership has invested in a tax shelter, it must give you a copy of its Form 8271 with your Schedule K-1. Use the information on this Form 8271 to complete your Form 8271.

If the partnership itself is a registration-required tax shelter, use the information on Schedule K-1 (name of the partnership, partnership identifying number, and tax shelter registration number) to complete your Form 8271.

Item H

If the box in Item H is checked, you are a partner in a publicly traded partnership and must follow the rules discussed on page 4 under **Publicly traded partnerships.**

Lines 1 Through 25

The amounts shown on lines 1 through 25 reflect your share of income, loss, credits, deductions, etc., from partnership business or rental activities without reference to limitations on losses or adjustments that may be required of you because of:

1. The adjusted basis of your partnership interest,

2. The amount for which you are at risk, or

3. The passive activity limitations. For information on these provisions, see

Limitations on Losses, Deductions, and Credits beginning on page 2.

If you are an individual and the passive activity rules do not apply to the amounts shown on your Schedule K-1, take the amounts shown in column (b) and enter them on the lines on your tax return as indicated in column (c). If the passive activity rules do apply, report the amounts shown in column (b) as indicated in the line instructions below.

If you are not an individual, report the amounts in column (b) as instructed on your tax return.

The line numbers in column (c) are references to forms in use for calendar year 1996. If you file your tax return on a calendar year basis, but your partnership files a return for a fiscal year, enter the amounts shown in column (b) on your tax return for the year in which the partnership's fiscal year ends. For example, if the partnership's tax year ends in February 1997, report the amounts in column (b) on your 1997 tax return.

If you have losses, deductions, or credits from a prior year that were not deductible or usable because of certain limitations, such as the basis rules or the at-risk limitations, take them into account in determining your net income, loss, or credits for this year. However, except for passive activity losses and credits, do not combine the prior-year amounts with any amounts shown on this Schedule K-1 to get a net figure to report on any supporting schedules, statements, or forms attached to your return. Instead, report the amounts on the attached schedule, statement, or form on a year-by-year basis.

If you have amounts other than those shown on Schedule K-1 to report on Schedule E (Form 1040), enter each item on a separate line of Part II of Schedule E.

Income

Line 1—Ordinary Income (Loss) From Trade or Business Activities

The amount reported for line 1 is your share of the ordinary income (loss) from the trade or business activities of the partnership. Generally, where you report this amount on Form 1040 depends on whether the amount is from an activity that is a passive activity to you. If you are an individual partner filing your 1996 Form 1040, find your situation below and report your line 1 income (loss) as instructed, after applying the basis and at-risk limitations on losses:

1. Report line 1 income (loss) from partnership trade or business activities in which you materially participated on Schedule E (Form 1040), Part II, column (i) or (k).

2. Report line 1 income (loss) from partnership trade or business activities in which you did not materially participate, as follows:

a. If income is reported on line 1, report the income on Schedule E, Part II, column (h). However, if the box in Item H is checked, report the income following the

Page 5

rules for **Publicly traded partnerships** on page 4.

b. If a loss is reported on line 1, follow the Instructions for Form 8582, to determine how much of the loss can be reported on Schedule E, Part II, column (g). However, if the box in Item H is checked, report the loss following the rules for **Publicly traded partnerships** on page 4.

Line 2—Net Income (Loss) From Rental Real Estate Activities

Generally, the income (loss) reported on line 2 is a passive activity amount for all partners. However, the income (loss) on line 2 is not from a passive activity if you were a real estate professional (defined on page 3) and you materially participated in the activity.

If you are filing a 1996 Form 1040, use the following instructions to determine where to enter a line 2 amount:

1. If you have a loss from a passive activity on line 2 and you meet **all** of the following conditions, enter the loss on Schedule E (Form 1040), Part II, column (g): ,

a. You actively participated in the partnership rental real estate activities. (See **Active participation in a rental real estate activity** on page 4.)

b. Rental real estate activities with active participation were your only passive activities.

c. You have no prior year unallowed losses from these activities.

d. Your total loss from the rental real estate activities was not more than $25,000 (not more than $12,500 if married filing separately and you lived apart from your spouse all year).

e. If you are a married person filing separately, you lived apart from your spouse all year.

f. You have no current or prior year unallowed credits from a passive activity.

g. Your modified adjusted gross income was not more than $100,000 (not more than $50,000 if married filing separately and you lived apart from your spouse all year).

h. Your interest in the rental real estate activity is **not** held as a limited partner.

2. If you have a loss from a passive activity on line 2 and you **do not** meet all the conditions in **1** above, report the loss following the Instructions for Form 8582 to determine how much of the loss you can report on Schedule E (Form 1040), Part II, column (g). However, if the box in Item H is checked, report the loss following the rules for **Publicly traded partnerships** on page 4.

3. If you were a real estate professional and you materially participated in the activity, report line 2 income (loss) on Schedule E (Form 1040), Part II, column (i) or (k).

4. If you have income from a passive activity on line 2, enter the income on Schedule E, Part II, column (h). However, if the box in Item H is checked, report the

Page 6

income following the rules for **Publicly traded partnerships** on page 4.

Line 3—Net Income (Loss) From Other Rental Activities

The amount on line 3 is a passive activity amount for all partners. Report the income or loss as follows:

1. If line 3 is a loss, report the loss following the Instructions for Form 8582. However, if the box in Item H is checked, report the loss following the rules for **Publicly traded partnerships** on page 4.

2. If income is reported on line 3, report the income on Schedule E (Form 1040), Part II, column (h). However, if the box in Item H is checked, report the income following the rules for **Publicly traded partnerships** on page 4.

Line 4—Portfolio Income (Loss)

Portfolio income or loss is not subject to the passive activity limitations. Portfolio income includes income not derived in the ordinary course of a trade or business from interest, dividends, annuities, or royalties and gain or loss on the sale of property that produces these types of income or is held for investment. Column (c) of Schedule K-1 tells individual partners where to report this income on Form 1040.

The partnership uses line 4f to report portfolio income other than interest, dividend, royalty, and capital gain (loss) income. It will attach a statement to tell you what kind of portfolio income is reported on line 4f.

If the partnership has a residual interest in a real estate mortgage investment conduit (REMIC), it will report on the statement your share of REMIC taxable income (net loss) that you report on Schedule E, Part IV, column (d). The statement will also report your share of any "excess inclusion" that you report on Schedule E, Part IV, column (c), and your share of section 212 expenses that you report on Schedule E, Part IV, column (e). If you itemize your deductions on Schedule A (Form 1040), you may also deduct these section 212 expenses as a miscellaneous deduction subject to the 2% adjusted gross income floor on Schedule A, line 22.

Line 5—Guaranteed Payments to Partners

Generally, amounts on this line are not passive income, and you should report them on Schedule E (Form 1040), Part II, column (k) (e.g., guaranteed payments for personal services).

Line 6—Net Gain (Loss) Under Section 1231 (Other Than Due to Casualty or Theft)

If the amount on line 6 is from a rental activity, the section 1231 gain (loss) is generally a passive activity amount. Likewise, if the amount is from a trade or business activity and you did not materially participate in the activity, the section 1231 gain (loss) is a passive activity amount.

However, an amount on line 6 from a rental real estate activity is not from a passive activity if you were a real estate professional (defined on page 3) and you materially participated in the activity.

● If the amount is not from a passive activity, report it on line 2, column (g) or (h), whichever is applicable, of **Form 4797,** Sales of Business Property. You do not have to complete the information called for in columns (b) through (f). Write "From Schedule K-1 (Form 1065)" across these columns.

● If gain from a passive activity is reported on line 6, report the gain on line 2, column (h), of Form 4797.

● If a loss from a passive activity is reported on line 6, see **Passive loss limitations** in the Instructions for Form 4797. You will need to report the loss following the Instructions for Form 8582 to determine how much of the loss is allowed on Form 4797. However, if the box in Item H is checked, report the loss following the rules for **Publicly traded partnerships** on page 4.

Line 7—Other Income (Loss)

Amounts on this line are other items of income, gain, or loss not included on lines 1 through 6. The partnership should give you a description and the amount of your share for each of these items.

Report loss items that are passive activity amounts to you following the Instructions for Form 8582. However, if the box in Item H is checked, report the loss following the rules for **Publicly traded partnerships** on page 4.

Report income or gain items that are passive activity amounts to you as instructed below.

The instructions given below tell you where to report line 7 items if such items are not passive activity amounts.

Line 7 items may include the following:

● Partnership gains from the disposition of farm recapture property (see Form 4797) and other items to which section 1252 applies.

● Income from recoveries of tax benefit items. A tax benefit item is an amount you deducted in a prior tax year that reduced your income tax. Report this amount on line 21 of Form 1040 to the extent it reduced your tax.

● Gambling gains and losses.

1. If the partnership was **not** engaged in the trade or business of gambling, **(a)** report gambling winnings on Form 1040, line 21, and **(b)** deduct gambling losses to the extent of winnings on Schedule A, line 27.

2. If the partnership was engaged in the trade or business of gambling, **(a)** report gambling winnings in Part II of Schedule E, and **(b)** deduct gambling losses to the extent of winnings in Part II of Schedule E.

● Any income, gain, or loss to the partnership under section 751(b). Report this amount on Form 4797, line 11.

- Specially allocated ordinary gain (loss). Report this amount on Form 4797, line 11.

- Net gain (loss) from involuntary conversions due to casualty or theft. The partnership will give you a schedule that shows the amounts to be entered on **Form 4684,** Casualties and Thefts, line 34, columns (b)(i), (b)(ii), and (c).

- Net short-term capital gain or loss and net long-term capital gain or loss from Schedule D (Form 1065) that is **not** portfolio income (e.g., gain or loss from the disposition of nondepreciable personal property used in a trade or business activity of the partnership). Report a net short-term capital gain or loss on Schedule D (Form 1040), line 5, column (f) or (g), and a net long-term capital gain or loss on Schedule D (Form 1040), line 13, column (f) or (g).

- Any net gain or loss from section 1256 contracts. Report this amount on line 1 of **Form 6781,** Gains and Losses From Section 1256 Contracts and Straddles.

Deductions

Line 8—Charitable Contributions

The partnership will give you a schedule that shows the amount of contributions subject to the 50%, 30%, and 20% limitations. For more details, see the Form 1040 instructions.

If property other than cash is contributed and if the claimed deduction for one item or group of similar items of property exceeds $5,000, the partnership must give you a copy of **Form 8283,** Noncash Charitable Contributions, to attach to your tax return. Do not deduct the amount shown on this form. It is the partnership's contribution. Instead, deduct the amount shown on line 8 of your Schedule K-1 (Form 1065).

If the partnership provides you with information that the contribution was property other than cash and does not give you a Form 8283, see the Instructions for Form 8283 for filing requirements. Do not file Form 8283 unless the total claimed deduction for all contributed items of property exceeds $500.

Charitable contribution deductions are not taken into account in figuring your passive activity loss for the year. Do not enter them on Form 8582.

Line 9—Section 179 Expense Deduction

Use this amount, along with the total cost of section 179 property placed in service during the year from other sources, to complete Part I of **Form 4562,** Depreciation and Amortization. Use Part I of Form 4562 to figure your allowable section 179 expense deduction from all sources. Report the amount on line 12 of Form 4562 allocable to a passive activity from the partnership following the Instructions for Form 8582. However, if the box in Item H is checked, report this amount following the rules for **Publicly traded partnerships** on page 4. If the

amount is not a passive activity deduction, report it on Schedule E (Form 1040), Part II, column (j).

Line 10—Deductions Related to Portfolio Income

Amounts entered on this line are deductions that are clearly and directly allocable to portfolio income (other than investment interest expense and section 212 expenses from a REMIC). Generally, you would enter line 10 amounts on Schedule A (Form 1040), line 22. See the Instructions for Schedule A, lines 22 and 27, for more information. However, enter deductions allocable to royalties on Schedule E (Form 1040), line 18. For the type of expense, write "From Schedule K-1 (Form 1065)."

These deductions are not taken into account in figuring your passive activity loss for the year. Do not enter them on Form 8582.

Line 11—Other Deductions

Amounts on this line are deductions not included on lines 8, 9, 10, 17e, and 18b, such as:

- Itemized deductions (Form 1040 filers enter on Schedule A (Form 1040)).

Note: *If there was a gain (loss) from a casualty or theft to property not used in a trade or business or for income-producing purposes, the partnership will notify you. You will have to complete your own Form 4684.*

- Any penalty on early withdrawal of savings.

- Soil and water conservation expenditures. See section 175 for limitations on the amount you are allowed to deduct.

- Expenditures for the removal of architectural and transportation barriers to the elderly and disabled that the partnership elected to treat as a current expense. The deductions are limited by section 190(c) to $15,000 per year from all sources.

- Any amounts paid during the tax year for insurance that constitutes medical care for you, your spouse, and your dependents. On line 26 of Form 1040, you may be allowed to deduct up to 30% of such amounts, even if you do not itemize deductions. If you do itemize deductions, enter on line 1 of Schedule A (Form 1040) any amounts not deducted on line 26 of Form 1040.

- Payments made on your behalf to an IRA, Keogh, or a simplified employee pension (SEP) plan. See Form 1040 instructions for lines 23a and 23b to figure your IRA deduction. Enter payments made to a Keogh or SEP plan on Form 1040, line 27. If the payments to a Keogh plan were to a defined benefit plan, the partnership should give you a statement showing the amount of the benefit accrued for the tax year.

- Interest expense allocated to debt-financed distributions. The manner in which you report such interest expense

depends on your use of the distributed debt proceeds. See Notice 89-35, 1989-1 C.B. 675, for details.

- Interest paid or accrued on debt properly allocable to your share of a working interest in any oil or gas property (if your liability is not limited). If you did not materially participate in the oil or gas activity, this interest is investment interest reportable as described below; otherwise, it is trade or business interest.

The partnership should give you a description and the amount of your share for each of these items.

Investment Interest

If the partnership paid or accrued interest on debts properly allocable to investment property, the amount of interest you are allowed to deduct may be limited.

For more information and the special provisions that apply to investment interest expense, get **Form 4952,** Investment Interest Expense Deduction, and **Pub. 550,** Investment Income and Expenses.

Line 12a—Interest Expense on Investment Debts

Enter this amount on Form 4952, line 1, along with your investment interest expense from Schedule K-1, line 11, if any, and from other sources to determine how much of your total investment interest is deductible.

Lines 12b(1) and (2)—Investment Income and Investment Expenses

Use the amounts on these lines to determine the amounts to enter in Part II of Form 4952.

Caution: *The amounts shown on lines 12b(1) and (2) include only investment income and expenses included on lines 4a, 4b, 4c, 4f, and 10 of this Schedule K-1. The partnership should attach a schedule that shows the amount of any investment income and expenses included on any other lines of this Schedule K-1. Be sure to take these amounts into account, along with the amounts on lines 12b(1) and 12b(2) and your investment income and expenses from other sources, when figuring the amounts to enter in Part II of Form 4952.*

Credits

Caution: *If you have credits that are passive activity credits to you, you must complete Form 8582-CR (or Form 8810 for corporations) in addition to the credit forms referenced below. See the Instructions for Form 8582-CR (or Form 8810) for more information.*

Also, if you are entitled to claim more than one general business credit (e.g., investment credit, work opportunity credit, credit for alcohol used as fuel, research credit, low-income housing credit, enhanced oil recovery credit, disabled access credit, renewable electricity production credit, Indian employment credit, credit for employer social security

Page 7

and Medicare taxes paid on certain employee tips, orphan drug credit, and credit for contributions to selected community development corporations), you must complete Form 3800, General Business Credit, in addition to the credit forms referenced below. If you have more than one credit, see the instructions for Form 3800 for more information.

Line 13a—Low-Income Housing Credit

Your share of the partnership's low-income housing credit is shown on line 13a. Any allowable credit is entered on **Form 8586,** Low-Income Housing Credit.

The partnership will report separately on line 13a(1) that portion of the low-income housing credit for property placed in service before 1990 to which section 42(j)(5) applies. All other low-income housing credits for property placed in service before 1990 will be reported on line 13a(2). Line 13a(3) will report the low-income housing credit for property placed in service after 1989 to which section 42(j)(5) applies. All other low-income housing credits for property placed in service after 1989 will be reported on line 13a(4).

Keep a separate record of the amount of low-income housing credit from each of these sources so that you will be able to correctly compute any recapture of low-income housing credit that may result from the disposition of all or part of your partnership interest. For more information, see the Instructions for Form 8586.

Line 13b—Qualified Rehabilitation Expenditures Related to Rental Real Estate Activities

The partnership should identify your share of the partnership's rehabilitation expenditures from each rental real estate activity. Enter the expenditures on the appropriate line of **Form 3468,** Investment Credit, to figure your allowable credit.

Line 13c—Credits (Other Than Credits Shown on Lines 13a and 13b) Related to Rental Real Estate Activities

The partnership will identify the type of credit and any other information you need to compute credits from rental real estate activities (other than the low-income housing credit and qualified rehabilitation expenditures).

Line 13d—Credits Related to Other Rental Activities

The partnership will identify the type of credit and any other information you need to compute credits from rental activities other than rental real estate activities.

Line 14—Other Credits

The partnership will identify the type of credit and any other information you need to compute credits other than on lines 13a through 13d. Expenditures qualifying for the **(a)** rehabilitation credit from other than

Page 8

rental real estate activities, **(b)** energy credit, or **(c)** reforestation credit will be reported to you on line 25.

Credits that may be reported on line 13c, 13d, or 14 (depending on the type of activity they relate to) include the following:

● Credit for backup withholding on dividends, interest income, and other types of income. Include the amount the partnership reports to you in the total that you enter on Form 1040, line 52.

● Nonconventional source fuel credit.

● Qualified electric vehicle credit (Form 8834).

● Unused credits from cooperatives.

● Work opportunity credit (Form 5884).

● Credit for alcohol used as fuel (Form 6478).

● Credit for increasing research activities (Form 6765).

● Enhanced oil recovery credit (Form 8830).

● Disabled access credit (Form 8826).

● Renewable electricity production credit (Form 8835).

● Empowerment zone employment credit (Form 8844).

● Indian employment credit (Form 8845).

● Credit for employer social security and Medicare taxes paid on certain employee tips (Form 8846).

● Orphan drug credit (Form 8820).

● Credit for contributions to selected community development corporations (Form 8847).

The passive activity limitations may limit the amount of credits on lines 13a, 13b, 13c, 13d, and 14 (other than the credit for backup withholding) that you may take. Lines 13a, 13b, 13c, and 13d credits are related to the rental activities of the partnership and are generally passive activity credits to all partners. However, amounts on lines 13a, 13b, and 13c are not passive activity credits if you were a real estate professional (defined on page 3) and you materially participated in the activity. Line 14 credits (other than the credit for backup withholding) are related to the trade or business activities of the partnership and are passive activity credits to all partners who did not materially participate in the trade or business activity. In general, credits from passive activities are limited to the tax attributable to passive activities.

But if you actively participated in a rental real estate activity, you may be able to use passive activity credits on line 13c against tax on other income. The amount of these credits you can use is limited to their deduction equivalent up to $25,000 (net of losses from rental real estate activities deductible against up to $25,000 of other income).

You may also claim passive activity credits on lines 13a and 13b against tax on other income, subject to the same $25,000 limitation, even if you did not actively participate in a rental real estate activity. Line 13d credits are limited to tax

attributable to passive activities. The $25,000 deduction equivalent does not apply to line 13d and line 14 credits.

Self-Employment

If you and your spouse are both partners, each of you must complete and file your own **Schedule SE (Form 1040),** Self-Employment Tax, to report your partnership net earnings (loss) from self-employment.

Line 15a—Net Earnings (Loss) From Self-Employment

If you are a general partner, reduce this amount before entering it on Schedule SE (Form 1040) by any section 179 expense deduction claimed, unreimbursed partnership expenses claimed, and depletion claimed on oil and gas properties. Do not reduce net earnings from self-employment by any separately stated deduction for health insurance expenses.

If the amount on this line is a loss, enter only the deductible amount on Schedule SE (Form 1040). See **Limitations on Losses, Deductions, and Credits** beginning on page 2.

If your partnership is an options dealer or a commodities dealer, see section 1402(i).

If your partnership is an investment club, see Rev. Rul. 75-525, 1975-2 C.B. 350.

Line 15b—Gross Farming or Fishing Income

If you are an individual partner, enter the amount from this line, as an item of information, on Schedule E (Form 1040), Part V, line 41. Also use this amount to figure net earnings from self-employment under the farm optional method on Schedule SE (Form 1040), Section B, Part II.

Line 15c—Gross Nonfarm Income

If you are an individual partner, use this amount to figure net earnings from self-employment under the nonfarm optional method on Schedule SE (Form 1040), Section B, Part II.

Adjustments and Tax Preference Items

Use the information reported on lines 16a through 16e (as well as your adjustments and tax preference items from other sources) to prepare your **Form 6251,** Alternative Minimum Tax—Individuals; **Form 4626,** Alternative Minimum Tax—Corporations; or Schedule I of **Form 1041,** U.S. Income Tax Return for Estates and Trusts.

Lines 16d(1) and 16d(2)—Gross Income From, and Deductions Allocable to, Oil, Gas, and Geothermal Properties

The amounts reported on these lines include only the gross income from, and deductions allocable to, oil, gas, and geothermal properties that are included on line 1 of Schedule K-1. The partnership should have attached a schedule that shows any income from or deductions allocable to such properties that are included on lines 2 through 11 and line 25 of Schedule K-1. Use the amounts reported on lines 16d(1) and 16d(2) and the amounts on the attached schedule to help you determine the net amount to enter on line 14f of Form 6251.

Line 16e—Other Adjustments and Tax Preference Items

Enter the information on the schedule attached by the partnership for line 16e on the applicable lines of Form 6251.

Foreign Taxes

Use the information on lines 17a through 17g and attached schedules to figure your foreign tax credit. For more information, get **Form 1116,** Foreign Tax Credit (Individual, Estate, Trust, or Nonresident Alien Individual), and the related instructions; **Form 1118,** Foreign Tax Credit—Corporations, and the related instructions; and **Pub. 514,** Foreign Tax Credit for Individuals.

Other

Lines 18a and 18b—Section 59(e)(2) Expenditures

The partnership will show on line 18a the type of qualified expenditures to which an election under section 59(e) may apply. It will identify the amount of the expenditure on line 18b. If there is more than one type of expenditure, the amount of each type will be listed on an attachment. Generally, section 59(e) allows each partner to elect to deduct certain expenses ratably over the number of years in the applicable period rather than deduct the full amount in the current year. Under the election, you may deduct circulation expenditures ratably over a 3-year period. Research and experimental expenditures and mining exploration and development costs qualify for a writeoff period of 10 years. Intangible drilling and development costs may be deducted over a 60-month period, beginning with the month in which such costs were paid or incurred. If you make this election, these items are not treated as adjustments or tax preference items for purposes of the alternative minimum tax. Make the election on Form 4562.

Because each partner decides whether to make the election under section 59(e), the partnership cannot provide you with the amount of the adjustment or tax preference item related to the expenses listed on line 18b. You must decide both how to claim the expenses on your return and compute the resulting adjustment or tax preference item.

Line 19—Tax-Exempt Interest Income

You must report on your return, as an item of information, your share of the tax-exempt interest received or accrued by the partnership during the year. Individual partners should report this amount on Form 1040, line 8b. Increase the adjusted basis of your interest in the partnership by this amount.

Line 20—Other Tax-Exempt Income

Increase the adjusted basis of your interest in the partnership by the amount shown on line 20, but do not include it in income on your tax return.

Line 21—Nondeductible Expenses

The nondeductible expenses paid or incurred by the partnership are not deductible on your tax return. Decrease the adjusted basis of your interest in the partnership by this amount.

Line 22—Distributions of Money (Cash and Marketable Securities)

Line 22 shows the distributions the partnership made to you of cash and certain marketable securities. The marketable securities are included at their fair market value on the date of distribution (minus your share of the partnership's gain on the securities distributed to you). If the amount shown on line 22 exceeds the adjusted basis of your partnership interest immediately before the distribution, the excess is treated as gain from the sale or exchange of your partnership interest. Generally, this gain is treated as gain from the sale of a capital asset and should be reported on the Schedule D for your return. However, the gain may be ordinary income. For details, see Pub. 541.

The partnership will separately identify **(a)** the fair market value of the marketable securities when distributed (minus your share of the gain on the securities distributed to you) and **(b)** the partnership's adjusted basis of those securities immediately before the distribution. Decrease the adjusted basis of your interest in the partnership (but not below zero) by the amount of cash distributed to you and the partnership's adjusted basis of the distributed securities. Advances or drawings of money or property against your distributive share are treated as current distributions made on the last day of the partnership's tax year.

Your basis in the distributed marketable securities (other than in liquidation of your interest) is the smaller of **(a)** the partnership's adjusted basis in the securities immediately before the distribution increased by any gain recognized on the distribution of the securities, or **(b)** the adjusted basis of your partnership interest reduced by any cash distributed in the same transaction and increased by any gain recognized on the distribution of the securities. If you received the securities in liquidation of your partnership interest, your basis in the marketable securities is equal to the adjusted basis of your partnership interest reduced by any cash distributed in the same transaction and increased by any gain recognized on the distribution of the securities.

If, within 5 years of a distribution to you of marketable securities, you contributed appreciated property (other than those securities) to the partnership and the fair market value of those securities exceeded the adjusted basis of your partnership interest immediately before the distribution (reduced by any cash received in the distribution), you may have to recognize gain on the appreciated property. See section 737 for details.

Line 23—Distributions of Property Other Than Money

Line 23 shows the partnership's adjusted basis of property other than money immediately before the property was distributed to you. Decrease the adjusted basis of your interest in the partnership by the amount of your basis in the distributed property. Your basis in the distributed property (other than in liquidation of your interest) is the smaller of **(a)** the partnership's adjusted basis immediately before the distribution. or **(b)** the adjusted basis of your partnership interest reduced by any cash distributed in the same transaction. If you received the property in liquidation of your interest, your basis in the distributed property is equal to the adjusted basis of your partnership interest reduced by any cash distributed in the same transaction.

If you contributed appreciated property to the partnership within 5 years of a distribution of other property to you, and the fair market value of the other property exceeded the adjusted basis of your partnership interest immediately before the distribution (reduced by any cash received in the distribution), you may have to recognize gain on the appreciated property. See section 737 for details.

Lines 24a and 24b—Recapture of Low-Income Housing Credit

A section 42(j)(5) partnership will report recapture of a low-income housing credit on line 24a. All other partnerships will report recapture of a low-income housing credit on line 24b. Keep a separate record of recapture from each of these sources so that you will be able to correctly compute any recapture of low-income housing credit that may result from the disposition of all or part of your partnership interest. For more information, get **Form 8611,** Recapture of Low-Income Housing Credit.

Supplemental Information

Line 25

Amounts shown on line 25 include:

1. Taxes paid on undistributed capital gains by a regulated investment company. Form 1040 filers enter your share of these taxes on line 57, check the box for Form 2439, and add the words "Form 1065."

2. Number of gallons of each fuel used during the tax year in a use qualifying for the credit for taxes paid on fuels and the applicable credit per gallon. Also your share of the credit allowed for the purchase of qualified diesel-powered highway vehicles. Use this information to complete **Form 4136,** Credit for Federal Tax Paid on Fuels.

3. Your share of gross income from the property, share of production for the tax year, etc., needed to figure your depletion deduction for oil and gas wells. The partnership should also allocate to you a share of the adjusted basis of each partnership oil or gas property. See Pub. 535 for how to figure your depletion deduction.

4. Recapture of the section 179 expense deduction. If the recapture was caused by a disposition of the property, include the amount on Form 4797, line 18. The recapture amount will be limited to the amount you deducted in earlier years.

5. Recapture of certain mining exploration expenditures (section 617).

6. Any information or statements you need to comply with requirements under section 6111 (regarding tax shelters) or section 6662(d)(2)(B)(ii) (regarding adequate disclosure of items that may cause an understatement of income tax on your return).

7. Preproductive period farm expenses. You may be eligible to elect to deduct these expenses currently or capitalize them under section 263A. Get **Pub. 225,** Farmer's Tax Guide, and Temporary Regulations section 1.263A-4T(c).

8. Any information you need to compute the interest due under section 453(l)(3) with respect to the disposition of certain

timeshares and residential lots on the installment method. If you are an individual, report the interest on Form 1040, line 51. Write "453(l)(3)" and the amount of the interest on the dotted line to the left of line 51.

9. Any information you need to compute the interest due under section 453A(c) with respect to certain installment sales. If you are an individual, report the interest on Form 1040, line 51. Write "453A(c)" and the amount of the interest on the dotted line to the left of line 51.

10. Any information you need to compute the interest due or to be refunded under the look-back method of section 460(b)(2) on certain long-term contracts. Use **Form 8697,** Interest Computation Under the Look-Back Method for Completed Long-Term Contracts, to report any such interest.

11. Any information you need relating to interest expense that you are required to capitalize under section 263A for production expenditures. See Regulations sections 1.263A-8 through 1.263A-15 for more information.

12. Any information you need to compute unrelated business taxable income under section 512(a)(1) (but excluding any modifications required by paragraphs (8) through (15) of section 512(b)) for a partner that is a tax-exempt organization.

Note: *A partner is required to notify the partnership of its tax-exempt status.*

13. Your share of expenditures qualifying for the **(a)** rehabilitation credit from other than rental real estate activities, **(b)** energy credit, or **(c)** reforestation credit. Enter the expenditures on the appropriate line of Form 3468 to figure your allowable credit.

14. Investment credit properties subject to recapture. Any information you need to figure your recapture tax on **Form 4255,** Recapture of Investment Credit. See the Form 3468 on which you took the original credit for other information you need to complete Form 4255.

You may also need Form 4255 if you disposed of more than one-third of your interest in a partnership.

15. Any information you need to figure your recapture of the qualified electric vehicle credit. See Pub. 535 for details, including how to figure the recapture.

16. Any information you need to figure your recapture of the Indian employment credit. Generally, if the partnership terminated a qualified employee less than 1 year after the date of initial employment, any Indian employment credit allowed for a prior tax year by reason of wages paid or incurred to that employee must be recaptured. For details, see section 45A(d).

17. Any other information you may need to file your return not shown elsewhere on Schedule K-1.

The partnership should give you a description and the amount of your share for each of these items.

Printed on recycled paper

*U.S. Government Printing Office: 1996 — 407-268

APPENDIX C

Sample Agreement Forms

he forms in this appendix can be used for various agreements that may be needed in forming and maintaining a partnership.

PARTNERSHIP AGREEMENT

1. Foreword

AGREEMENT made this _____ day of _____ , 19 _____ , between _____ residing at _____ , and _____ , residing at _____ , as follows:

2. Partnership Name and Business

The parties hereby form a partnership that will operate under the name _____ and will engage in the business of _____ .

3. Location of Business

The partnership's principal office shall be located at _____ and/or such other place as the partners may unanimously agree.

4. Commencement of Partnership

The partnership will commence on and continue until terminated as hereinafter set forth.

5. Capital Contributions

Each partner shall contribute $ _____ to the partnership. The sum of the partners' contributions, totaling $ _____ will be the partnership capitalization. Additional capital will be contributed by the partners, whenever it may be required in the business of the partnership, in the same proportion in which such partners share in profits and losses.

6. Capital Accounts

The partnership shall maintain an individual capital account for each partner, which shall be maintained in an amount not below the capital contribution set forth above. Should any partner's capital account fall below this amount, the partner's share of partnership profits due the partner shall be paid to his or her capital account, and, if that is not enough to reach the necessary capital amount, the partner must immediately pay the amount of any deficiency to the partnership.

7. Share of Profits and Losses

Partnership net profits and losses will be shared (equally, proportionately to their capital contribution) by the partners.

8. Partnership Withdrawals: Compensation

Partners will not receive salaries but may draw from partnership receipts, net after provision for debts, $ _____ per _____ . The withdrawals, however, will not be permitted to impair the capital accounts of the partnership.

9. Annual Accounting

The partnership's books and records will be maintained at its principal office, and all partners may have access thereto at any time. The records will be maintained on a cash basis, will be closed and balanced as of December 31 each year, and will be audited annually as of such date. If a partner has withdrawn more than another partner during such year, the excess will be repaid to the partnership. If there are net profits, in excess of debts, liabilities, and necessary working capital, it will be divided (equally, proportionately to capital contribution, etc.) and paid to the partners.

10. Management and Operations of the Partnership

The partners will spend their full time and use their best efforts on the partnership business and will equally manage same. Partnership funds will be deposited in a bank account chosen by a majority of the partners, with all withdrawals therefrom to be signed by (two partners). Partnership records are to be maintained at the partnership's principal place of business and are to be available to partners for inspection at all reasonable times.

The following transactions require the unanimous written agreement of all of the partners: (1) transactions requiring the partnership to spend in excess of $ _____ , and (2) borrowing money that requires the granting of any security interest in partnership assets.

11. Incapacity

If for any reason a partner is unable to perform his partnership duties for a continuous period in excess of _____ months, the other partners may compel the withdrawal of such partner from the partnership. Such withdrawal

shall take effect immediately upon receipt of written notice from the remaining partners, and the partner's rights shall be the same as if he had served notice of an intent to retire.

12. Misconduct or Delinquency

If a partner, due to misconduct or failure to attend to the affairs of the partnership, shall seriously damage the partnership business, a majority of the senior partners (determined by either length of service, number of votes, or required capital contribution) may determine that said partner shall be required to withdraw from the partnership. The partner shall, upon being given written notice of such determination, be deemed to have withdrawn on the date stipulated in the notice and shall not thereafter participate in future partnership profits. Losses attributable to the partner's misconduct or inattention will be charged against the partner's capital account prior to settlement of the partner's capital interest.

13. Retirement or Withdrawal

Upon prior written notice _____ days prior to the end of any (calendar, fiscal) year, a partner may retire. The remaining partner(s) may terminate, or elect to continue the business, in which case the remaining partner(s) can, at their option, purchase the interest of the retiring partner at the fair market value of the partner's interest, as determined by the partnership's independent accountant at the end of the month in which such written notice is given. Notice of intention to exercise the purchase option shall be given, in writing, to the retiring partner within _____ days of receipt of the notice of retirement. The partnership name will (not) be changed to remove the name of the retiree. If the option to purchase is not exercised, the partnership will be liquidated as promptly as reasonably possible, and the partners will share (equally, or in any other method), profits or losses during the liquidation period, and the liquidation proceeds shall, after satisfaction of capital accounts, be divided (equally, etc.).

14. Goodwill

It is hereby agreed that any goodwill of the firm shall have no value and shall thereby be excluded from the total assets that can be distributed.

15. Noncompetition Requirement

A partner who retires or withdraws from the partnership may not engage in a business competitive to the business of the partnership for a period of _____ years from the date of the partner's retirement or withdrawal.

16. Death

If a partner dies during the term of the partnership, the survivor(s) shall either purchase decedent's partnership interest or liquidate the business. Notice of election to purchase decedent's partnership interest must be served, in writing, upon decedent's legal representative within _____ days of appointment of such representative. Payment for decedent's interest, if purchased by surviving partners pursuant hereto, shall be at a price determined as if decedent had retired. The partnership is not obligated to change or remove the name of the decedent. Payments for decedent's share shall be made to his legally appointed representative. If none is appointed, the partnership will retain the amount of the payment in trust for such purpose until appointment is made. The partnership is not obligated to remove the name of the decedent from the name of the partnership.

17. Vacation

Partners each will be entitled to an annual vacation of _____ weeks. Unused vacation time will be (not be) accumulated for use in future years.

18. Termination of Partnership

The partnership may be terminated at any time, upon agreement of any of the partners. All assets, including the partnership name, will be sold with reasonable diligence, and the proceeds, after payment of all partnership obligations, distributed so as to (1) equalize the partnership capital accounts, (2) equalize the partnership income accounts, and (3) distribute the balance (equally, proportionately, etc.) to each partner as they are so entitled.

19. Signatures

IN WITNESS WHEREOF, the parties have signed (and sealed) this agreement.

_____

_____

AGREEMENT TO ADMIT NEW PARTNER

1. Date and Parties

Agreement made this _____ day of _____ 19 _____ by *(names and addresses of new and present partners)*.

2. Purpose

WHEREAS *(partners)* have been doing business as a partnership, with principal offices at _____ , the partnership consisting of *(general statement)*; and _____ , as a new partner, has agreed to buy a _____ % interest in the partnership by paying to the partnership $ _____ (or by contributing to the partnership the following assets: _____ . The parties hereto have agreed to continue the partnership among all parties named in this agreement.

The parties also agree as follows:

3. Partnership Agreement Binding

Except as changed by this agreement, the partnership agreement dated _____ , 19 _____ , a copy of which is attached hereto, shall be fully binding on all parties hereto and shall be for the benefit of all parties who have signed this agreement.

4. Conduct of Affairs

The partnership affairs shall be conducted as if _____ *(new partner)* had been an original partner.

5. Division of Profits and Losses

From and after the date of this agreement, all net profits and net losses of the partnership will be divided equally (or proportion as appropriate) between the parties to this agreement.

6. Partnership Assets

All partnership assets as of this date hereof shall continue as the assets of the new partnership. The new partnership hereby assumes full responsibility for all debts and liabilities of the original partnership.

7. Inventory and Capital Accounts

An inventory shall be taken of all assets and liabilities as of the date of this agreement, and the original partnership accounts shall be closed, and new accounts shall be entered to reflect the ownership by _____ *(new partner)* of a _____ % interest in the assets and liabilities of the new partnership.

IN WITNESS WHEREOF, the parties have signed this agreement.

_____

_____

(Signature of parties)

AGREEMENT GIVING NOTICE TO WITHDRAW

1. Date and Parties

Agreement made this _____ day of _____ 19 _____
by *(names and addresses of the present partners)*.

2. Purpose

Unless physically prevented from doing so, a partner must give notice to all
partners of his/her intention to withdraw from the partnership effective
_____ *(specify date)*. The withdrawing partner also agrees to give
required notice to all outside third parties of his/her withdrawal as of the date
of intended withdrawal. Upon proper notice to all required parties, the withdrawing partner shall no longer be responsible for all partnership liabilities
incurred after the date of withdrawal.

IN WITNESS WHEREOF, the parties have signed this agreement.

_____

_____

(Signature of parties)

SAMPLE LIMITED PARTNERSHIP AGREEMENT

1. Foreword

Agreement made this _____ day of _____ , 19 _____, by and among *(name and address)* and *(name and address)* as general partners, and *(name and address)* and *(name and address)* as limited partners.

2. Intent of the Parties

The parties agree to form a limited partnership pursuant to the laws of the State of _____ . The purpose of the partnership shall be to *[any service type activity, oil or mineral production etc., to acquire for the partnership a certain property known as (address) (the "property")].*

3. Term of Partnership

The partnership term shall be from _____ 19 _____ , to 20 _____ , excepting that the partnership may be dissolved prior thereto in the event of:

1. Partnership disposition of all of its property; or

2. The selection of (a majority of) the general partners to dissolve the partnership as provided in paragraph _____ hereof; or

3. The retirement, death, incapacity, bankruptcy, resignation, or other termination of a general partner as set forth in paragraph_____ .

4. Principal Office

The partnership's principal office will be located at *(address)* or at such other place as the general partners may designate.

5. General and Limited Partners

The general partners are:

1. A *(name and address)* _____

2. B *(name and address)* _____

The limited partners are:

1. C *(name and address)* _____

2. D *(name and address)* _____

6. Capital Contributions

The partners shall each contribute to the partnership capital the following amounts:

Partner	Contribution
A	$_____
B	$_____
C	$_____
D	$_____

7. Share of Profit or Loss

Partnership net profits and net losses and the proceeds of any sale, or other receipts of the partnership, are subject only to the limited partners' liability limitation to the amount of their investment and are to be apportioned among the partners as follows:

Partner	%
A	_____
B	_____
C	_____
D	_____

For the purpose of this agreement, net partnership profits shall be determined according to generally accepted accounting principles. Partnership net profits will be distributed at intervals determined in the sole discretion of the general partners.

8. Limited Partner's Liability and Rights of Assignment

Limited Partner's liability for losses shall not, in any event, exceed that partner's total partnership capital contribution. Losses in excess of such amount are to be borne by the general partners solely and proportionately to said general partner's share of profits as set forth in this agreement.

Limited partners may assign their partnership interest with the consent of the general partners upon the furnishing of documents reasonably required by the general partners.

9. General Partners' Fees, Salaries, etc.

Except as otherwise specifically provided in this agreement, partners, whether general or limited, shall receive no salaries for their services as partners, nor will any partner, general or limited, be paid interest on a partnership capital contribution.

10. Management of the Partnership

The general partners shall be equally authorized to participate in partnership management and shall each devote the time reasonably required for such management. Limited partners will not participate in the management of the partnership. Consent of a majority of the general partners will be required for all management decisions except those requiring unanimous vote according to the Uniform Partnership Act of this state.

11. Withdrawal of Limited Partner

Limited partners may withdraw their capital contribution in the event of partnership termination, provided that (1) all partnership liabilities have been paid or (2) the partnership has retained assets sufficient for payment, excepting liabilities to the partners for their partnership capital contributions. Limited partners shall not have the right, except as specifically stated otherwise, to receive property other than cash in repayment of their capital contributions.

12. Competition

The partners, whether general or limited, may engage in or interact with, directly or indirectly, business ventures of any kind, without limitation, so long as these activities do not compete with the business of the partnership.

13. Books and Records

The partnership records shall be maintained at the partnership's principal office or at some other place that the general partners, by majority vote, may select. Partnership records shall be maintained on a basis of the calendar year, and annual statements of the results of partnership operation and partnership shares shall be promptly prepared by the accountants for the partnership and promptly distributed to all partners.

All partnership funds will be deposited in a bank account designated by the general partners.

14. General Partner's Death, Retirement, etc.

If a general partner dies, resigns, or is adjudicated bankrupt or incompetent, the partnership may, at the election of all the remaining general partners, be dissolved and liquidated or may be continued. The election of the remaining general partners to continue the partnership, as provided for herein, shall be made within days of the death, retirement, or adjudication of bankruptcy or incompetency of any general partner.

15. Limited Partner's Death

A limited partner's death will not cause the termination of the partnership. The deceased limited partner's legal representative will have all of the rights of the deceased subject to this agreement.

16. Termination of the Partnership

The partnership will terminate and be dissolved as elsewhere herein provided or whenever a determination to terminate and dissolve is made by a majority of _____ days prior written notice to each of the limited partners. In such event, the general partners will liquidate the partnership and distribute the proceeds in the following priority:

1. In payment of partnership's liabilities;

2. A fund shall be set up for any possible remaining liabilities that may occur, such fund to be determined by the partnership's accounts and held in escrow by the attorney selected to represent the partnership in all matters relating to the dissolution of the firm;

3. Repayment, prorata, of any loans or advances made to the partnership by any partners thereof; and

4. The balance to be distributed to all the partners as follows: (a) cash shall be distributed to each partner in satisfaction of his partnership interest as set forth in paragraph (share of profit and loss) and (b) partnership assets may be distributed in kind, with each partner receiving an undivided interest therein, subject to its related liabilities. The interest of each partner in the distribution shall be based on his distributive share of profit and loss.

A reasonable time shall be allowed for the orderly liquidation of the assets of the partnership and the discharge of liabilities to creditors so that the general partners may minimize the normal losses that usually occur upon a liquidation. Each partner is to receive a statement prepared by the partnership's Certified Public Accountants, setting forth the assets and liabilities of the partnership at the date of complete liquidation. When the distribution plan is completed the partnership's attorney-at-law will file a Certificate of Cancellation of the partnership as required by state law.

17. General Partner's Liability Limitation

Except as stated in this limited partnership agreement, general partners are not personally liable for the return of any portion of a limited partner's capital contribution. The return of any partner's capital contribution will be exclusively from the assets of the partnership.

18. Notices

Any notices required in this limited partnership agreement must be in writing and sent by certified mail to the parties at the addresses stated in this partnership and to the partnership at its principal office.

19. Signature

IN WITNESS WHEREOF, the parties have signed this agreement on the date above written.

The General Partners:

1. A _____

2. B _____

The Limited Partners:

1. C _____

2. D _____

AGREEMENT AS TO VALUATION
OF A PARTNER'S INTEREST

Upon written notice to all partners, the value of the partnership shall be determined by the partnership's outside independent accountant using the _____ *(select method such as liquidation or replacement value)* on the date selected by all the current partners for either admitting or buying out a departing partner's interest.

Such method shall also be used in valuing a deceased partner's interest at the date of his/her death.

IN WITNESS WHEREOF, the parties have signed this agreement.

_____

_____

_____

_____

(Signature of parties)

Useful Literature

Apostolou, N., *Keys to Business and Personal Financial Statements* (Barron's Educational Series, Inc., Hauppauge, NY, 1991).

Barfield, R., Sylvia Titus, and G.T. Friedlob, *Barron's Business Library: Business Communications* (Barron's Educational Series, Inc., Hauppauge, NY, 1992).

Capela, John and S. Hartman, *Dictionary of International Business Terms* (Barron's Educational Series, Inc., Hauppauge, NY, 1996).

Crumbley, D.L. and Jack P. Friedman, *Barron's Guide to Tax Terms* (Barron's Educational Series, Inc., Hauppauge, NY, 1995).

Crumbley, D.L., Jack P. Friedman, and S.B. Anders, *Dictionary of Tax Terms* (Barron's Educational Series, Inc., Hauppauge, NY, 1994).

De Vries, Mary A., *Barron's Business Thesaurus* (Barron's Educational Series, Inc., Hauppauge, NY, 1996).

DeThomas, A. and W.B. Fredenberger, *Barron's Business Library: Writing a Convincing Business Plan* (Barron's Educational Series, Inc., Hauppauge, NY, 1995).

Downing, D., *Barron's Business Library: Computers and Business Tasks* (Barron's Educational Series, Inc., Hauppauge, NY, 1991).

Downing, D. and J. Clark, *Business Review Series: Business Statistics* (Barron's Educational Series, Inc., Hauppauge, NY, 1997).

Dungan, C. and Ridings, *Barron's Business Library: Business Law* (Barron's Educational Series, Inc., Hauppauge, NY, 1990).

Eisen, P., *Business Review Series: Accounting* (Barron's Educational Series, Inc., Hauppauge, NY, 1994).

Emerson, Robert and J. Hardwicke, *Business Review Series: Business Law, 3rd ed.* (Barron's Educational Series, Inc., Hauppauge, NY, 1997).

Fox, Stephen A., *Keys to Buying a Franchise* (Barron's Educational Series, Inc., Hauppauge, NY, 1991).

Fox, Stephen A., *Keys to Buying and Selling a Business* (Barron's Educational Series, Inc., Hauppauge, NY, 1991).

Friedman, Jack P., *et al.*, *Dictionary of Business Terms, 2nd ed.* (Barron's Educational Series, Inc., Hauppauge, NY, 1994).

Geffner, A.B., *How to Write Better Business Letters, 2nd ed.* (Barron's Educational Series, Inc., Hauppauge, NY, 1995).

Jonnard, C., *Keys to Starting an Export Business* (Barron's Educational Series, Inc., Hauppauge, NY, 1996).

Peterson, Mark A., *The Complete Entrepreneur* (Barron's Educational Series, Inc., Hauppauge, NY, 1996).

Pincus, Marilyn, *Everyday Business Etiquette* (Barron's Educational Series, Inc., Hauppauge, NY, 1996).

Siegel, Joel G. and Jae K. Shim, *Accounting Handbook, 2nd ed.* (Barron's Educational Series, Inc., Hauppauge, NY, 1995).

Siegel, Joel G. and Jae K. Shim, *Keys to Managing Your Cash Flow* (Barron's Educational Series, Inc., Hauppauge, NY, 1992).

Siegel, Joel G. and Jae K. Shim, *Keys to Starting a Small Business* (Barron's Educational Series, Inc., Hauppauge, NY, 1991).

Sinclair, Carol, *Keys for Women Starting or Owning a Business* (Barron's Educational Series, Inc., Hauppauge, NY, 1991).

INDEX